Nexus LSAT Curriculum Highlights

Cutting-Edge Techniques

- ✓ Full curriculum revision completed in 2014
- ✓ Techniques focus on the LSAT trends from 2012-2014
- ✓ Skill Group focus builds robust LSAT abilities

Advanced Practice

- ✓ Targeted drills teach you core skills on simplified questions
- ✓ Three kinds of problem sets with different focuses for each problem type
- ✓ Skill Group diagnostics, practice sets, and tests hone and measure your skills

Serious Customization

- ✓ Depth of topics covered fits your course length
- ✓ Problem sets match your LSAT abilities and work "your edge"
- ✓ Verified Improvement System: master each important skill before moving on

Praise for Power Tutoring

My Nexus LSAT tutor helped me increase my score to the 99th percentile by targeting my weaknesses. I recommend Nexus LSAT to anyone serious about succeeding on the LSAT, whether they are starting off or trying to improve a previous score.

> — DAVID, New Jersey
> +8 points after a Kaplan classroom course, 172 Official Score
> Attending Columbia Law School

Nexus LSAT proved to be the best money I've ever spent! I went from thinking about a tier 3 school to now applying to TOP 14.

> — JOSH, North Carolina
> +16 points, 169 Official Score

I was struggling with the Games section in particular, and Nexus helped me focus on raising my score in that area while also improving my other sections. I know I wouldn't have been able to get a 172 without them!

> — ROBYN, New Mexico
> +11 points, 172 Official Score

I raised my score 15 points from my first practice test to my actual LSAT, and I scored in the 98th percentile! I can't begin to express how thorough this program is. I shopped around for LSAT prep programs, and there isn't a value out there even close to the Nexus LSAT tutoring. I would recommend them to anyone who wants to excel on this test.

> — GREG, Nevada
> +15 points, 170 Official Score

Nexus LSAT was perfect for me, and I highly recommend it. When I took the LSAT, I was working full time and needed a program that would fit my schedule and give me results – Nexus LSAT was it! I was able to work at a pace that fit my life, focus on the sections that were tougher for me, and have the assistance of a private tutor.

> — HANNAH, New York
> +14 points, 165 Official Score

Before my Nexus LSAT course, I never imagined I could feel so prepared and confident going into the LSAT. Nexus' approach was so thorough and comprehensive, however, that I actually looked forward to test day; I knew I was ready. That feeling of confidence is a true testament to the effectiveness of the Nexus program.

— LAUREN, Massachusetts
+10 points, 171 Official Score
Harvard Law School

Nexus' intense, personalized course schedule was just what I needed to lift my score ten points. Constantly communicating with my Tutor helped me to focus and stay on track, resulting in a score in the 96th percentile. I would recommend Nexus LSAT to anyone who's serious about getting into a great law school.

— NICK, Wisconsin
+10 points, 168 Official Score

Power Tutoring was a crucial asset for my LSAT prep. The curriculum content was challenging and rewarding; the problem sets were exceptional and really improved my skills quickly. My Nexus Tutor was very accessible and the daily guidance constantly refined how I was prepping. I'm extremely happy with my LSAT score.

— RACHEL, Texas
+19 points, 173 Official Score

After being unhappy with my first LSAT score, I wanted to feel confident retaking the test. My Nexus LSAT Tutor made sure that I was as prepared as possible, and created a specialized study schedule that fit needs. Any question or concern I had while going through the materials was quickly answered, and my Tutor made sure that I was focused on the areas of the test where I needed the most review. When the time came to retake the test, I knew I could handle any question the LSAT threw me and ended up significantly improving my score. I would recommend this program to anyone looking to get an individualized and in depth LSAT prep experience.

— CALI, Washington DC
+9 points, 169 Official Score
Harvard Law School

The best aspect of the Nexus course was the material and the methodology. The course uses a method that is ideal for scoring well on any test: learning and building skills, drilling those skills, applying those skills on a small scale, and then executing those skills on a grand scale.

— PRIUM, New Jersey
+13 points, 163 Official Score

Linking

Logical Reasoning Module 1

Linking is written and edited by Thomas Hall, Ryan Fliss, and Tom Nading.
Special thanks to Patrick Kurz for helping with usability and design.
Nexus Publishing, Telluride CO 81435.

Continuous effort — not strength or intelligence — is the key to unlocking our potential.
—Winston Churchill

Contents

Linking Module Introduction

Linking is the first of five Modules in the Logical Reasoning curriculum:

1. Linking

2. Flaws

3. Understand Flaw

4. Describe Argument

5. Compare Arguments

Each Logical Reasoning Module focuses solely on Logical Reasoning. The full Nexus LSAT curriculum also includes a Setup Module, three Games Modules, three Reading Comprehension Modules, an Advanced Practice Module, and an Explanation Module, a total of 14 Modules.

The Linking Skill Group

The overall focus of the Linking Module is to teach you how to correctly link two pieces of information (or concepts). These links occur when you find an inference by linking two pieces of information or when you see a missing link in an argument. Those skills correspond to the two problem types in this Module: Inference problems and Justify problems. For each type, you will learn powerful techniques and then reinforce them with targeted drills and three types of problem sets. This is the most advanced technique reinforcement in a LSAT curriculum.

This Module also teaches two general LSAT skills: conditionals and argument parts. These general skills are useful on Inference and Justify problems, and these problem types are a great place to practice these skills. You will also work with conditionals and argument parts across the LSAT, including in the Games and Reading Comprehension sections. These skill chapters reflect the most recent trends in the LSAT. Unfortunately, most LSAT curricula do not teach conditionals accurately.

Part of Power Tutoring

All Modules are designed to be used as a part of Power Tutoring. Your PrepNexus schedule contains Sessions that walk you through this Module optimally. Your Tutor will also guide you through this Module to ensure that you learn and improve quickly.

Drills, Problems, and Length

The Linking Module contains 25 drill problems and 119 official Logical Reasoning problems from recent tests. It takes the average student 11.5 hours to read the chapters and complete and review all the problems. Power Tutoring is built on custom scheduling. Your Tutor will tailor how you interact with this Module, the pace at which you work, and what parts of it you complete.

Chapters

1. Logical Reasoning Introduction: Before you enter the Linking Skill Group, learn the importance of the Logical Reasoning (or LR) section, the parts of each LR problem, and the LR Skill Groups.

2. Linking Diagnostic: This timed problem set tests your initial abilities on Inference and Justify problems. Your tutor relies on this diagnostic to tailor your prep in the Linking Skill Group.

3. Conditionals: This is a general LSAT skill chapter. It will teach you how to understand and work with conditionals, a precise reasoning relationship. Conditionals show up across the LSAT and a great deal in the Linking Skill Group.

4. Inference: This is a problem type chapter. Inference problems ask you to draw a deduction from a group of facts. Learn techniques to approach these problems, and then practice them extensively with drills and three types of problem sets, each with unique goals.

5. Argument Parts: In this general skill chapter, you will learn how to identify the conclusion, support, and other parts of an argument. Identifying argument parts is a skill you will use on a majority of LR problems.

6. Justify: Justify problems ask you to link two unconnected concepts in an argument and make the argument valid. Learn and practice techniques for this common and important problem type.

7. Linking Practice Sets: Use these short problem sets to hone all the Linking Skills you have built in chapters three through six.

8. Linking Test: This timed problem set measures your improvement on the Linking Skill Group and helps your Tutor plan your upcoming Logical Reasoning prep.

Logical Reasoning Introduction

Learn about Logical Reasoning, the most important section on the LSAT. This chapter will prepare you to begin the Linking Skill group.

Chapter Contents

Logical Reasoning Basics

Stem

Stimulus

Choices

Logical Reasoning Skill Groups

Linking Skill Group Overview

Introduction

This chapter will introduce you to the Logical Reasoning (or LR) section of the LSAT. It will walk you through basic information about the LR section and then discuss the three parts of each Logical Reasoning problem: the stimulus, stem, and choices. This chapter concludes with a discussion on the four LR Skill Groups in this curriculum and a detailed overview of the Linking Skill Group.

Logical Reasoning Basics

To start, let's talk about the importance of the Logical Reasoning section, look at an example LR problem, and then talk about all there is to learn from the LR section.

Logical Reasoning is the most important kind of section on the LSAT. Of the four scored sections on the LSAT, *two* are LR sections. On a typical LSAT, one Logical Reasoning section has 25 problems, and the other LR section has 26 problems. That means you'll see 51 LR problems out of a total of 101 problems on the LSAT, so Logical Reasoning accounts for half of your LSAT score! For this reason, your Power Tutoring will focus a great deal on developing your Logical Reasoning skills. During your prep, always remember that Logical Reasoning is king.

Problem Parts

Every Logical Reasoning problem has three parts: the stimulus, the stem, and the choices. Take a look at this example LR problem below:

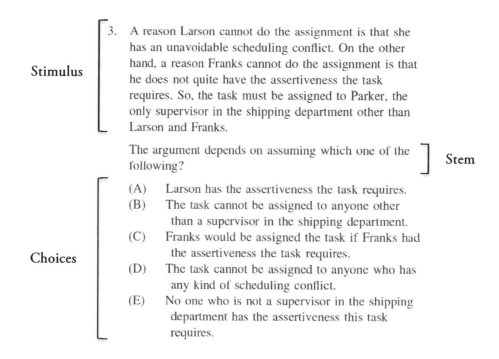

Stimulus

3. A reason Larson cannot do the assignment is that she has an unavoidable scheduling conflict. On the other hand, a reason Franks cannot do the assignment is that he does not quite have the assertiveness the task requires. So, the task must be assigned to Parker, the only supervisor in the shipping department other than Larson and Franks.

The argument depends on assuming which one of the following? Stem

Choices

(A)   Larson has the assertiveness the task requires.
(B)   The task cannot be assigned to anyone other than a supervisor in the shipping department.
(C)   Franks would be assigned the task if Franks had the assertiveness the task requires.
(D)   The task cannot be assigned to anyone who has any kind of scheduling conflict.
(E)   No one who is not a supervisor in the shipping department has the assertiveness this task requires.

The <u>stimulus</u> contains a paragraph or two to analyze, and the <u>stem</u> asks you a question about the stimulus. One out of the five <u>choices</u> correctly answers the question asked by the stem. The other four choices are incorrect.

Mentally Shift Gears

Each Logical Reasoning problem is a separate little puzzle. New information comes in the stimulus, a set of facts or an argument that you must analyze. In each LR problem, you're asked to perform a task with the information in the stimulus. The stem may ask you to infer a new fact, identify a missing link in the logic, describe a flaw in the argument, etc. The correct choice does that task correctly. There are a limited number of tasks, and each one represents one of the 12 different LR problem types.

Remember there are 51 LR problems per LSAT. That means you're going to have 51 stimuli to dissect, 51 tasks to perform with those stimuli, and 51 correct choices to locate. We will give you the tools you need to maximize your number of correct answers on each LR section. However, notice how much mental processing you'll need to do as you go through the two LR sections. You'll have to critically analyze 51 stimuli. That's a lot of gear-switching!

Deal with Pressure

And what's more, you have 35 minutes per section of 25 or 26 LR problems. So, not only are you mentally switching between tasks to answer each problem, but you also must do so within a tight time constraint. Taking this time pressure into account, it's important to be able to switch gears quickly and to pace yourself appropriately. You'll develop all these skills in your course so they'll be automatic on test day.

Just as the LR section tests your reasoning skills, it also tests your ability to deal with in-test stress. Facing 51 problems with unique stimuli that test your ability to do 12 different tasks, your brain is going to be jumping through a lot of hoops. But after our thorough and personalized course, you'll be ready for the challenges of the Logical Reasoning section. Just know as you move forward that the LSAT is mentally taxing, and the two LR sections are a great place to build your mental endurance and ability to stay calm under pressure.

The Smart Place to Start Prep

When students take their first diagnostic LSAT, it's common to score a lower percentage correct in the Logic Games section than the LR section because Games is initially the most foreign section. Even so, most students have far more points to gain in the LR section because there are two LR sections per LSAT, and each LR section has more problems than the Games section. A typical Games section has 23 problems, compared to the 51 LR problems.

Because Logical Reasoning comprises half of the LSAT, it is a powerhouse for improving your score. It's also great for building universal LSAT skills such as breaking down arguments, working with abstract logic, understanding conditionals, pacing, switching gears, and keeping a cool head under the pressure of the test. Thus, your foray into LSAT prep starts with this important section.

Order of Approach

In this LR curriculum, you will learn to approach the parts of a Logical Reasoning problem in this order: read the stem first, then analyze the stimulus, and finally work the choices. Let's look at each of the three parts in detail, starting with the question stem.

Stem

The question stem assigns your task for the problem; it asks you to perform a certain action with the information in the stimulus. Consider the stem from the example problem we looked at earlier:

> The argument depends on assuming which one of the following?

This stem asks you to find an assumption in the stimulus.

When you approach a LR problem, *always read the question stem first*. When you know what to do with the stimulus, you can approach it more effectively because you'll know what to look for in the stimulus. The alternative approach is to read the stimulus, read the stem, and then return to the stimulus to do the task. That is a less efficient method of approaching an LR problem although some LSAT companies (ahem, Testmasters) will teach you that method.

Stems boil down to 12 different actions you need to complete, and these are the 12 different LR problem types. Certain indicator words in the stem tell you the problem type. When you can identify the different types, then you know which techniques apply to each problem.

In the example LR problem from before, the stem asks you to determine an assumption integral to the argument. This is a Necessary Assumption problem, and there are specific techniques to use and patterns that show up in this problem type. The moment you understand your task from the stem, you call to mind those techniques and patterns. This is a key for improvement on the LR section. Once you recognize a problem type, you can use the techniques that help you solve it accurately and quickly.

Stem Stamp

When you identify the problem type, write the type abbreviation next to the stem (we will teach you the abbreviations). This is called a Stem Stamp. This shorthand annotation is a simple and effective means of reminding yourself exactly what type of actions to take for a problem type. The abbreviation also makes sure you only need to read the question stem once.

For instance, the stem below is for a Necessary Assumption problem because it asks you to select the assumption that's required for the argument to be true. Naturally, the abbreviation for Necessary Assumption problems is "na," so the stem stamp will look like this:

na   The argument depends on assuming which one of the following?

As for lowercase versus uppercase, write whichever comes naturally to you. Throughout the curriculum we use lowercase, but this is arbitrary—the only one that's "better" is whichever you prefer.

Using Stem Stamps will help you use the proper techniques for each LR problem. Because you Stem stamp every Necessary Assumption problem the same way, each time you stamp a new stem you mentally activate the techniques for that type. This is also true for the other 11 types of problem you'll face. We'll reinforce the stem-technique connection in several of the problem sets that follow the techniques for each problem type.

Stimulus

The stimulus contains the meat of an LR problem, a paragraph or two of new information you need to analyze. Here's the stimulus from the example problem before:

> A reason Larson cannot do the assignment is that she has an unavoidable scheduling conflict. On the other hand, a reason Franks cannot do the assignment is that he does not quite have the assertiveness the task requires. So, the task must be assigned to Parker, the only supervisor in the shipping department other than Larson and Franks.

When you get to the stimulus, you'll already know your task from reading the question stem. As a consequence, you'll know exactly how to work with the new information. Let's turn to specific aspects of stimuli, starting with arguments versus fact groups.

Arguments vs. Fact Groups

Logical Reasoning stimuli come in two broad flavors: arguments or fact groups. Arguments have a conclusion; there's a "main point." Other parts of the argument support that conclusion. Here's a simple argument:

> The LSAT score is by far the most important element of a law school application. Therefore, if you want to get into a great law school, you should study hard to get a great LSAT score.

The conclusion in this argument is that you should study hard to get a good LSAT score. The statement about how important the LSAT is in law school admissions provides support for the conclusion. Essentially, it helps to justify the conclusion. We'll take a deeper look at the conclusion and support dynamic shortly.

A fact group is just a group of related facts or statements. Here is an example:

> Active volcanoes in Iceland can have a severe impact on global weather. Last year, the storm pattern called El Niño was the largest it's been in years.

Unlike an argument, there's no conclusion in a fact group, so there is no support either. You could *infer* a main point by adding up the information present to conclude something not stated. With the fact group above, for example, you can infer that Icelandic volcanoes are responsible for the extreme El Niño last year. However, the fact group itself never says that.

Arguments are much more common than fact groups. About 80% of stimuli are arguments, and only 20% are fact groups. Arguments inherently have more complex logical relationships, so it makes sense that the LSAT writers use them as the foundation of LR questions a great deal more often than fact groups.

The difference between arguments and fact groups becomes important when you are asked to perform tasks on a stimulus. The good news is that arguments appear *exclusively* with certain problem types, while fact groups appear exclusively with different problem types. The techniques for each problem type naturally address whether or not the stimulus is an argument or fact group.

Let's turn now to specific elements of an argument: the *conclusion* and its *support*.

Argument Parts: Conclusion and Support

Later in this Module, there is an in-depth chapter on argument parts. This section offers a quick overview of argument parts to prime your understanding.

Arguments are made up of a conclusion and evidence provided as support for the conclusion. The <u>conclusion</u> is the argument's main point; it's the central idea of the argument.

The <u>support</u> for the conclusion is any justification or evidence for the conclusion. Sometimes in LR stems or choices, you'll see the support referred to as "premises." That's just a fancy way of saying "support." A "premise" refers to one piece of support, and "premises" refers to several pieces of support.

Here is a simple argument:

> We shouldn't take the dogs to the park today because the park is covered in fresh snow.

The conclusion is "we shouldn't take the dogs to the park today." The support, or justification, for that idea is that "the park is covered in fresh snow." The support gives you a reason to believe the conclusion.

The arguments in LR stimuli are longer and much more complex. Often, it is not easy to identify the different argument parts. To do so, read the argument carefully, and watch the flow of information. When you are finished reading it, identify the conclusion. The rest of the argument should build to it. Then, locate the support as a check to see that you have identified the conclusion correctly. This process will be covered in greater depth later in this Module.

After you analyze the stimulus, the next step in working an LR problem is to evaluate the choices.

Choices

Every problem on the LSAT presents you with five answer choices. Logical Reasoning, Logic Games, and Reading Comprehension questions all follow this pattern. Working the choices is an incredibly important skill to build. In this section, we'll give broad guidance on how to best work the choices on an LR problem.

Here are the choices from the earlier example problem:

(A)   Larson has the assertiveness the task requires.
(B)   The task cannot be assigned to anyone other than a supervisor in the shipping department.
(C)   Franks would be assigned the task if Franks had the assertiveness the task requires.
(D)   The task cannot be assigned to anyone who has any kind of scheduling conflict.
(E)   No one who is not a supervisor in the shipping department has the assertiveness this task requires.

Only one of these choices is correct; the other four are all incorrect. It may seem like there's a lot of information to wade through here, but you'll see that, by implementing the proper techniques, you can cut through it all relatively quickly.

Sometimes the stem will ask you to select which of the choices is *most* correct as if there are degrees of correctness. This is misleading because there is only one correct answer. The other four choices are definitely wrong. Our curriculum will give you everything you need to figure out exactly which choice is correct and which four are not.

Eliminate

On many LR problem types, a key technique to locate the correct answer is to first identify and eliminate the choices that are definitely *not* the correct answer. This process is called <u>elimination</u>, and it's the first step for dealing with many Logical Reasoning choices. It's often easier to see why incorrect choices are wrong than why the correct choice is right, so elimination narrows down the choices that you must analyze in depth. This technique improves your accuracy.

There will usually be two to four choices that clearly do not fulfill the problem's task. We call these duds. Through elimination, you cross these off and reduce the total number of choices you must consider. With a solid understanding of the stimulus and task, you can often eliminate four choices, leaving only the correct answer.

If you don't eliminate any choices, you are prone to select the first attractive choice that comes along. *The LSAT-writers are aware of this bad habit.* They will try to use this against you at times, perhaps providing an early answer choice that's very attractive while the correct answer choice comes at the end of the list as (D) or (E).

Using elimination to weed out the clearly incorrect choices first ensures that you consider all of the choices. When you dedicate a little time to analyze how each of the choices may be incorrect, you won't accidentally miss the correct choice because you selected another choice and moved on before getting to it.

In our Problem Set explanations, we cross off the incorrect answers just as you will in the elimination process:

(A)   Larson has the assertiveness the task requires.
(B)   The task cannot be assigned to anyone other than a supervisor in the shipping department.
(C)   Franks would be assigned the task if Franks had the assertiveness the task requires.
(D)   The task cannot be assigned to anyone who has any kind of scheduling conflict.
(E)   No one who is not a supervisor in the shipping department has the assertiveness this task requires.

In the example above, the majority of the choices were eliminated. (B) and (E) both made it out of the Elimination step because they're both possible correct choices. In the end, (B) won out in the Confirmation step, which we'll turn to now.

Confirm

Once you've eliminated choices, you'll be left with one or two choices that need to be considered further. If there are two choices, you'll have to analyze the two to decide which is the correct answer. There are different ways to confirm a correct answer depending on the problem type, but a useful rule of thumb is to check each remaining choice against the task and the stimulus. If you are left with a single choice after the elimination step, then your job is to confirm that it correctly answers the question.

Only one choice will effectively perform the task asked by the stem, and that is, of course, the correct choice. Circle the choice and move onto the next problem.

Be Critical

Always keep a critical eye on the choices. Picture the <u>LSAT writers</u>, the people designing the problems and choices, as spiders trying to trap you in their webs. They do their best to trick you in each question. They're actually taught how to build effective "distractors" into the questions they write.

One such distraction is creating two choices that are very similar even though they are opposites of each other. If you're looking for one of these choices, you might accidentally select the choice that contains the opposite of what you need to complete the task. For instance, you need to strengthen the argument, and the writers provide a very attractive choice that uses the correct elements of the argument to *weaken* the argument's conclusion. If you forget your task for a moment, you might be tempted to select this choice because it addresses the argument in a way you expected.

Many test takers will take the bait and mark this trap choice as correct. They fall right into the writers' web. But don't worry, we'll teach you how identify and handle all of their common traps. Simply using the eliminate and confirm steps will get you started on the right foot.

With an understanding of the three parts of an LR problem and how to approach them, let's now look at the specific skills that will be tested as you work through the Logical Reasoning section.

Logical Reasoning Skill Groups

The different types of problems you'll see on the Logical Reasoning section require you to use one of four key skills: Linking, Understanding Flaws, Describe Arguments, and Compare Arguments. All problem types are grouped according to the skill they test. For instance, Inference and Justify problems both test your ability to *link* pieces of information. Thus, they are together in the Linking Module, so you can develop your higher-level linking skills as you learn and practice the specific techniques for each problem type.

The beauty of the Skill Group system is that you build broad LSAT skills as you learn specific techniques for each problem type. Progress takes place on two fronts. As you learn and practice the Inference techniques, you're learning what to do when you see an Inference problem, and you're also developing your Linking skills. When you get to Justify problems, you develop your Justify techniques, and at the same time you improve, refine, and revisit the same Linking skills you began to develop in the Inference chapter. This process takes place in each of the four LR Skill Groups. Let's briefly take a look at each now.

Linking

Linking is the first Skill Group. There are two problem types that ask you to use your Linking skill set. Each of these types presents you with information, and you must link pieces of that information to get the correct answer—hence the name "Linking."

<u>Inference</u> problems ask you to understand a fact group and select the choice that can be properly inferred from that information.

<u>Justify</u> problems ask you to understand an argument, locate the gap in its reasoning, and then find the choice that links the information on both sides of the gap (like putting in a clasp to link up two sides of a broken chain). In so doing, you link the two unlinked concepts in the argument and make it airtight.

Linking problems make up 25% of the Logical Reasoning section. On a typical LSAT, you can expect about 13 problems from the Linking Skill Group across the two LR sections.

Understand Flaw

The Understand Flaw Skill Group is by far the largest. These problem types make up 46% of the LR section (about 23 problems). In this group, your success rides on your ability to spot and understand the <u>flaw</u> in the argument. There's a limited number of ways that a stimulus can be flawed. Seven types of flaws appear over and over again in LR arguments, so spotting and describing the flaw in an argument is not as hard as it might sound. We will discuss each of the ways an argument can be flawed in depth in the second LR Module.

As for the different tasks you're asked to perform with the flawed arguments, there are four different problem types in the Understand Flaw Skill Group:

Flaw problems are straightforward; you must describe how the argument is flawed. Once you find the flaw, you're one very short step from the correct choice.

Weaken/Strengthen problems ask you to either Weaken or Strengthen the argument. This is done easily if you leverage the flaw in the argument. The flaw is a weak point in the argument, right? To make an argument weaker (in a Weaken problem), you'll select the choice that points out or uses the flaw to weaken the argument.

Necessary Assumption problems ask you to select the choice that states an assumption that is required for the argument to be true. This crucial assumption is directly linked to the flaw in the argument. After all, an assumption is information that an argument assumes to be true without explicitly stating it.

Explain the Paradox problems asks you to explain how a pair of facts in the stimulus, which seem to conflict with each other, are both actually true. Your ability to Explain the Paradox hinges on seeing the way the information is misrepresented to seem conflicting when it is not.

Describe Argument

The Describe Argument Skill Group is made up of problems that ask you to describe parts of an argument or the structure of the entire argument. These three problem types make up 13% of the LR section (~7 problems).

Conclusion problems ask you to identify the argument's conclusion. In order to do so, you must understand the reasoning of the argument.

Role problems ask you to precisely describe the role of a specific part of an argument. You might be asked to describe the role of a support piece, background information, or the argument's conclusion.

Argument Structure problems ask you to describe (you guessed it) the argument's structure. The correct choice to an Argument Structure problem describes how the argument proceeds in abstract terms, so it might say something like "the argument offers a supporting premise, which leads to a second premise, which, taken together, lead to the conclusion."

Compare Arguments

The final Skill Group, Compare Arguments, requires you to understand and work with two or more arguments. The three types in this Skill Group make up about 16% of the LR sections (~8 problems).

Matching problems, a notorious problem type, ask you to understand the argument in the stimulus and then find the choice that has a similar reasoning structure. Each choice is an argument, only one of which matches the argument's reasoning in the stimulus.

Disagree/Agree problems ask you to compare two speakers' arguments to determine what piece of information that they disagree or agree about.

Principle problems ask you to compare a principle to its application or to distill a principle from a situation. They are a bit of an outlier in this group.

Manageable Patterns

Looking at the LR section as a test of these four key skills makes it much more manageable. Even though there are 51 LR problems, the LSAT writers can only be so creative. They adhere to a strict set of patterns when they create problems. The writers might try to hide their patterns, but we've reverse-engineered them through deep analysis of recent LSATs (and perhaps we understand them better than the writers do themselves). This is the knowledge, the patterns, and the techniques to beat them that the curriculum Modules teach you.

How the Skill Groups Are Taught

Let's talk about how the curriculum teaches you a Skill Group. First, you take a Diagnostic to measure your starting abilities for the Skill Group. It is composed of the problem types in the group. Your diagnostic score helps your Tutor optimize how you spend your prep time across the different Skill Groups, so take each Skill Group Diagnostic seriously in order to provide accurate data for your Tutor.

After we have a baseline measure of your abilities for the Skill Group, it's time to improve them. To do this, you will complete chapters that teach you the problem types and skills tested by the Skill Group. For example, the Linking Group has these four chapters: Conditionals (a skill), Inference Problems (a problem type), Argument Parts (a skill), and Justify Problems (a problem type).

The problem type chapters have extensive and varied practice to help you master the type. This practice includes drills and three different kinds of problem sets. The variety of practice not only boosts your skills rapidly, but it also keeps your prep stimulating and engaging.

After you complete all the chapters for a Skill Group, you will practice all the types in the Skill Group to further reinforce the skills you have built. Finally, you will take a Skill Group Test to measure your progress. This score should be markedly higher than that of your Skill Group Diagnostic. The Tests represent important milestones in your prep. Your Tutor will use your results from each test to determine where to give you additional practice in the Skill Group later in your course.

Linking Skill Group Overview

Before we discuss the chapters in this Skill Group, it's important to understand a basic idea that goes into any act of Linking. In order to link, you must first have two unconnected concepts. Those concepts are then linked together using a third concept, the link. For instance, your friend says, "I'm about to play in a football game. We need to buy skittles!" Those are two concepts that don't really connect. But then he adds the link, "During football games, I eat skittles at half time for energy." This information ties the other two pieces together logically.

The two problem types in the Linking Skill Group test your ability to understanding linking. Let's take a brief look at each skill and type chapter in this Module.

Conditionals (Skill)

A Conditional is a specific logical relationship where you're told that one condition will lead to another condition. An example is "if it rains, the soccer game will be canceled." The first condition is it raining. When that condition is met, that "triggers" the second condition, the game being canceled. Using the conditional, we know for a fact that, if it rains, then the game will be canceled. There is a lot more to conditionals that you will learn in the upcoming chapter.

The Conditionals chapter teaches you how to understand and work with conditionals, including how to link several conditionals together. This is important background knowledge because conditionals often crop up on Inference and Justify problems, and they also appear in other LR types and in the Games section. Consequently, this is an important introductory chapter.

Inference (Problem Type)

Recall that Inference problems ask you to identify which piece of information can be properly inferred, or deduced, from the information provided. The stimulus is a fact group, and you must see a valid link formed from two facts within it that gives rise to a third, previously unstated fact. In the choices, you're given a number of potential inferences, and only one is correct.

This chapter will teach you techniques to approach Inference problems and then thoroughly hone your skills with drills and three Inference problem sets.

Argument Parts (Skill)

This chapter teaches you how to identify the conclusion and support in complex arguments. Targeted drills support the techniques for understanding arguments. This is a skill that you will use on 80% of LR problems, all those that have arguments for stimuli. You start to practice breaking down arguments in full problems in the Justify chapter.

Justify (Problem Type)

In Justify problems, your task is to justify the argument's reasoning by finding the choice that links two key pieces of the argument together, typically a support piece and the argument's conclusion. While this may seem like an argument skill—and it is, at least in part—it's also very much a Linking skill. Like the Inference chapter, this chapter will teach you the patterns to recognize in Justify problems and then hone your skills through drills and problem sets.

Logical Reasoning Introduction Review

Every content-based chapter in the curriculum includes a Review section. These are a great way to check your understanding after reading the chapter.

Logical Reasoning Basics

- LR is the most important section because the two LR sections make up half of your LSAT score.

- The LR challenges you to do different tasks and stay calm under timing pressure. This section builds core LSAT skills, so it is a good place to start your LSAT prep.

- Approach each LR problem by reading the stem first to understand your task, then analyzing the stimulus with your task in mind, and finally working the choices.

Stem

- The stem asks you to perform an action with the stimulus.

- Read the stem first, before the stimulus, when you complete an LR problem. Knowing your task informs how you approach the stimulus.

- A Stem Stamp is an abbreviation for the problem type that you write next to the stem. Writing the Stem Stamp mentally activates the techniques for the problem type.

Stimulus

- The stimulus is a paragraph or two of new information to analyze.

- Most stimuli are arguments, which means they have a conclusion and support. About one in five stimuli are fact groups: a set of related facts that has no main point.

Choices

- For each LSAT question, there is a single correct answer choice that correctly does the task asked for in the stem. There are four definitely incorrect choices.

- When working the choices, first eliminate those that are clearly incorrect. This ensures that you see every choice, and it is often easier to see why an incorrect choice is wrong than why the correct choice is right.

- After the eliminate step, you might be left with two choices. Use the stimulus and analysis of the choices to confirm the correct one. If you are left with a single choice after the confirm step, just make sure that it is correct.

- Be critical on the choices. The LSAT writers create tempting incorrect choices.

Logical Reasoning Skill Groups

- There are four main skills tested on the Logical Reasoning section, and these group together related problem types and skills.

- <u>Linking</u> – Work with linking concepts in the stimulus, either in an Inference or a Justify problem.

- <u>Understand Flaw</u> – Spot and understand the flaw in an argument. Problem types in this Skill Group include Flaw, Weaken/Strengthen, Necessary Assumption, and Explain the Paradox.

- <u>Describe Argument</u> – Describe an argument or one of its parts. These problem types include Conclusion, Role, and Argument Structure.

- <u>Compare Arguments</u> – Compare arguments in a Matching, Disagree/Agree, or Principle problem.

2 Linking Diagnostic

Complete a timed diagnostic to measure your current Linking abilities. Your Tutor will use this information to optimize your Logical Reasoning prep.

Chapter Contents
Skill Group Diagnostic Introduction
Linking Diagnostic

Skill Group Diagnostics

Each Skill Group begins with a Skill Group Diagnostic. These short tests of 7-10 problems are a mix of Logical Reasoning problem types from the upcoming Skill Group. For instance, this Linking Diagnostic is made of Inference and Justify problems. In this way, Skill Group Diagnostics measure your initial abilities on each Skill Group before you hone your skills on the Skill Group.

Used to Optimize Your Prep

This baseline score helps your Tutor guide your prep as you learn a Skill Group. If you are relatively weak on this Linking Skill Group, for example, you will be assigned deeper practice to be sure that you boost these important skills. Your Tutor needs to know your starting abilities for each Skill Group to guide you through the prep for that Skill Group most effectively.

The Skill Group Diagnostics also measure your improvement at the end of a Skill Group. After you work through all the chapters on the skills and types in a Skill Group, you will take the Skill Group Test. Your Tutor will compare your Test score to your Diagnostic score. The Diagnostics and Tests have the same average problem difficulty, so the results on each are directly comparable. This gives your Tutor a precise understanding of how much your skills developed during the Skill Group prep. If a certain skill is lagging behind your normal rate of improvement, we know you need to focus on developing that skill or adjust your prep in other ways.

Pacing and Timing

During the official LSAT, you may only use an analog watch to pace yourself on each section; digital watches are not allowed. The LSAT administrators are worried you'll have a James Bond style digital watch that is taking pictures of each page of the test and emailing them to your friends who will soon take the test in the Hawaii time zone.

For every timed exercise throughout your prep, you should use an analog watch to pace yourself. This will make sure you are comfortable pacing that way on your official LSAT. Generally, you want your practice to match the official test experience as closely as possible. This is one example of that. If you don't have an analog watch, go buy one! There are inexpensive options on Amazon.

To make pacing with an analog watch easy, set the minute hand on your watch to 12 at the beginning of a section. That way, you can easily see how many minutes have elapsed during the section because there's no need to subtract the current time from your start time. This is a great pacing habit for the official LSAT.

During the official LSAT, your proctor will call out when time is done. This is an external source of notification for the end of a section. Your watch will not give you that, so you need to mimic that, too. Set a timer on your phone or a digital kitchen timer to alert you when time is up on this Linking Diagnostic. Pace with your watch, but set a timer to know when time is up.

Once you have your watch, timer, and a pencil ready, begin the Diagnostic.

Linking Diagnostic

Directions

- <u>Time Limit:</u> There is a 13-minute time limit for this 10-problem set. Pace with your watch and set a timer. Guess on any problems you do not reach, just as you will on the official LSAT.

- <u>Don't rush:</u> Give each question you attempt a thorough analysis.

- <u>Bubble Sheet:</u> Like all timed sets, fill in your answers in the bubble sheet for this Test Set.

- <u>Review:</u> Do not review the problems in this set. We are only interested in the score here.

1. Parent: Pushing very young children into rigorous study in an effort to make our nation more competitive does more harm than good. Curricula for these young students must address their special developmental needs, and while rigorous work in secondary school makes sense, the same approach in the early years of primary school produces only short-term gains and may cause young children to burn out on schoolwork. Using very young students as pawns in the race to make the nation economically competitive is unfair and may ultimately work against us.

   Which one of the following can be inferred from the parent's statements?

   (A) For our nation to be competitive, our secondary school curriculum must include more rigorous study than it now does.

   (B) The developmental needs of secondary school students are not now being addressed in our high schools.

   (C) Our country can be competitive only if the developmental needs of all our students can be met.

   (D) A curriculum of rigorous study does not adequately address the developmental needs of primary school students.

   (E) Unless our nation encourages more rigorous study in the early years of primary school, we cannot be economically competitive.

2. Counselor: Hagerle sincerely apologized to the physician for lying to her. So Hagerle owes me a sincere apology as well, because Hagerle told the same lie to both of us.

   Which one of the following principles, if valid, most helps to justify the counselor's reasoning?

   (A) It is good to apologize for having done something wrong to a person if one is capable of doing so sincerely.

   (B) If someone tells the same lie to two different people, then neither of those lied to is owed an apology unless both are.

   (C) Someone is owed a sincere apology for having been lied to by a person if someone else has already received a sincere apology for the same lie from that same person.

   (D) If one is capable of sincerely apologizing to someone for lying to them, then one owes that person such an apology.

   (E) A person should not apologize to someone for telling a lie unless he or she can sincerely apologize to all others to whom the lie was told.

3. "Hot spot" is a term that ecologists use to describe those habitats with the greatest concentrations of species found only in one place—so-called "endemic" species. Many of these hot spots are vulnerable to habitat loss due to commercial development. Furthermore, loss of endemic species accounts for most modern-day extinctions. Thus, given that only a limited number of environmental battles can be waged, it would be reasonable for organizations dedicated to preserving species to _____.

Which one of the following most logically completes the argument?

(A) try to help only those species who are threatened with extinction because of habitat loss

(B) concentrate their resources on protecting hot spot habitats

(C) treat all endemic species as equally valuable and equally in need of preservation

(D) accept that most endemic species will become extinct

(E) expand the definition of "hot spot" to include vulnerable habitats that are not currently home to many endangered species

4. The government is being urged to prevent organizations devoted to certain views on human nutrition from advocating a diet that includes large portions of uncooked meat, because eating uncooked meat can be very dangerous. However, this purported fact does not justify the government's silencing the groups, for surely the government would not be justified in silencing a purely political group merely on the grounds that the policies the group advocates could be harmful to some members of society. The same should be true for silencing groups with certain views on human nutrition.

Which one of the following principles most helps to justify the reasoning in the argument?

(A) The government should not silence any group for advocating a position that a significant proportion of society believes to be beneficial.

(B) The government ought to do whatever is in the best interest of society.

(C) One ought to advocate a position only if one believes that it is true or would be beneficial.

(D) The government ought not to silence an opinion merely on the grounds that it could be harmful to disseminate the opinion.

(E) One ought to urge the government to do only those things the government is justified in doing.

5. There are 70 to 100 Florida panthers alive today. This represents a very large increase over their numbers in the 1970s, but their population must reach at least 250 if it is to be self-sustaining. Their current habitat is not large enough to support any more of these animals, however.

If the statements above are true, which one of the following must also be true?

(A) Some part of the panthers' current habitat is only of marginal quality.

(B) If the population of Florida panthers ever exceeds 250, it will be self-sustaining.

(C) Unless Florida panthers acquire a larger habitat, their population will not be self-sustaining.

(D) The population of Florida panthers will never increase much beyond its current level.

(E) Today, Florida panthers occupy a larger habitat than they did in the 1970s.

6. Editorial: One of our local television stations has been criticized for its recent coverage of the personal problems of a local politician's nephew, but the coverage was in fact good journalism. The information was accurate. Furthermore, the newscast had significantly more viewers than it normally does, because many people are curious about the politician's nephew's problems.

Which one of the following principles, if valid, would most help to justify the reasoning in the editorial?

(A) Journalism deserves to be criticized if it does not provide information that people want.

(B) Any journalism that intentionally misrepresents the facts of a case deserves to be criticized.

(C) Any journalism that provides accurate information on a subject about which there is considerable interest is good journalism.

(D) Good journalism will always provide people with information that they desire or need.

(E) Journalism that neither satisfies the public's curiosity nor provides accurate information can never be considered good journalism.

7. Small experimental vacuum tubes can operate in heat that makes semiconductor components fail. Any component whose resistance to heat is greater than that of semiconductors would be preferable for use in digital circuits, but only if that component were also comparable to semiconductors in all other significant respects, such as maximum current capacity. However, vacuum tubes' maximum current capacity is presently not comparable to that of semiconductors.

If the statements above are true, which one of the following must also be true?

(A) Vacuum tubes are not now preferable to semiconductors for use in digital circuits.

(B) Once vacuum tubes and semiconductors have comparable maximum current capacity, vacuum tubes will be used in some digital circuits.

(C) The only reason that vacuum tubes are not now used in digital circuits is that vacuum tubes' maximum current capacity is too low.

(D) Semiconductors will always be preferable to vacuum tubes for use in many applications other than digital circuits.

(E) Resistance to heat is the only advantage that vacuum tubes have over semiconductors.

8. One child pushed another child from behind, injuring the second child. The first child clearly understands the difference between right and wrong, so what was done was wrong if it was intended to injure the second child.

Which one of the following principles, if valid, most helps to justify the reasoning in the argument?

(A) An action that is intended to harm another person is wrong only if the person who performed the action understands the difference between right and wrong.

(B) It is wrong for a person who understands the difference between right and wrong to intentionally harm another person.

(C) Any act that is wrong is done with the intention of causing harm.

(D) An act that harms another person is wrong if the person who did it understands the difference between right and wrong and did not think about whether the act would injure the other person.

(E) A person who does not understand the difference between right and wrong does not bear any responsibility for harming another person.

9. Members of the VideoKing Frequent Viewers club can now receive a special discount coupon. Members of the club who have rented more than ten videos in the past month can receive the discount coupon only at the VideoKing location from which the member last rented a movie. Members of the Frequent Viewers club who have not rented more than ten videos in the past month can receive the coupon only at the Main Street location. Pat, who has not rented more than ten videos in the past month, can receive the special discount coupon at the Walnut Lane location of VideoKing.

    If all of the statements above are true, which one of the following must be true?

    (A)   The only people who can receive the special discount coupon at the Main Street location are Frequent Viewers club members who have not rented more than ten videos.

    (B)   Some members of the Frequent Viewers club have not rented more than ten videos.

    (C)   Some members of the Frequent Viewers club can receive the special discount coupon at more than one location of VideoKing.

    (D)   Some people who are not members of the Frequent Viewers club can receive the special discount coupon.

    (E)   If Pat rents a movie from the Main Street location, then she will not receive the special discount coupon.

10. Ethicist: Only when we know a lot about the events that led to an action are we justified in praising or blaming a person for that action—as we sometimes are. We must therefore reject Tolstoy's rash claim that if we knew a lot about the events leading up to any action, we would cease to regard that action as freely performed.

    Which one of the following, if assumed, enables the conclusion of the ethicist's argument to be properly drawn?

    (A)   People should not be regarded as subject to praise or blame for actions that were caused by conditions beyond their control.

    (B)   Whether an act is one for which the person doing it is genuinely responsible is not determined by how much information others possess about that act.

    (C)   We can be justified in praising or blaming a person for an action only when we regard that action as freely performed.

    (D)   The responsibility a person bears for an action is not a matter of degree; however, our inclination to blame or praise whoever performed the action varies with the amount of information available.

    (E)   If we do not know much about the events leading up to any given action, we will regard that action as freely performed.

END OF SET

Linking Diagnostic Answer Key

Correct the set with the Answer Key below. Do not review these problems because you will reuse them later in your course. That practice will be less valuable later if you thoroughly analyze these problems now.

1. D
2. C
3. B
4. D
5. C
6. C
7. A
8. B
9. D
10. C

3 Conditionals

A conditional is a specific logical relationship between two conditions where one condition triggers the other to occur. Understanding conditionals is a key Logical Reasoning skill. You will work with conditionals on many problem types and often in Inference and Justify problems, which is why you are learning them now.

Chapter Contents

Conditional Logic
Conditional Indicators
Sufficient Indicators
Necessary Indicators
When to Diagram Conditionals
Quantifiers
Diagram Drill

Skill Tags

Sufficient Condition
Necessary Condition
Contrapositive
Contrapositive Choice

Introduction

This chapter will introduce a type of reasoning called Conditional Reasoning. Knowledge of conditionals is a skill that will help you often throughout the Logical Reasoning section, and it is also important on the Logic Games section of the exam. Roughly four to eight Logical Reasoning stimuli feature conditionals on each LSAT (~12% of the LR section), so we're teaching you this skill early. You will get to use your conditional reasoning abilities on the upcoming Inference and Justify problem types.

Conditional Logic

Conditional logic is a type of reasoning that is dependent on certain *conditions* being met. These conditions are often discussed with language such as 'if' and 'then.' A conditional relationship provides a guarantee; *if* one of the conditions is met, *then* the other condition will occur as well. Consider this example of a conditional relationship:

> If I can afford this sofa, I'll buy it.

This is a conditional precisely because one condition triggers another condition. "Affording to buy the sofa" triggers the act of buying it. There are two types of conditions: sufficient and necessary.

Sufficient and Necessary conditions are inherently linked; you can't have one without the other. A sufficient condition is one that's *enough* to bring about the outcome, while a necessary condition is something that's *required* by the particular situation.

A note on terminology: *sufficient* and *necessary* may seem like unnecessary jargon to describe these two ideas. Why not 'enough' and 'required' or something more conversational? Truth be told, we'd like a simpler alternative as well. However, the words sufficient and necessary show up in LSAT choices from time to time, and they can be confusing if you're not familiar and comfortable with them. Because of that, we're using the terms you'll see on the test, so when your test rolls around you'll be as comfortable with conditionals as possible.

Let's look at an example for clarification of sufficient and necessary conditions.

> If Steve goes outside, he will bring an umbrella.

This situation is very straightforward. There are two elements connected in a conditional relationship: outside and umbrella. Here's how you could diagram this relationship:

> Outside → Umbrella

> Sufficient → Necessary

"Outside" is the catalyst for "umbrella." It is "sufficient" to bring about the result, the necessary condition. Notice that these conditions are either going to happen or they won't. Steve can't partially go outside or sort of bring an umbrella. He is either outside or he is not, and he either leaves the umbrella behind or takes it with him. This relationship states that, when "outside" happens, it triggers "umbrella" to happen. If the sufficient (first) condition is met, then you know the necessary (second) condition is also met.

The <u>conditional diagram</u> is an excellent tool for visualizing a conditional relationship. It features both the sufficient and necessary conditions, and it takes a matter of seconds to write in the margin next to the stimulus.

In any conditional relationship, the sufficient condition is on the *left* of the diagram, and the necessary condition, the 'outcome,' is on the *right*. In our example, 'going outside' is sufficient, or enough, to bring about the condition in which Steve brings his umbrella. 'Going outside' is a catalyst for the second condition; it is the first domino in a line, and the umbrella is the second.

The second domino needs the first to fall before it can fall. He could bring an umbrella when he's not outside—he could just bring it everywhere around the house, in his office, and have it by his side at the local watering hole. Of course, these scenarios, based on the information we know from the conditional relationship, are all just speculation. But if the first domino does fall, then you know the second domino will fall, too. If Steve is outside, then you know *for a fact* he has his umbrella because of the conditional relationship.

Because the sufficient condition is always on the left and the necessary is always on the right, you can perform a sort of 'fill-in-the-blanks' for the trickier conditional relationships. If you're not quite sure which is the sufficient or necessary condition and which should go on which side of the arrow, you can use the context to help you out.

> I only bring my umbrella if I go outside.

With this statement, "only" is an indicator of a necessary condition (we'll get into all the buzzwords soon). So, you can put "umbrella" on the right side of the diagram and then fill in the other side with the remaining condition.

> Outside → Umbrella

Buzzwords are extremely helpful for conditionals; they not only indicate that a conditional relationship is used in the reasoning, but they also tell you which condition is sufficient and which is necessary. Consider how the word "never" factors into the conditional diagram if we add it to the example above:

> I never bring my umbrella if I go outside.

> Outside → –Umbrella

This diagram tells you in very few strokes of the pencil that, "If I'm outside, I do not have an umbrella."

In conditional diagramming, use a dash (–) to denote a negative condition (i.e. "not," "no," or "never") as in the example above. The dash allows you to properly read the relationship in all its positive or negative glory. It allows the diagram above to say, "If outside, then no umbrella." If it helps, think of the dash as a "negative" sign like the one used to denote negative numbers.

Inferences and the Contrapositive

Conditional statements allow you to infer certain outcomes based on the given information. First, though, it's important to note what these relationships do *not* tell you.

> If Steve goes outside, he will bring an umbrella.

> Outside → Umbrella

The conditional arrow only points in one direction, and it is only in that direction that you have your guarantee. This relationship thus tells you what happens when Steve goes outside, and that is all. When Steve goes outside, he brings an umbrella.

If Steve has an umbrella, does that mean he must be outside? No. All you know is what happens when Steve is outside. He could bring an umbrella around with him when he's inside a building, but you wouldn't know that from this conditional statement. The only thing you can infer is that, any time Steve *does not* have an umbrella, he is *not* outside. If the second condition is not met, you know the first did not occur because the first triggers the second. As a consequence, you get the negative version of this relationship:

> –Umbrella → –Outside

This is the <u>contrapositive</u>, the negative version, of the example. Every conditional relationship has a contrapositive relationship. For any conditional, you can infer the contrapositive by following these steps:

- Negate each conditions
- Reverse their locations in the diagram

By creating the contrapositive, the negated necessary condition becomes sufficient and vice versa. The contrapositive essentially says, "If the result did not occur, then the catalyst also did not occur." So, this contrapositive is read, "If Steve does not have an umbrella, he is not outside" or "Steve won't go outside without his umbrella." This is technically the same statement as the first, but it's just the contrapositive version.

Let's look at the implications of a different example:

> If it's not raining, I like to take an hour-long walk every morning.

> –Rain → Walk

If there's no rain, you know you can find me walking around at some point in the morning.

If it is raining, does that mean I won't go for a walk? No, it doesn't, but many test takers fall into conditional traps like this one. It appeals to your common sense that, if it's raining, I would not go for a walk, but this conditional statement does not say what happens when it rains, just what happens when it does rain. Maybe when it rains I go for a walk 50% of the time or one time in ten—you don't know. All you know is what happens when it does not rain.

The contrapositive, the negative version of this conditional statement, looks like this:

−Walk → Rain

Again, negate each term and then reverse their order to get the contrapositive.

This statement tells you that, when I do not go for a walk, it was raining. It does not tell you that I never go for a walk when it's raining. Instead, it just indicates some circumstances under which I would not go for a walk.

When crafting the contrapositive, you negate each side. Notice how that process happens in the example above, which features a negative condition. To negate the negative condition "no rain," all you have to do is make it into the positive statement "rain." In other words, you're negating the negative, which gives you a positive.

After all, the word 'contrapositive' is composed of two parts: contra-, which means opposite, and -positive, which is a form of the word 'position.' In taking the contrapositive, you're taking the 'opposite-position,' the negated and switched version of the conditional relationship.

Contrapositive of a Multi-Variable Condition

As you just saw, finding the contrapositive of a conditional relationship involves flipping the sufficient and necessary conditions and negating their signs. This process gets complicated when you have more than two variables in one condition.

For instance, try to craft the contrapositive for this statement:

If the food is hot and I'm in a good mood, then I'll eat.

The regular diagram would look like:

Hot food & Good mood → Eat

But how would the contrapositive shake out with that first sufficient clause, which contains two variables: "hot food" and "good mood"?

It turns out that, when you flip and negate a conditional relationship that has two variables in one condition, you also need to reverse the way the two variables are connected. In the example above, the two variables "hot food" and "good mood" are connected with "and," which means that both conditions must be met for the necessary condition to be met as well.

The contrapositive will connect both variables (which are now negated) with the opposite of "and," "or." The same is true when taking the contrapositive of a multi-variable condition that connects two variables with "or." The contrapositive would connect the negated variables with "and" instead.

The conditional relationship above thus has a contrapositive that looks like:

−Eat → −Hot food *or* −Good mood

If the speaker doesn't eat, then you know the food wasn't hot or she wasn't in a good mood, but you don't know *for certain* that both the food wasn't hot *and* she wasn't in a good mood. Because you don't know whether one, the other, or both of the variables were not met, you must use "or" instead of "and."

This is a small feature of conditional reasoning that, once learned, is easy to remember. It doesn't show up super often, so you'll only get to use it every now and then on the LSAT.

Contrapositive Choices

Some choices in LSAT problems use the contrapositive to try to trip you up. Instead of the answer you're looking for, the one that you've envisioned or that you're expecting, the LSAT writers will include the contrapositive of that answer.

Instead of this positive answer:

> The cable bridge is more beautiful than the concrete bridge.

You might find its contrapositive:

> (A)   The concrete bridge is not more beautiful or equal in beauty to the cable bridge.

As you can tell from just this one example, contrapositive choices can be confusing in their wording. Whenever a contrapositive is the correct choice to a problem, we will mark that problem with the tag "Contrapositive Choice."

When to Use Contrapositives

For the majority of the Logical Reasoning section, you don't need to worry too much about inferring contrapositives.

In the LR section, contrapositives mainly come into play in the choices, where the LSAT writers try to trip you up by making the correct choice—instead of simply stating the conditional relationship—state the contrapositive. Don't be too quick to eliminate a choice just because it's negative when you're expecting a positive—it may be the contrapositive of what you're expecting. If you suspect a negative choice is the answer but are unsure, simply take its contrapositive. In doing so, you re-word the relationship so it's positive and easier to understand. As a result, you will be able to determine if it's correct or incorrect more easily.

Contrapositives also show up on the Analytical Reasoning section of the LSAT (often referred to as the Logic Games section). In that section, any inferences you can make help you to understand the scenario at hand better. Don't worry about the Games, though. For now, know that the contrapositive has one main purpose in the LR section: evading tricky choices.

Mini-Drill: Conditional Diagrams

Try your hand at diagramming conditionals and their contrapositives with the relationships below.

Directions

- First, write the standard diagram.

- Negate each condition and reverse their order to get the contrapositive.

1. If the restaurant serves fish, I'll order an entrée that has fish.

2. If we have a large meeting, the boss never brings her notepad.

3. Whenever I bike, I can't help but smile.

Note that this last relationship doesn't use the standard if-then statement—and it doesn't have to. Conditional statements can come in many different forms, and this is one instance of a variation on the if-then structure.

The explanations to this drill are on the next page.

Mini-Drill Explanations

The following conditional relationships are represented by their diagrams and contrapositives:

1. If the restaurant serves fish, I'll order an entrée that has fish.

Serves fish → Order fish
−Order fish → −Serves fish

This contrapositive only tells you that, if I don't order fish, it's because the restaurant doesn't serve fish. Some test takers get eager with contrapositives and infer information that's not actually there. With this contrapositive, they may think that it means, if the restaurant doesn't serve fish, I won't try to order fish, or if I don't order fish, it could be because I didn't want fish. But, both of these inferences are not supported by this conditional relationship.

The first fails to "flip" or switch the conditions when forming the contrapositive. You don't know what I'll do when the restaurant *doesn't* serve fish; you just know what happens when the restaurant serves fish or when I don't order fish (the contrapositive).

Likewise, the only thing you know as a fact if I don't order the fish is that the restaurant could not have had fish on the menu. If they did have it on the menu, I 100% would have ordered it. The fact that I didn't order it means they 100% did not have it on the menu. That's all you know. To say that I didn't order the fish because I didn't feel like eating fish is to ignore the 100% guarantee in the conditional relationship that, if there is fish on the menu, I will order that fish.

2. If we have a large meeting, the boss never brings her notepad.

Large meeting → −Notepad
Notepad → −Large meeting

This contrapositive tells you that, if the boss brings her notepad, you know she can't be attending a large meeting.

3. Whenever I bike, I can't help but smile.

Bike → Smile
−Smile → −Bike

This contrapositive states that, if I'm not smiling, I must not be on my bike because every time I'm on my bike I'm a-smiling. Note that it doesn't mean that I only smile when I'm on my bike—it just tells you what I do when I am on my bike with no mention of my smiling habits off-bike.

Conditional Indicators

This section will introduce you to the specific meaning of certain conditional indicators, such as the sufficient indicator "if" and the necessary indicators "only" and "only if."

The traditional conditional statement is an "if..., then..." statement, but not all conditional reasoning on the LSAT is indicated so clearly with these words.

Some relationships use indirect conditional words, such as *every* or *all*, as in "Every time I go to the store, I get a biscuit" or "All cab drivers know their way around the city." These sentences can be restated in the if-then structure to make their conditional nature more obvious. "If I go to the store, then I get a biscuit," and "If you're a cab driver, then you know your way around the city."

Other times, there are no conditional indicators at all. Consider the threat "Snitches get stitches. "It's not readily obvious, but this phrase contains conditional logic. If you snitch (tell the authorities about someone's crime), then you will get stitches. That is a guarantee.

It's important to note the unidirectional, or one-way, nature of the if-then statement. If you're a snitch, then you get stitches, yes. But if you have stitches, does that mean you're a snitch? Of course it doesn't.

I fell and cut my hand, resulting in ten stitches. Someone who doesn't understand conditional reasoning would ask me, "So, who'd you snitch on?" That person is confusing *one way* to bring about an outcome as *the only way* to bring about that outcome. That's a common flaw in LSAT stimuli. Obviously, there are many more ways to get stitches beyond snitching.

On the other hand, if this person knew I had snitched on someone, then he would have been justified in asking, "So, where are your stitches?" The conditional relationship guarantees that, "if you snitch, you will get stitches."

Sufficient Indicators

These words indicate a sufficient condition, the trigger or catalyst on the left side of the conditional diagram.

If

"If" is the poster child of conditional reasoning. It's the most obvious giveaway of conditional logic on the LSAT, and for that reason you can expect to see it rarely—the LSAT writers don't like to show their cards if they can help it. The clause that follows "if" is the sufficient condition, the trigger, to bring about an outcome.

While it's uncommon to see a simple "if-then" statement on the LSAT, it's common to see "if" combined with other conditional terms such as "only" or "or." When combined with "only," "if" gets a bit more complicated. By itself, "if" indicates sufficiency, but with "only" it indicates a necessary condition, as in the phrase "only if." More on this soon. For now, just remember that "if" alone is a sufficient condition.

Unless

"Unless" is the secret weapon of the LSAT writers. It is the trickiest of all conditional buzzwords. But if you remember a simple rule, you'll always know how to understand and diagram the conditional relationship. That rule is short, sweet, and hard to forget.

Replace "unless" with "if… not." Let us explain why this works.

"Unless" is an inherently negative word. It indicates a sufficient condition, but, because of the negativity contained in "unless," that sufficient condition must be negated when diagrammed. Any time you see it on the LSAT, replace it with "if… not" or "if… no." This technique allows you to diagram the "unless" statements without a hitch.

Let's turn to an example to see the "unless"/"if… not" conversion in action:

> You can't sew unless you have a needle.

To put that in simpler terms, change unless to "if" and add "no" or "not" to include the negativity from "unless."

> You can't sew *if* you do *not* have a needle.

That's easier! Diagramming this modified relationship gives you:

> –Needle → –Sew

See how much simpler that is? "Unless" can be confusing, but you don't have to let it slow you down at all. Any time you see it, cross it out and write 'if not' where it best fits in the sentence. You'll keep your momentum and be one step closer to that great LSAT score.

Every, Any, All, When, Whenever

These are technically quantifiers because they indicate quantity or amount, but they have conditional implications as well. Each of these words indicates a sufficient condition, as they're introducing the catalyst, the first domino. Consider these examples:

> Every time you talk, I can't help but daydream.
>
> Whenever you talk, I daydream.
>
> Any time you talk, I daydream.

These statements all have the same diagram:

> You talk → I daydream

No, None

"No" and "none" are negative words that introduce a sufficient condition just as "all" or "every" can indicate a sufficient condition. For instance, consider the adage:

> No news is good news.

This could be re-phrased in the classic if-then conditional structure as:

> If we've not received any news, then that's good news.

> –News → Good news

In this example, you can see how "no" and "none" function to introduce the sufficient condition of a conditional relationship.

Diagramming

Any time you see one of these indicators, the following clause is the sufficient condition, so put that clause on the left side of the diagram. As you know by now, this diagram uses a one-way left-to-right arrow that never changes its direction. To take the contrapositive, switch and negate the conditions.

This consistent system will make sure that you never accidentally switch the conditions around or misplace a negative and misrepresent the relationship as a consequence.

Conditional Imposter: "Even if"

When used in an argument, the phrase "even if" has no conditional implications.

"Even if" is used to say, "Regardless of whether X happens, Y may or may not happen." This phrase is therefore not used to indicate any kind of relationship. It just says that, "even if" something happens, that condition has no implications on the outcome. Consider this example:

> Even if it rains, I'll go for a run.

How would you diagram that? You can't. You might be tempted to put rain on the left, and run on the right, but that would mean, "If it rains, then I'll go for a run," or, in other words, "every time it rains, I will go for a run." But the statement has no such guarantee; it just states that I'd go for a run even in the rain.

Thus, from a conditionals perspective, ignore 'even if' when it comes up in an argument.

Necessary Indicators

These buzzwords tell you which condition is the necessary condition, the "result" in your conditional diagram.

Then

"Then" is the other half of the "if-then" statement. When you see "then" you know you're looking at the resulting condition, the necessary condition. "Then" is almost always paired with "if."

> If you go to the party, then I'll go too.

In this example, your attendance ensures mine; your going is sufficient or enough to get me to go, too. Note that I could still go even if you don't go to the party, but, if you do go, then I'll definitely go.

Only and Only If

Both "only" and "only if" indicate a *required condition*.

"Only if" is straightforward. It is your friend because it corresponds directly with the necessary condition. When you see "only if" used in an LSAT stimulus, whatever comes after it should go on the right side of the diagram. This is a key distinction because "if" on its own typically means a sufficient condition. The "only" modifies "if," though, so you end up with a *necessary* condition—"only" indicates that the given circumstances are required for the outcome. As a result, "only if" gives you the necessary condition.

Consider this example:

> I will buy the TV **only if** the price is right.

> Buy TV → Right price

You know that, if I bought the TV, the price must have been right. Some test takers get confused as to where to place the different conditions, but you'll be fine if you remember that whatever comes right after 'only if' is a necessary condition.

"Only" can be a bit trickier. Most of the time, it comes before the necessary condition just like "only if." Sometimes, however, it comes in a weird spot. Check out this statement:

> The only drink I like better than coffee is tea.

The "only drink" in question here is tea, not coffee—the statement says that coffee is good, and the only thing better than coffee is tea. See how "only" is removed from the word it should be connected to, "tea?" This is one way LSAT writers may trick you. The diagram for this example would look like this:

> Better than Coffee → Tea

This diagram could be read, "If it's better than coffee, then it must be tea."

Remember, though, that this use of "only" is in the minority. Most of the time, it will come before the necessary condition as is the case for "only if." Just be on the lookout when you see "only" used conditionally because it might be thrown in there to trip you up as opposed to helping you.

Mini Drill: Contrapositive Diagrams

Directions

- Diagram the following relationships based on their indicators.
- Once you have the conditional diagram, negate each condition and reverse their order to get the contrapositive.
- Answers to this mini-drill are on the next page.

1. I grab a carton of eggs whenever I go to the store.

2. If it's too hot outside, I'll stay indoors all day long.

3. Only when I wake up early am I able to be productive.

4. Unless there's some drastic change in weather, I'll walk to the library today.

Mini Drill Explanations

Check your diagrams with the correct ones below. The indicator is represented in **boldface**.

1. I grab a carton of eggs **whenever** I go to the store.

> Store → Eggs
> −Eggs → −Store

"Whenever" is a sufficient condition indicator. Putting this statement into if-then terms gives you "if I go to the store, then I will get eggs." Both "when" and "whenever" are temporal ways of saying "if." They link an action (when or if a condition is met—i.e. going to the store) with an outcome (i.e. grabbing the eggs).

2. **If** it's too hot outside, I'll stay indoors all day long.

> Too hot → Inside
> −Inside → −Too hot

Classic "if" conditional statement here. There's no "then," but do you really need the "then" if you have the "if?" It's an either/or situation with indicators—if you have just one of them, that tells you whether the given condition is sufficient or necessary, so you know the status of the other condition, too.

3. **Only** when I wake up early am I able to be productive.

> Productive → Wake early
> −Wake early → −Productive

"Only" acts as the necessary condition indicator here. Note the usage of "when," which is essentially like saying, "Only if I wake up early am I productive."

4. **Unless** there's some drastic change in weather, I'll walk to the library today.

> If there's no change in the weather, I'll walk to library. Got it.
> −Weather change → Walk
> −Walk → Weather change

Switching out "unless" with "if... not" gives you a different statement, one that's much simpler to diagram. You shouldn't necessarily write out the whole new statement; we've just done that here to show you what it would look like.

When to Diagram Conditionals

This section gives context to everything you have just learned about conditionals; it tells you in what situations you should diagram conditionals.

Diagramming conditionals is an extremely helpful skill for a good LSAT score. In the Logical Reasoning section, you'll come across conditional logic in one to three problems per section.

When you work through a section, you shouldn't diagram the majority of the conditionals you see, though, because diagramming takes a lot of time and is rarely necessary. Only rarely will you use a conditional diagram on an LR problem. Diagramming is useful to learn before you encounter conditionals because it helps you understand which condition is sufficient and which is necessary. Moreover, this skill helps you spot indicators, and consequently it makes seeing how conditions relate all the more simple.

But, the goal here is to spot and understand conditionals. For the vast majority of Logical Reasoning problems that have conditional logic, no diagram is necessary as you complete the problem. Conditional relationships in the LR section tend to be pretty simple, so keep the diagram in your head until it gets too complex. When it is complex, nevertheless, by all means write it down on paper if that is necessary to solve the problem.

Diagramming is powerful because it helps you understand easily and quickly how two elements interact in a relationship. This task is much harder without a well-developed *ability* to diagram, but only very rarely should you actually use those diagramming skills *during* an LR section.

Review, however, is a different story. When you review a LR problem with conditionals, diagram the conditionals to your heart's content. During review, you have all the time in the world, so go right ahead and draw a diagram or several if you think it will help you better understand a problem. This is actually great practice.

Quantifiers

Quantifiers are words that indicate quantity or amount such as "none," "some," "most," and "all." We saw some of these in the section on conditional buzzwords. Quantifiers can indicate a conditional relationship, and knowing what amount they refer to automatically is a great skill to have in your skill belt. Let's quickly review these words and their incredibly specific amounts.

In the real world, quantifiers are thrown around without regard. People say "all the time," like, literally all the time. On the LSAT, however, words such as "all," "most," or "some" refer to very specific quantity ranges. For instance, "most" always refers to an amount greater than 50% while "some" can refer to any amount greater than 0% and up to 100%. The chart below shows the values associated with each of these terms.

All, Always	100%
Most, Most of the time	51% – 99%, greater than half but not all
Many, Several times	>1% (not 100%)
Some, Sometimes	>0% (not 100%)
None, Never	0%

Quantifier Combinations

Quantifiers can get confusing when they're combined. For instance, if some ducks lay blue eggs and some ducks lay yellow eggs, you can't say whether any ducks that lay blue eggs also lay yellow ones. The amount "some" only tells you that more than 0% of ducks lay blue and yellow eggs. The actual amount could be 2% that lay yellow and 1% that lay blue (with some other combination of colors rounding out the rest of the set). In this scenario, there's absolutely no reason to believe that that 2% overlaps with the other 1%. When *some* and *some* combine, they don't lead to any inferences about the two groups.

Now, that example would be different if you knew that *most* ducks lay blue eggs and *most* ducks lay yellow eggs. "Most" refers to an amount greater than half, so you're guaranteed to have at least *some* overlap between those two groups. Even if it's split so that 51% of ducks lay yellow eggs and 51% lay blue, there's still that 1% of overlap, so you can infer that some ducks (i.e. >0%) lay both blue eggs and yellow eggs.

The bottom line is that, unless there's a specification as to what quantity "some" contains (which there almost never ever is on the LSAT), you have no way to know the amount, so you must assume that it is the least possible amount. To assume a specific amount (say, greater than 50% for 'some') is to move beyond the data provided, which is a grave error on the LSAT.

This is what we mean when we talk about Quantifier Combination: two quantifiers are used to make statements about the same subject, leading to an inferred amount. In the first example about ducks, the two quantifiers are "some" and "some," and they were "most" and "most" in the second example.

When you have "some" of the set that does X and "some" that does Y, you can't say whether any do X and Y. When you have "most" that do X and "most" that do Y on the other hand, you can deduce that at least "some" do both X and Y. In both instances, the quantifiers are "combined" or added together to infer a third quantifier.

This chart details how different quantifiers combine:

All	+	All	=	All
All	+	Most	=	Most
Most	+	Most	=	Some
None	+	None	=	None

Note that the only logically valid combinations are with "all" and "most." "All" and "all," "all" and "most," and "most" and "most" each have enough overlap that you can infer that at least some of one category is also in the other category. Any time the quantifier "some" is featured in any combination with another quantifier, there is no logical inference you can draw about the overlapping amounts.

Let's take a look at some examples:

Most of my coworkers drive cars with a manual transmission. Most of my coworkers drive to work.

This is a "most" + "most" conditional combination. So, you know that some (at least one) of my coworkers drive a manual transmission car to work.

Some of the people in the movie ate popcorn. Some of the popcorn was poisonous!

Based on the given information, there's no way to be sure if anyone got poisonous popped corns. Any conclusion that says otherwise is wrong.

Conditionals Review

Conditional Logic

Two conditions are connected in a relationship

- Sufficient condition: the catalyst or trigger. This condition ensures that the second occurs.

- Necessary condition: the result or outcome. This is the second half of a conditional relationship. It's "required" to take place if the first condition (sufficient) is met.

- Sufficient → Necessary

- Sufficient conditions are always on the left of the one-sided arrow, and necessary is always on the right.

- Mark negative conditions with a dash: Eat → –Hungry

- There will always be a contrapositive to infer from a conditional.

  o Flip the position of the conditions and reverse their polarity. If they were positive, they will be negative and vice versa.

  o If a condition contains multiple variables, you must switch the connecting word as well.

    ▪ "And" gets switched to "or".

    ▪ "Or" gets switched to "and".

Conditional Indicators

- These are words that tell you that you are dealing with a conditional.

- Example language: "every, all, must, if, when, only, unless."

Sufficient Indicators

- "If" – Your standard conditional indicator, introduces the sufficient condition.

- "Unless" – Switch out with "if… not," and the conditional relationship becomes much clearer.

- "Every, any, all, when, whenever" – These are all straightforward, and they appear before the sufficient condition.

Necessary Indicators:

- "Then" – The other half of the if-then conditional statement, "then" rarely appears with "if."

- "Only if" – Introduces necessary condition.

- "Only" – Introduces necessary condition like "only if," but it can be out of place (i.e. it isn't necessarily next to the clause it modifies). Put the statement into the "if-then" structure to clarify if you're unsure.

When to Diagram Conditionals

- During review and on untimed practice early in your prep, diagram conditionals as much as necessary to build your skills.

- Only diagram a conditional during a timed section if you absolutely must in order to understand the stimulus.

Quantifiers

- All (100%), most (>50%), many/some (>1%), none (0%)

Diagram Drill

This drill will reinforce the conditional skills you have built while reading this chapter.

Directions

- There are several conditional relationships below.
- Diagram the relationship with the sufficient condition on the left and necessary on the right.
  - ○ Look for indicators to speed up the diagramming process.
- Then, flip the positions of the conditions and negate them to get the contrapositive.

Set 1

1. The only way I'll get a good grade is if I study all night.

2. If you can't stand the heat, get out the kitchen.

3. I have a good day only if I'm able to sleep in.

4. You must be 18 or older to attend this concert.

END OF SET

Set 1 Explanations

1. The **only** way I'll get a good grade is if I study all night.

$$Good\ grade \rightarrow Study\ all\ night$$
$$-Study\ all\ night \rightarrow -Good\ grade$$

This is an example of a tricky "only." The statement says, "The only way…is if I study all night." Essentially, it says, "Only if I study all night will I get a good grade." If you ask yourself what "only" connects to, you'll be pointed in the right direction. Here, the statement says that, in order to get a good grade, the only thing to be done—the thing that's required for the good grade—is to study all night. See how that can be a bit tricky? The "only" here is actually connected to the clause "…if I study all night," making that the necessary condition. This is the trickiest that conditionals get; the rest are much more straightforward.

2. **If** you can't stand the heat, get out the kitchen.

$$-Stand\ heat \rightarrow Leave\ kitchen$$
$$-Leave\ Kitchen \rightarrow Stand\ heat$$

"If" is your sufficient indicator here. The contrapositive tells you, "If not leave kitchen, then you can stand the heat." Love that caveman talk…

3. I have a good day **only if** I'm able to sleep in.

$$Sleep\ in \rightarrow Good\ day$$
$$-Good\ day \rightarrow -Sleep\ in$$

"Only if" indicates the necessary condition: sleeping in. The contrapositive says, "If I don't have a good day, then I must not have slept in."

4. You **must** be 18 or older to attend this concert.

$$Attend\ concert \rightarrow 18\ or\ older$$
$$-18\ or\ older \rightarrow -Attend\ concert$$

"Must" is an indicator that we didn't talk about, but it should make sense because it indicates something that's required, and consequently it points to the necessary condition. "Must" is uncommon as a conditional indicator, but it's just a variation of "required" or "necessary." Keep that in mind, and it shouldn't give you any problem.

Set 2

1. Unless you have something positive to say, don't speak at all.

2. Only people under 30 can hear a certain high-pitched frequency.

3. The best things in life aren't free.

4. If he eats shellfish, he will die.

5. Every time I walk around the block I get barked at by at least five dogs.

6. If you want to gain weight, you need to eat more.

7. Her knees pop when she jumps.

8. Every time I go to a concert, my ears hurt the next day.

END OF SET

Set 2 Explanations

1. **Unless** you have something positive to say, don't speak at all.

$$-Positive \rightarrow -Speak$$
$$Speak \rightarrow Positive$$

Switching "Unless" to "if… not" gives you: "If you do not have something positive to say, don't speak at all." The diagram is simple once you have that clearer understanding. The contrapositive tells you, "If you speak, then it must be positive."

2. **Only** people under 30 can hear a certain high-pitched frequency.

$$Hear\ high\ pitch \rightarrow Under\ 30$$
$$-Under\ 30 \rightarrow -Hear\ high\ pitch$$

"Only" indicates the necessary condition here. There's no "if" in the sentence, but, if you were to add it in, it would go right after only: "Only if you're under 30 can hear a certain high pitch." So, "under 30" is the necessary condition, and hearing the high pitch is the sufficient condition. Another way to think of it is that it's *required* that you be under 30 years old in order to hear the high pitch.

3. The best things in life aren't free.

$$Best \rightarrow -Free$$
$$Free \rightarrow -Best$$

This relationship has no indicators. That shouldn't be a problem, though. Put it into the "if-then" structure if it gives you any trouble. "If it's one of the best things in life, then it's not free." This makes diagramming much simpler. The contrapositive makes sense, too. "If it's free, then it can't be one of the best things in life."

4. **If** he eats shellfish, he will die.

$$Eat\ shellfish \rightarrow Dead$$
$$-Dead \rightarrow -Eat\ shellfish$$

"If" is your sufficient condition indicator, and this relationship is very clear. Don't give him shellfish, unless you want him dead. The contrapositive says, "If he isn't dead, he must not have eaten shellfish."

5. **Every** time I walk around the block I get barked at by at least five dogs.

$$Walk \rightarrow Bark$$
$$-Bark \rightarrow -Walk$$

"Every" indicates the sufficient condition: walking around the block. Whenever that happens, the dogs must bark at our walker. If they aren't barking, the contrapositive tells us the person must not be walking around the block.

6. **If** you want to gain weight, you need to eat more.

$$Gain\ weight \rightarrow Eat$$
$$-Eat \rightarrow -Gain\ weight$$

This is a classic "if" conditional statement where the "if" points right at the sufficient condition: gaining weight. It's necessary that you eat more calories in order to gain weight; that's a fact of science. I guess you could technically drink more calories to gain weight… but you get the idea.

7. Her knees pop **when** she jumps.

$$Jumps \rightarrow Knees\ pop$$
$$-Knees\ pop \rightarrow -Jump$$

"When" marks the sufficient condition: jumping. You could rephrase this in an "if-then" structure as "if she jumps, then her knees pop." The contrapositive tells you, "If her knees don't pop, then she must not have jumped."

8. **Every** time I go to a concert, my ears hurt the next day

$$Concert \rightarrow Ears\ hurt$$
$$-Ears\ hurt \rightarrow -Concert$$

"Every" indicates the sufficient condition: going to a concert. The statement tells you that whenever this person goes to a concert, they're 100% going to come away with hurt ears. The contrapositive says, "If my ears don't hurt, then I must not have gone to a concert last night."

Inference

Inference problems ask you to find a choice that is well supported by the facts in the stimulus, typically through a deduction (link) between two concepts. This is your first problem type chapter, and it has some new parts to build your skills, including problem sets.

Chapter Contents

Stem

Stimulus

Choices

Proven Choice Drill

Technique Set

Logically Completes Subtype

Challenge Set

Test Set

Problem Type Information

Stimulus type: Fact Group

Stimulus skills: Understand the facts

Can Envision Correct Answer: Rarely

Choice skills: Identify whether a choice is proven

Problem Type Tags

Obvious Inference

Logically Completes subtype

Parallel Situation

Prove and Move

Introduction

Inference problems ask you to find the choice proven by a fact-group stimulus. The proven choice is an <u>inference</u>: a new piece of information that you infer, or deduce, from connecting two pieces of provided information. Much of the work on Inference problems comes in analyzing each choice and checking the choice against the stimulus. Inference problems are common; expect to see about seven Inference problems in two LR sections.

Stem

The most common type of Inference problem asks you what "must be true," what is "most strongly supported," or what is "properly inferred" based on the stimulus.

- The statements above, if true, **most strongly support** which one of the following?

- If the essayist's statements are true, then which one of the following **must also be true**?

- Which one of the following can be **properly inferred** from the statements above?

As you can see, the stem-stamp for Inference problems is an "I."

These standard Inference problems make up 80% of all Inference problems. Their stems ask you what additional, new information the stimulus supports. In other words, you must determine which inference can be drawn from the facts in the stimulus. The other 20% of inference problems fall into the Logically Completes subtype, which will be covered later in this chapter.

Stimulus

Inference stimuli are Fact Groups: a set of related facts, *not* arguments. The stimuli are composed of statements on a subject with no conclusion and no hierarchy among the statements (i.e. no single statement is more important than another). The stimuli can be packed with information, and the lack of argument structure can make that information challenging to absorb. Do not fret; you will learn to read Inference stimuli effectively. Let's look at the steps.

Step 1 – Read the Stimulus Carefully

Read the facts that make up the stimulus carefully so that you understand the subject and, as much as possible, the specific facts it contains. Think of each stimulus as a set of support pieces for an unknown inference, the correct choice. You must understand the support so that when you see the inference in the choices it will make sense to you.

Take your time reading Inference stimuli, especially if they are full of information or conditionals. The more challenging Inference problems will have dense stimuli. Get a good understanding of the information on your first read through. Be thorough, but do not take too long reading the stimulus. You will need a lot of time to analyze the choices, more time than you'll need for most LR problem types.

Inferences

An inference is new information derived from linking two pieces of information from the stimulus. Here is an example of a stimulus and its inference:

> The dog next door to me used to always bark late at night. However, the owner recently bought him a bark collar that is 100% effective at stopping dogs barking. The owner has been using the collar on her dog nightly.
>
> Inference: The dog is no longer barking late at night.

The fact that the bark collar is 100% effective combines with the fact that the neighbor is using the collar. Linking those facts creates the inference that the dog is no longer barking at night.

Logic Chain Inference

If the stimulus contains a <u>Logic Chain</u> with a series of connected links, it is not uncommon for the correct choice to be the inference that the links connect. For example, let's say that we can sum up the Logic Chain in an Inference stimulus with these parts:

- Owning a dog makes the owner more loving
- Being more loving leads to having less conflict in personal relationships

The inference would be that the first link in the chain (owning a dog) leads to the last link (having less conflict in personal relationships). Whenever you see a Logic Chain in a stimulus, the Obvious Inference for that Inference problem is the first link leading to the last. Be on the lookout for these situations.

Step 2 – Look for an Obvious Inference

After you finish reading an Inference stimulus, pause for a moment. Spend a few seconds looking for an Obvious Inference that can be drawn by connecting parts of the stimulus. An <u>Obvious Inference</u> is one that jumps out at you. If there are two important conditionals mentioned in the stimulus, they may link to form an Obvious Inference. The example above about the barking dog features a simple stimulus that has an Obvious Inference. Because the collar works all the time and the owner is using it, the dog is no longer barking. The stimulus seems to be building to that inference, which is often a quality of Obvious Inferences.

Only spend a few moments looking for an inference. The longer, more complex Inference stimuli could support several inferences and not have a single Obvious Inference. On these Inference problems, you will need to devote a lot of time to analyzing the choices, so you don't want to waste time looking for an inference. Here is an example of a stimulus that has many possible inferences:

> Unusually large and intense forest fires swept the tropics in 1997. The tropics were quite susceptible to fire at that time because of the widespread drought caused by an unusually strong El Niño, an occasional global weather phenomenon. Many scientists believe the strength of the El Niño was enhanced by the global warming caused by air pollution.

The easier Inference problems tend to have an Obvious Inference. The moderate and difficult problems are less likely to have an Obvious Inference. Most difficult Inference problems do not have an obvious inference. Instead, they have a couple possible inferences, none of which stand out as obvious or especially important. In general, a little less than half of Inference problems have an Obvious Inference.

Read Inference stimuli for understanding. Don't spend much energy looking for an Obvious Inference. If you happen to see one, though, that is great. Taking your Obvious Inference into the choices will help you analyze the choices more quickly.

Choices

Most of the effort on Inference problems comes in analyzing the choices, in seeing whether a choice is a valid inference based on the stimulus or not. This is different from most of the Find Flaw problem types, where much of the effort comes in analyzing an argument and finding the flaw within it. Once you have that flaw, you can analyze the choices against your knowledge of the flaw. But unless there is an Obvious Inference, you'll need to analyze the choices intently on an Inference problem.

Proving a Valid Inference

On Inference problems, you can use the stimulus to prove a choice correct or incorrect as depicted in the diagram below:

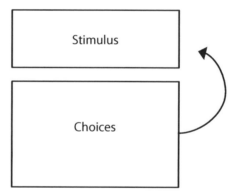

When you see that a choice is a valid inference, you know that it must be the correct answer to the problem. That is an empowering feeling when you're analyzing the choices. Here is an example of a choice that is 100% proven by the stimulus:

> Daisy loves the NFL and is a huge Denver Broncos fan. She also likes to be active. The only time she is ecstatic on Sunday nights is if the Broncos win and she was active during the day. However, she is only active on Sundays if she goes on a long hike. Unfortunately, whenever Daisy goes on a long hike, the Broncos lose.

> (A)   Daisy is never ecstatic on Sundays.

The stimulus says that, in order for Daisy to be ecstatic, the Broncos must win and she must be active. But if she is active, then she went on a long hike, and the Broncos lose whenever she does that. So, the stimulus tells us that both of the requirements for Daisy to be ecstatic on a Sunday will *never be met*. This proves choice (A); she is never ecstatic on Sundays.

Compare the Choices to the Stimulus

Analyzing each choice to see if it is proven takes time. This is because on Inference problems you often do not have any idea what the correct choice will look like after reading the Fact Group stimulus. You can't envision the correct answer ahead of time unless you saw an Obvious Inference. This is very different from many of the other LR problem types. On a Flaw problem, you will generally know the exact flaw in the argument after reading the stimulus. Then, you use the flaw as a lens to work through the choices. That is typically not the case on Inference problems because generally there are many possible inferences in the fact group and no one inference will stand out. Working each choice to see if it is in fact a proven inference takes time and requires precision in your thinking.

There is a subtle strategy shift for Inference choices that comes from the extra time and energy required to work the choices. Let's first look at an overview of the correct and incorrect choices and then learn a powerful strategy for working the choices that saves time called "Prove and Move."

Correct Choice

Of course, the correct choice on an Inference problem is an inference. The answer combines two pieces of information from the stimulus to say something semi-new and 100% valid. Please read this Inference stimulus:

> For many centuries it was believed that only classical Euclidean geometry could provide a correct way of mathematically representing the universe. Nevertheless, scientists have come to believe that a representation of the universe employing non-Euclidean geometry is much more useful in developing certain areas of scientific theory. In fact, such a representation underlies the cosmological theory that is now most widely accepted by scientists as accurate.

This is the correct choice:

> (B)   Scientists generally do not now believe that classical Euclidean geometry is uniquely capable of giving a correct mathematical representation of the universe.

This choice is an inference based on these facts:

- Scientists used to believe that only Euclidean geometry could represent the universe in a mathematically correct way.
- Now scientists believe that a representation of the universe employing non-Euclidean geometry is more useful in certain ways and such a representation underlies the theory that is most widely accepted.

When we put these facts together, we see that (B) is proven. Scientists do not think that *only* Euclidean geometry can give a correct mathematical view of the universe. Some other representation of the universe does not use Euclidean geometry, and it is now considered the most useful representation.

The correct choice doesn't need to feel big or important based on the stimulus. (B) is a pretty good example of that because it sounds fairly conservative. All the correct choice needs to do is be a valid inference; it needs to be *proven by the statements in the stimulus*. Sometimes the inference will sound simple or slight, and that is perfectly fine. If the inference sounds like a restatement of something in the stimulus, that just means it is a simple link. Here is an example based on the previous stimulus:

> Unusually large and intense forest fires swept the tropics in 1997. The tropics were quite susceptible to fire at that time because of the widespread drought caused by an unusually strong El Niño, an occasional global weather phenomenon. Many scientists believe the strength of the El Niño was enhanced by the global warming caused by air pollution.

> (B)   Air pollution is believed by some in the scientific community to have contributed to global warming.

Incorrect Choices

All four incorrect choices are *not* proven by the stimulus. They are not valid inferences, and they do not have the firm support from the stimulus that the correct choice has. However, incorrect choices will often *sound great* because they seem to connect information in the stimulus or they are plausible thoughts on a subject from the stimulus. That connection is, of course, not actually supported by the facts in the stimulus.

Learning how to eliminate a choice because it is not proven by the stimulus is a key skill on Inference problems. A re-analysis of the facts related to the information in the choice will tell you if the choice has proof. That often means rereading certain parts of the stimulus.

Let's look at a few common types of incorrect choices to see how to eliminate them using the stimulus.

Many incorrect choices are Plausible Choices. They might make sense and sound supported based on the info in the passage, but you see that the choice is unproven when you look deeper. These choices are very common and can be tempting. Here is an example of a Plausible Incorrect choice based on the same stimulus about representing the universe:

> For many centuries it was believed that only classical Euclidean geometry could provide a correct way of mathematically representing the universe. Nevertheless, scientists have come to believe that a representation of the universe employing non-Euclidean geometry is much more useful in developing certain areas of scientific theory. In fact, such a representation underlies the cosmological theory that is now most widely accepted by scientists as accurate.

> (C)   Non-Euclidean geometry is a more complete way of representing the universe than is Euclidean geometry.

(C) sounds reasonable and supported, but is it actually proven? No. The stimulus tells us that a representation of the universe based on non-Euclidean geometry is "more useful in developing certain areas of scientific theory." That concept is not the same as being a *more complete* way of representing the universe. The information about the Non-Euclidean representation of the universe sounds like it supports (C) until you take a critical look at the stimulus. Be precise when you analyze Inference choices.

Other incorrect choices might discuss a New Concept, which is a subject not talked about in the stimulus. These choices are not proven because the stimulus does not give you information about them. If the stimulus doesn't talk about a concept, then a choice that talks about that concept cannot be correct. Here is an example of a choice that has a few New Concepts:

> (A)   Scientists who use Euclidean geometry are likely to believe that progress in mathematical theory results in progress in natural science.

The stimulus never talks about what scientists who use Euclidean geometry believe nor does it talk specifically about the concept of progress in natural science. (A) has New Concepts that cannot be proven by the stimulus, so it is incorrect.

The caveat here is that an inference might sound new because it is new information, but it's actually new information strongly supported by other information in the stimulus. When you analyze a choice with a valid inference, look to see how it is backed by the facts in the stimulus. Be careful when writing off a choice as a New Concept. A truly New Concept does not have support in the stimulus.

Now that you know what the correct and incorrect choices will look like, let's go over the techniques for working the choices.

Start With (E)

There are tons of (E), (D), and (C) correct answers to Inference problems. The test-writers do this because they know that analyzing the choices takes a long time for Inference problems, and test-takers tend to analyze the choices in descending order from (A) to (E). Planting the correct answer towards the end of the choices means that difficult Inference problems will take longer on average for students to complete. That adds difficulty to the LR section, and adding difficulty is something the test-writers are always looking to do.

You can save time analyzing the choices by starting your analysis with (E) and working your way to (A). Starting with (E) helps you get to the correct answer more quickly, and then Prove and Move.

It's important to resist using your knowledge that Inference problems tend to have later choices to help you decide between two choices. (E) should not be a more tempting answer solely because Inference problems often have (E) as the correct answer. Focus on the validity of the choices, and select the choice that is proven by the stimulus or the last choice standing after you eliminate the other four choices.

Step 1 – Eliminate Unproven Choices

On Inference problems, elimination takes more time for each choice. If you didn't find an Obvious Inference after reading the stimulus, you probably don't have a strong idea what the correct choice will look like as you move into the choices. That knowledge of what to look for in the correct choice is what typically enables you to eliminate an incorrect choice quickly. On a flaw problem, you can eliminate a choice quickly if it does not match the flaw you identified. On Inference problems, you do not have that "envisioned answer" tool in your pocket about half the time.

For each choice you analyze, you need to carefully check whether it is proven. On some choices, you might need to refer back to reread the relevant parts of the stimulus to see if the choice is an inference, and do not expect the correct choice to always sound appealing. Often, you have to dig into a choice and use your knowledge of the stimulus before you see that the choice is in fact a valid inference.

All of this means that analyzing the choices on an Inference problem can take more time than usual.

Prove and Move

If you find a choice that you are very confident is proven as you eliminate incorrect choices, you can choose to select that choice and move on to the next problem without analyzing the remaining choices. We call this technique <u>Prove and Move</u>. Taking the time to eliminate the other choices does not make sense if you have found a choice that the stimulus proves true. You know that choice must be the correct answer because the correct answer is the only one that's valid. Properly implemented, the Prove and Move technique can save you time when completing Inference problems.

Here is how Prove and Move works: Let's say that you are eliminating the incorrect choices on an Inference problem, working up from (E) of course. You have eliminated choices (E) and (D). As you analyze (C), you determine that it is a proven inference based on a link in the stimulus, so you are very confident that (C) is correct. In that case, select (C), and then move on to the next problem without even looking at (B) or (A).

If you analyze a choice and are not sure whether it is correct or incorrect, keep the choice as you typically do on the eliminate step. Then, continue eliminating the choices until you find a proven inference or you have eliminated all the incorrect choices. In other words, if you can't Prove to yourself that the choice is correct, don't Move on to the next problem.

The Prove and Move technique is aggressive because it allows you to select an answer without spending time on every choice. The reward for the technique is saving time for the other problems in the LR section. Nevertheless, that time savings is worthless if you use Prove and Move to quickly select an *incorrect choice*. If you find that you are missing a lot of Inference problems during your practice, especially during the eliminate step, analyze every choice.

Step 2 – Confirm the Correct Choice

If you did not feel comfortable using Prove and Move on a problem, then you find yourself on the confirm step. On more difficult Inference problems, the correct choice will often be worded in an unexpected way, so it may be challenging to see that the choice is an inference. When this is the case, eliminating all the other choices in the eliminate step will help enormously. The last choice standing must be correct.

If you are choosing between two choices, look for the safest inference, the one with the tightest connection between the stimulus information. Remember, the correct choice does not need to be groundbreaking or important; it only needs to be proven by the stimulus. Sometimes, the correct choice simply *restates* or rephrases one piece of information from the stimulus. These correct choices are not really inferences, but they are indeed proven. Here is a fabricated example of a choice that restates information from the stimulus about Euclidean geometry:

> For many centuries it was believed that only classical Euclidean geometry could provide a correct way of mathematically representing the universe. Nevertheless, scientists have come to believe that a representation of the universe employing non-Euclidean geometry is much more useful in developing certain areas of scientific theory. In fact, such a representation underlies the cosmological theory that is now most widely accepted by scientists as accurate.

> (E)   There was a long period of time when Euclidean geometry was the most popular way to represent the universe mathematically.

(E) merely restates the first sentence of the stimulus. It is not groundbreaking, but it is proven. For that reason, it is correct.

Proven Choice Drill

The Proven Choice drill teaches you how to evaluate whether a choice is proven by the stimulus, a crucial Inference skill.

Directions

For each of the stimuli below, please complete these two steps:

1) Read the fact-group stimulus carefully.

2) Analyze each of the three choices given, working from (E) upward. Under the choice, write why it is unproven or proven. If a choice is unproven, label it as either a Plausible Incorrect or a New Concept (if either of those applies). If the choice is proven, write how it is an inference from information in the stimulus.

Set 1

1. Cardiologist: Coronary bypass surgery is commonly performed on patients suffering from coronary artery disease when certain other therapies would be as effective. Besides being relatively inexpensive, these other therapies pose less risk to the patient since they are less intrusive. Bypass surgery is especially debatable for single-vessel disease.

   (A) Bypass surgery is riskier than all alternative therapies.

   (C) Bypass surgery should be performed when more than one vessel is diseased.

   (E) Sometimes there are equally effective alternatives to bypass surgery that involve less risk.

2. Beginning in the 1950s, popular music was revolutionized by the electrification of musical instruments, which has enabled musicians to play with increased volume. Because individual musicians can play with increased volume, the average number of musicians per band has decreased. Nevertheless, electrification has increased rather than decreased the overall number of musicians who play popular music professionally.

   (C) The number of professional musicians in some bands has increased.

   (D) The total number of professional bands has increased as a result of electrification.

   (E) Many professional musicians play in more than one band.

END OF SET

Set 1 Explanations

1. Cardiologist: Coronary bypass surgery is commonly performed on patients suffering from coronary artery disease when certain other therapies would be as effective. Besides being relatively inexpensive, these other therapies pose less risk to the patient since they are less intrusive. Bypass surgery is especially debatable for single-vessel disease.

The stimulus describes therapies that are superior to bypass surgery in various ways. It then concludes with a case where Bypass surgery is particularly questionable. There is no Obvious Inference here, which is not surprising because there are many facts in the stimulus.

    (E)   Sometimes there are equally effective alternatives to bypass surgery that involve less risk.

We begin working the choices with (E), and in this case (E) is proven. The stimulus says that certain other therapies "would be as effective" and "pose less risk to the patient" than bypass surgery. Linking those two pieces of information proves this choice as a valid inference.

    (C)   Bypass surgery should be performed when more than one vessel is diseased.

This is a Plausible Incorrect choice. We are told that bypass surgery is very debatable (less than ideal) for single vessel disease, but that does not mean that it is *optimal* for multi-vessel disease.

    (A)   Bypass surgery is riskier than all alternative therapies.

This is also a Plausible Incorrect choice that is not proven by the stimulus. We are told that bypass surgery is more risky than certain other therapies. That does not mean it is more risky than *all* other therapies.

2. Beginning in the 1950s, popular music was revolutionized by the electrification of musical instruments, which has enabled musicians to play with increased volume. Because individual musicians can play with increased volume, the average number of musicians per band has decreased. Nevertheless, electrification has increased rather than decreased the overall number of musicians who play popular music professionally.

The stimulus talks about several effects of the electrification of musical instruments. Since the 50's, the average size of a band has decreased even as the number of pro musicians has increased. There is no Obvious Inference here.

    (E)   Many professional musicians play in more than one band.

This choice is a New Concept. The stimulus never talks about musicians playing in more than one band, and the stimulus does not contain information that links to support (E).

    (D)   The total number of professional bands has increased as a result of electrification.

We know that there are more professional musicians now, *and* the average size of a band has gone down. That means that there must be more bands now than before to support the greater number of pro musicians. (D) may sound like a New Concept, but it is a valid inference.

    (C)   The number of professional musicians in some bands has increased.

(C) sounds *very* Plausible, but it is not proven. We know that there are more musicians now, but that doesn't relate to this statement about the size of some bands. We know that the *average size* of a band has decreased. Based on the stimulus, it is possible that the number of musicians in a band has not increased in a single band. It sounds strange to say that possibility, so (C) is a great example of a Plausible Choice that is not actively proven by the stimulus.

Set 2

3. The economy is doing badly. First, the real estate slump has been with us for some time. Second, car sales are at their lowest in years. Of course, had either one or the other phenomenon failed to occur, this would be consistent with the economy as a whole being healthy. But, their occurrence together makes it quite probable that my conclusion is correct.

(C)   If the real estate market is healthy, then it is likely that the economy as a whole is healthy.

(D)   If the economy is in a healthy state, then it is unlikely that the real estate and car sales markets are both in a slump.

(E)   The bad condition of the economy implies that both the real estate and the car sales markets are doing badly.

4. Researcher: We studied two groups of subjects over a period of six months. Over this period, one of the groups had a daily routine of afternoon exercise. The other group, the control group, engaged in little or no exercise during the study. It was found that those in the exercise group got 33 percent more deep-sleep at night than did the control group. Exercising in the afternoon tends to raise body temperature slightly until after bedtime, and this extra heat induces deeper sleep.

(C)   The best way to get increased deep-sleep is to induce a slight increase in body temperature just before bedtime.

(D)   No one in the control group experienced a rise in body temperature just before bedtime.

(E)   Raising body temperature slightly by taking a warm bath just before bedtime will likely result in increased deep-sleep.

END OF SET

Set 2 Explanations

3.   The economy is doing badly. First, the real estate slump has been with us for some time. Second, car sales are at their lowest in years. Of course, had either one or the other phenomenon failed to occur, this would be consistent with the economy as a whole being healthy. But, their occurrence together makes it quite probable that my conclusion is correct.

This Inference stimulus is an argument, which is very rare, but that doesn't change how you should deal with it. The stimulus says that the economy is doing badly, and the evidence is that there is a real estate slump *and* car sales are down. If only one of these things was happening, then that would mean the economy is healthy, but both occurring at the same time indicates that the economy is doing badly. There is no Obvious Inference here.

(E)   The bad condition of the economy implies that both the real estate and the car sales markets are doing badly.

(E) is a Plausible Incorrect choice. It has a conditional error; it reverses the relationship of the evidence to the conclusion. The fact that the real estate and car markets are doing badly implies that the economy is doing poorly, not the other way around.

(D)   If the economy is in a healthy state, then it is unlikely that the real estate and car sales markets are both in a slump.

(D) is proven. It is a restatement of this sentence: "Had either one or the other phenomenon failed to occur, this would be consistent with the economy as a whole being healthy." Remember that sometimes the correct answer to an Inference problem is just a restatement of a piece of information from the stimulus, instead of an inference that links two pieces of information.

(C)   If the real estate market is healthy, then it is likely that the economy as a whole is healthy.

(C) sounds plausible, but it is not proven. The stimulus says that, when exactly one of the markets is *unhealthy*, that fact indicates that the economy as a whole is healthy. With (C), it could be that the real estate market is healthy and the car market is also healthy, a situation where we do not know how the economy as a whole is doing.

4.   Researcher: We studied two groups of subjects over a period of six months. Over this period, one of the groups had a daily routine of afternoon exercise. The other group, the control group, engaged in little or no exercise during the study. It was found that those in the exercise group got 33 percent more deep-sleep at night than did the control group. Exercising in the afternoon tends to raise body temperature slightly until after bedtime, and this extra heat induces deeper sleep.

The stimulus talks about the results of a study relating exercise to sleep quality. The study learned that people who exercised slept more soundly, an effect due to a rise in body temperature after bedtime. There is no Obvious Inference.

Notice that all four of these drill problems did not have an Obvious Inference. This is a reminder that many Inference problems will not have an inference that stands out. Only the easier Inference problems do, and the test-writers don't want to give these to you too often.

(E)   Raising body temperature slightly by taking a warm bath just before bedtime will likely result in increased deep-sleep.

The final sentence of the stimulus is "this extra heat induces deeper sleep." So, a warm bath will likely result in increased deep-sleep. (E) is a reasonable inference, but perhaps not a choice where you would Prove and Move. It doesn't feel quite *that* proven.

(D)   No one in the control group experienced a rise in body temperature just before bedtime.

(D) is a New Concept because the stimulus doesn't talk about the body temperature of the *control group*. We know that the exercise group had a rise in temperature, but it is unsupported to say that *no one* in the control group had a rise in body temp before bedtime.

(C)   The best way to get increased deep-sleep is to induce a slight increase in body temperature just before bedtime.

(C) is a Plausible Incorrect choice. The stimulus does not support it. We learn that a slight increase in body temperature is one way to get deeper sleep, but the stimulus never says it is the *best* way. Perhaps a relaxing bedtime routine is actually the best way to get increased deep-sleep, not a slight increase in body temp.

Returning to (E), we see that it is correct.

Inference Review

Inference problems ask you to find the choice that makes a valid inference from the information in the stimulus.

Stem

- There is some variety in Inference stems. Look for these phrases: "most strongly supported," "must be true," and "properly inferred."

- Stem stamp = "I"

Stimulus

- The stimuli are Fact Groups, so read them to understand the facts and how they relate, not to find argument structure or a flaw.

- Step 1 – Read carefully and understand the facts.

- Step 2 – After you read the stimulus, look for an Obvious Inference.

    o An <u>Obvious Inference</u> is a link between two pieces of information that jumps out at you.

    o If there is a Logic Chain (A → B → C), the correct choice may be A → C.

    o Don't spend much time on this envisioning step. Difficult Inference problems don't have an Obvious Inference.

Choices

- Step 1 – Eliminate unproven choices.

    o Begin analyzing the choices with (E).

        ▪ Prove and Move: If you find a choice that you are confident is proven, select the choice and move on without analyzing the remaining choices.

    o Eliminate Plausible Incorrect choices that sound reasonable but are not proven.

    o New Concept incorrect choices talk about something that the stimulus does not discuss.

- Step 2 - Confirm the correct choice.

    o You will be able to prove the correct choice by checking it against the stimulus.

    o The correct choice does not need to sound big or important. Safe and proven is all you need.

    o The correct choice may be worded unexpectedly or may sound like a New Concept until you see it is a valid inference.

Techniques Summary

- <u>Core Focus</u>: Start with (E) and use Prove and Move.

- Stimulus: Understand the facts and look for an Obvious Inference.

- Choices:

    o Start with (E).

    o Eliminate unproven choices.

    o If you find a proven choice, Prove and Move.

Problem Sets Introduction

The practice for Inference problems and all LR types is divided into three types of problem sets. Each set has a unique purpose. The first is the <u>Technique Set</u>, during which you will focus on properly implementing the Inference techniques you have learned on each problem you attempt. On average, these problems are of moderate difficulty. For the Technique Set, you will attempt each problem and then review it before moving onto the next problem.

The <u>Challenge Sets</u> give you challenging practice to build your Inference skills. They contain difficult problems. There is no time limit for the Sets, allowing you to aim for a high level of accuracy despite the difficulty of the problems.

The final problem set, the <u>Test Set</u>, allows you to show off your newly honed Inference skills under time pressure. The Test Set measures the skills that you have built in the first two sets on problems of moderate difficulty. You will attempt the entire Set in one go. There is a time limit for the Set.

At the end of these problem Sets, when you see an Inference problem it will be like greeting an old friend, and you'll know exactly what to do.

Inference Technique Set

The Technique Set is your chance to practice the Inference techniques and to learn how to answer this type of problem correctly. Here is an overview of this set:

- 8 problems completed one at a time.

- Attempt a problem and then review it.

- During a problem, read the Techniques Summary after stamping the stem.

- Review every problem by reading the explanation carefully.

Directions

- Technique Summary: The Techniques Summary from the Inference Review page is printed next to each of the eight problems you'll work in the Technique Set. For each problem, after you read the stem and stamp it, pause working the problem and read the Techniques Summary. This will ensure that the core techniques are fresh in your mind as you work the rest of the problem. As you read the stimulus and work the choices, actively apply the techniques.

- Time Limit: There is no time limit for completing the problems, so do your best to answer each correctly. Take your time on each, and be careful with the answer you select. You will work on your pacing with Inference problems in the Test Set at the end of this chapter.

- Review: For each problem, read the explanation intently to check that you used the techniques properly. Also, use the explanation to improve your understanding of how the problem works.

- Milk every drop of learning out of a problem and its explanation before moving on so that your skills build steadily during this set. As you get more comfortable with Inference problems, the problems in this Technique Set become more challenging. Thorough review throughout the set ensures that you are ready to ace the difficult problems at the end.

1. Large deposits of the rare mineral nahcolite formed in salty lakes 50 million to 52 million years ago during the Eocene epoch. Laboratory tests found that, in salty water, nahcolite can form only when the atmosphere contains at least 1,125 parts per million of carbon dioxide.

    The statements above, if true, most strongly support which one of the following?

    (A) For most of the time since the Eocene epoch, the level of carbon dioxide in the atmosphere has been lower than it was during most of the Eocene epoch.

    (B) Levels of carbon dioxide in the atmosphere fluctuated greatly during the Eocene epoch.

    (C) Lakes were more likely to be salty during periods when the level of carbon dioxide in the atmosphere was at least 1,125 parts per million.

    (D) The atmosphere contained at least 1,125 parts per million of carbon dioxide during at least some part of the Eocene epoch.

    (E) No significant deposits of nahcolite have formed at any time since the Eocene epoch.

Techniques Summary

- Core Focus: Start with (E) and use Prove and Move.

- Stimulus: Understand the facts and look for an Obvious Inference.

- Choices:
    o Start with (E).
    o Eliminate unproven choices.
    o If you find a proven choice, Prove and Move.

1. Large deposits of the rare mineral nahcolite formed in salty lakes 50 million to 52 million years ago during the Eocene epoch. Laboratory tests found that, in salty water, nahcolite can form only when the atmosphere contains at least 1,125 parts per million of carbon dioxide.

   The statements above, if true, **most strongly support** which one of the following?

   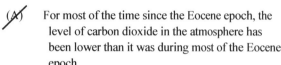

   (A) For most of the time since the Eocene epoch, the level of carbon dioxide in the atmosphere has been lower than it was during most of the Eocene epoch.

   (B) Levels of carbon dioxide in the atmosphere fluctuated greatly during the Eocene epoch.

   (C) Lakes were more likely to be salty during periods when the level of carbon dioxide in the atmosphere was at least 1,125 parts per million.

   (D) The atmosphere contained at least 1,125 parts per million of carbon dioxide during at least some part of the Eocene epoch.

   (E) No significant deposits of nahcolite have formed at any time since the Eocene epoch.

Type: Inference
Tag: Obvious Inference, Conditionals, Prove and Move

Stem - The stem asks you which choice the stimulus most strongly supports, so this is an Inference problem. Enter the stimulus to understand the facts it presents.

Stimulus – 1) Read the stimulus very carefully, watching where it flows. We learn that large deposits of nahcolite formed 50 to 52 million years ago (the Eocene epoch). Laboratory tests showed a requirement for its forming in salty water: the atmosphere must contain 1125 ppm carbon dioxide.

2) Look for an Obvious Inference. We are told nahcolite formed and a requirement for it to form., so we can infer that the requirement (1125 parts carbon dioxide in the atmosphere) was met during that time period. Whenever an outcome occurs, that means any requirement for that outcome must have been met. That is Conditionals 101.

Choices – 1) Eliminate choices that are not proven by the stimulus, starting with (E). Be on the lookout for our Obvious Inference. (E) – The stimulus says that nahcolite is a rare mineral, but it never implies that nahcolite has not formed since the time period discussed. (E) is not proven. (D) matches our Obvious Inference. If nahcolite requires at least 1125 ppm of carbon dioxide to form in those situations and it did form, then that atmospheric condition must have been around for at least some part of the Eocene epoch when it formed. (D) is proven. If you are quite confident in (D), you can use the Prove and Move technique to select (D) and move on without analyzing the other choices.

Let's analyze (C) through (A) for practice. (C) confuses a few pieces of information from the stimulus. There is no connection between lakes being salty and the carbon dioxide levels in the atmosphere, but there is a connection between nahcolite forming in salty lakes and the carbon dioxide in the atmosphere. (B) – This is a completely new concept because the stimulus never talks about the stability of carbon dioxide levels during the Eocene epoch. (A) – The stimulus gives us no information about carbon dioxide since the Eocene epoch.

Notice that there is no Confirm step here because we used the Prove and Move technique.

2. Forest fragmentation occurs when development severs a continuous area of forest, breaking it down into small patches. Some animals, such as white-footed mice, thrive in conditions of forest fragmentation, reaching their highest population densities in small forest patches. These mice are the main carrier of the bacteria that cause Lyme disease, a debilitating illness that is often transmitted from white-footed mice to humans by deer ticks.

Which one of the following is most strongly supported by the information above?

(A)   White-footed mice are very rarely found in unfragmented forests.

(B)   The population density for most species of small animals increases when a continuous area of forest becomes fragmented.

(C)   Forest fragmentation reduces the number and variety of animal species that an area can support.

(D)   Efforts to stop the fragmentation of forests can have a beneficial effect on human health.

(E)   Deer ticks reach their highest population densities in small forest patches.

Techniques Summary

- Core Focus: Start with (E) and use Prove and Move.

- Stimulus: Understand the facts and look for an Obvious Inference.

- Choices:

  o   Start with (E).

  o   Eliminate unproven choices.

  o   If you find a proven choice, Prove and Move.

2. Forest fragmentation occurs when development severs a continuous area of forest, breaking it down into small patches. Some animals, such as white-footed mice, thrive in conditions of forest fragmentation, reaching their highest population densities in small forest patches. These mice are the main carrier of the bacteria that cause Lyme disease, a debilitating illness that is often transmitted from white-footed mice to humans by deer ticks.

Which one of the following is **most strongly supported** by the information above?

 (A) White-footed mice are very rarely found in unfragmented forests.

 (B) The population density for most species of small animals increases when a continuous area of forest becomes fragmented.

 (C) Forest fragmentation reduces the number and variety of animal species that an area can support.

 (D) Efforts to stop the fragmentation of forests can have a beneficial effect on human health.

 (E) Deer ticks reach their highest population densities in small forest patches.

Type: Inference
Tag: Obvious Inference, Logic Chain

Stem – "Most strongly supported" tells you that this is an Inference problem. Get ready to understand the stimulus.

Stimulus – 1) Read the stimulus carefully. We learn that forest fragmentation causes white-footed mice populations to grow. These mice are the primary carrier of Lyme disease, which is often transmitted to humans. These mice have white feet? It's like they are wearing little socks! Cute.

2) Look for an Obvious Inference. The final sentence says that the mice are the main carrier of Lyme disease., and earlier we learned that forest fragmentation means more mice. Linking these two facts, we draw the inference that forest fragmentation leads to more Lyme disease. This is a Logic Chain: fragmentation → more mice → more Lyme disease.

Choices – 1) Eliminate incorrect choices, starting with (E). (E) – We are told that mice thrive in small patches of forest, but we are never told that ticks do. We don't know anything about where ticks thrive. (D) matches the Obvious Inference in a general way. Less forest fragmentation would mean fewer white-footed mice, which would mean less Lyme disease (a debilitating illness). So yes, less fragmentation could have a beneficial effect on human health. (D) looks good, but I'm not sure it justifies a Prove and Move. Keep it and continue analyzing the choices. (C) sounds plausible; breaking a forest into small patches seems like it would reduce the variety of animal species the area can support. However, the only effect that the stimulus mentions for forest fragmentation is that some animals thrive in those conditions. (B) – The stimulus says "some animals, such as white-footed mice" thrive when forest fragmentation occurs. It is a jump to say that most species of small animals will see that population increase. (A) is unproven. Just because white-footed mice see their highest population densities in fragmented forests does not mean they are rarely found in unfragmented forests.

2) Confirm. (D) is the only choice standing, and it is proven. The use of the phrase "can have" makes this choice safe. Stopping forest fragmentation *can have* a beneficial effect on human health by lowering white-footed mouse populations, which will limit Lyme disease. One key here is to see that Lyme disease affects human health. That is a valid translation, something that the correct choice may ask you to do on an Inference problem. This can make the correct choice more difficult to see.

Notice that we have a Logic Chain in the stimulus. The inference relies on that chain. The inference says that the first part of the chain (fragmentation) connects to the end of the chain (Lyme disease).

3. The size of northern fur seals provides a reliable indication of their population levels—the smaller the average body size of seals in a population, the larger the population. Archaeologists studied seal fossils covering an 800-year period when the seals were hunted for food by Native peoples in North America and found that the average body size of the seals did not vary significantly.

The statements above, if true, provide the most support for which one of the following?

(A) During the 800-year period studied, seal hunting practices did not vary substantially between different groups of Native peoples in North America.

(B) The body size of northern fur seals is not strongly correlated with the overall health of the seals.

(C) Before the 800-year period studied, the average body size of northern fur seals fluctuated dramatically.

(D) Native peoples in North America made an effort to limit their hunting of northern fur seals in order to prevent depletion of seal populations.

(E) Hunting by Native peoples in North America did not significantly reduce the northern fur seal population over the 800-year period studied.

Techniques Summary

- Core Focus: Start with (E) and use Prove and Move.

- Stimulus: Understand the facts and look for an Obvious Inference.

- Choices:

  o Start with (E).

  o Eliminate unproven choices.

  o If you find a proven choice, Prove and Move.

3. The size of northern fur seals provides a reliable indication of their population levels—the smaller the average body size of seals in a population, the larger the population. Archaeologists studied seal fossils covering an 800-year period when the seals were hunted for food by Native peoples in North America and found that the average body size of the seals did not vary significantly.

 The statements above, if true, **provide the most support** for which one of the following?

(A) During the 800-year period studied, seal hunting practices did not vary substantially between different groups of Native peoples in North America.

(B) The body size of northern fur seals is not strongly correlated with the overall health of the seals.

(C) Before the 800-year period studied, the average body size of northern fur seals fluctuated dramatically.

(D) Native peoples in North America made an effort to limit their hunting of northern fur seals in order to prevent depletion of seal populations.

(E) Hunting by Native peoples in North America did not significantly reduce the northern fur seal population over the 800-year period studied.

Type: Inference
Tag: Obvious Link, Prove and Move

Stem - The stem asks you what the statements support, which tells you this is an Inference problem. Get ready to read the stimulus carefully.

Stimulus – 1) Read the stimulus carefully. We learn that the average body size of fur seals predicts how big their population is. The smaller the body size, the bigger the population. This makes sense because the more seals in an area vying for food, the less each seal probably gets to eat. Next, the stimulus says that over 800 years, Native peoples hunted the seals, and the seals average body size did not change much during that period of time.

2) Look for an Obvious Inference. The final sentence of the stimulus supports the idea that the seal hunting over this period did not change with the size of seal populations much because the average body size did not change much.

Choices – 1) Eliminate choices, starting with (E). Keep an eye out for the Obvious Inference. (E) matches the inference well; the hunting did not significantly reduce the seal populations. If it had, the average body size of the seals would have increased because average animal size is inversely proportional to the overall population size. The stimulus told us that the average body did not vary much. (E) is correct and is ripe for Prove and Move.

For practice, lets analyze (A), a popular incorrect choice. (A) talks about seal hunting *practices* during the time period, but the stimulus doesn't. The size of the seal populations didn't change during that period, but the different groups of hunters could have changed how they hunted. The hunting practices could have changed without affecting the number of seals killed. (A) is unproven.

4. Over the last few decades, public outcries against pollution have brought about stricter regulations of emissions. The cities that had the most polluted air 30 years ago now have greatly improved air quality. This would not have happened without these stricter regulations.

   Which one of the following can be properly inferred from the statements above?

   (A) In the city with the worst air pollution today, the air quality is better than it was 30 years ago.

   (B) No city has worse air pollution today than it did 30 years ago.

   (C) Most of the public outcries against pollution came from people in the cities that had the most polluted air.

   (D) The most polluted cities today are not the cities that were the most polluted 30 years ago.

   (E) Public criticism led to an improvement in the air quality of the cities that had the most polluted air 30 years ago.

Techniques Summary

- <u>Core Focus</u>: Start with (E) and use Prove and Move.

- Stimulus: Understand the facts and look for an Obvious Inference.

- Choices:

  o Start with (E).

  o Eliminate unproven choices.

  o If you find a proven choice, Prove and Move.

4. Over the last few decades, public outcries against pollution have brought about stricter regulations of emissions. The cities that had the most polluted air 30 years ago now have greatly improved air quality. This would not have happened without these stricter regulations.

   Which one of the following can be **properly inferred** from the statements above?

   (A)   In the city with the worst air pollution today, the air quality is better than it was 30 years ago.

   (B)   No city has worse air pollution today than it did 30 years ago.

   (C)   Most of the public outcries against pollution came from people in the cities that had the most polluted air.

   (D)   The most polluted cities today are not the cities that were the most polluted 30 years ago.

   (E)   Public criticism led to an improvement in the air quality of the cities that had the most polluted air 30 years ago.

Type: Inference
Tag: Logic Chain, Obvious Inference, Prove and Move

Stem – "Properly inferred" tells you that this is an Inference problem.

Stimulus – 1) Read the stimulus carefully. We learn that public outcries led to stricter regulations on emissions. Those stricter regulations helped improve the air quality of cities with the most polluted air 30 years ago. This is a Logic Chain: Outcries → Regulations → Improvement

2) Look for an Obvious Inference. The stimulus is a Logic Chain, so the correct choice might link the first part of the chain with the last, something like "the public outcries improved the air quality of the most polluted cities."

Choices – 1) Eliminate unproven choices, starting with (E). (E) states our Obvious Inference. Public criticism (outcries) brought about the stricter regulations, and the regulations caused the improvements in air quality for the most polluted cities. So, the public criticism led to improved air quality, via the regulations. (E) makes a classic inference based on the Logic Chain in the support. A caused B and B caused C, so A caused C. (E) is logically proven and matches our Obvious Inference, so use the Prove and Move technique.

For practice, lets analyze (C) and (A). (C) – The stimulus does not say where the public outcries came from, only that they caused the stricter regulations. We know that the cities that were most polluted benefited from the outcries, but we don't know that the outcries mostly occurred there. (A) talks about the city with the worst air pollution today, which is a city we know nothing about. The stimulus only talks about cities with the worst pollution *30 years ago*, so (A) is unproven.

5. One should apologize only to a person one has wronged, and only for having wronged that person. To apologize sincerely is to acknowledge that one has acted wrongfully. One cannot apologize sincerely unless one intends not to repeat that wrongful act. To accept an apology sincerely is to acknowledge a wrong, but also to vow not to hold a grudge against the wrongdoer.

The statements above, if true, most strongly support which one of the following?

(A)   If one apologizes and subsequently repeats the wrongful act for which one has apologized, then one has not apologized sincerely.

(B)   One cannot sincerely accept an apology that was not sincerely offered.

(C)   If one commits a wrongful act, then one should sincerely apologize for that act.

(D)   An apology that cannot be sincerely accepted cannot be sincerely offered.

(E)   An apology cannot be both sincerely offered and sincerely accepted unless each person acknowledges that a wrongful act has occurred.

Techniques Summary

- <u>Core Focus</u>: Start with (E) and use Prove and Move.

- Stimulus: Understand the facts and look for an Obvious Inference.

- Choices:

  o   Start with (E).

  o   Eliminate unproven choices.

  o   If you find a proven choice, Prove and Move.

5. One should apologize only to a person one has wronged, and only for having wronged that person. To apologize sincerely is to acknowledge that one has acted wrongfully. One cannot apologize sincerely unless one intends not to repeat that wrongful act. To accept an apology sincerely is to acknowledge a wrong, but also to vow not to hold a grudge against the wrongdoer.

I

The statements above, if true, **most strongly support** which one of the following?

(A)   If one apologizes and subsequently repeats the wrongful act for which one has apologized, then one has not apologized sincerely.

(B)   One cannot sincerely accept an apology that was not sincerely offered.

(C)   If one commits a wrongful act, then one should sincerely apologize for that act.

(D)   An apology that cannot be sincerely accepted cannot be sincerely offered.

(E)   An apology cannot be both sincerely offered and sincerely accepted unless each person acknowledges that a wrongful act has occurred.

Type: Inference
Tag: Conditionals Heavy, Prove and Move

Stem – "Most strongly support" tells you that this is an Inference problem.

Stimulus – 1) Read the stimulus carefully. There are four dense conditionals regarding apologies. They could link in all kinds of ways meaning there are many possible inferences here.

2) Look for an Obvious Inference. There is no Obvious Inference; the stimulus has way too much information for that.

Choices – 1) Eliminate unproven choices, starting with (E). (E) says that both sincerely offering and accepting an apology requires both people to acknowledge that a wrongful act has occurred. Let's check back in with the stimulus to analyze. "To apologize sincerely is to acknowledge that one has acted wrongfully." Offering an apology sincerely does require acknowledgment of a wrongful act. And from the final sentence: "to accept an apology sincerely is to acknowledge a wrong." So, (E) is logically proven. You can employ the Prove and Move technique on this problem. It is unlikely that you would remember the support for this choice, so referring back to the stimulus is very helpful.

For learning purposes, let's analyze (A). The stimulus says that to apologize sincerely one has to "*intend* not to repeat that wrongful act." Intention is different than action. So, one could meet the requirement for a sincere apology and then still repeat the act, for whatever reason. (A) is not proven.

6. The airport's runways are too close to each other to allow simultaneous use of adjacent runways when visibility is poor, so the airport allows only 30 planes an hour to land in poor weather; in good weather 60 planes an hour are allowed to land. Because airline schedules assume good weather, bad weather creates serious delays.

    Which one of the following is most strongly supported by the information above?

    (A) In poor weather, only half as many planes are allowed to land each hour on any one runway at the airport as are allowed to land on it in good weather.

    (B) When the weather at the airport is good it is likely that there are planes landing on two adjacent runways at any given time.

    (C) If any two of the airport's runways are used simultaneously, serious delays result.

    (D) Airlines using the airport base their schedules on the assumption that more than 30 planes an hour will be allowed to land at the airport.

    (E) In good weather, there are few if any seriously delayed flights at the airport.

Techniques Summary

- Core Focus: Start with (E) and use Prove and Move.

- Stimulus: Understand the facts and look for an Obvious Inference.

- Choices:
    - Start with (E).
    - Eliminate unproven choices.
    - If you find a proven choice, Prove and Move.

6. The airport's runways are too close to each other to allow simultaneous use of adjacent runways when visibility is poor, so the airport allows only 30 planes an hour to land in poor weather; in good weather 60 planes an hour are allowed to land. Because airline schedules assume good weather, bad weather creates serious delays.

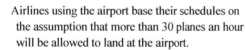

Which one of the following is **most strongly supported** by the information above?

(A)   In poor weather, only half as many planes are allowed to land each hour on any one runway at the airport as are allowed to land on it in good weather.

(B)   When the weather at the airport is good it is likely that there are planes landing on two adjacent runways at any given time.

(C)   If any two of the airport's runways are used simultaneously, serious delays result.

(D)   Airlines using the airport base their schedules on the assumption that more than 30 planes an hour will be allowed to land at the airport.

(E)   In good weather, there are few if any seriously delayed flights at the airport.

Type: Inference
Tag: Prove and Move

Stem – "Most strongly supported" = Inference problem.

Stimulus – 1) Read the stimulus carefully. We learn that this airport can only use its two runways simultaneously in good weather. In good weather, 60 planes can land an hour. In bad, only 30 can land. The stimulus finishes on the idea that bad weather creates delays because airline schedules assume good weather.

2) Look for an Obvious Inference. Nothing sticks out.

Choices – 1) Eliminate unproven choices, starting with (E). (E) – We know that there are delays in bad weather, but we don't know what happens in good weather. More planes can land each hour, but that doesn't mean there aren't delays. (E) is unproven. (D) – We know that the airline schedules assume good weather, and bad weather causes delays. For bad weather to cause delays, the airlines must assume that more than 30 planes can land each hour. Otherwise, the bad weather wouldn't cause any delays. (D) is logically proven, so it must be correct. Prove and Move.

Let's analyze (B) and (A). (B) talks about planes landing on both runways at the same time. The stimulus never talked about landing specifically. We only know that both runways could be *used* at the same time. (A) assumes that the airport alternates runway use during bad weather. Perhaps in bad weather only one runway is used and it gets as many planes per hour as it does during good weather.

7. People who are allergic to cats are actually allergic to certain proteins found in the animals' skin secretions and saliva; which particular proteins are responsible, however, varies from allergy sufferer to allergy sufferer. Since all cats shed skin and spread saliva around their environment, there is no such thing as a cat incapable of provoking allergic reactions, although it is common for a given cat to cause an allergic reaction in some—but not all—people who are allergic to cats.

Which one of the following statements is most strongly supported by the information above?

(A) Any particular individual will be allergic to some breeds of cat but not to others.

(B) No cat is capable of causing an allergic reaction in all types of allergy sufferers.

(C) Not all cats are identical with respect to the proteins contained in their skin secretions and saliva.

(D) The allergic reactions of some people who are allergic to cats are more intense than the allergic reactions of other allergy sufferers.

(E) There is no way to predict whether a given cat will produce an allergic reaction in a particular allergy sufferer.

Techniques Summary

- Core Focus: Start with (E) and Prove and Move.

- Stimulus: Understand the facts and look for an Obvious Inference.

- Choices:

  o Start with (E).

  o Eliminate unproven choices.

  o If you find a proven choice, Prove and Move.

7. People who are allergic to cats are actually allergic to certain proteins found in the animals' skin secretions and saliva; which particular proteins are responsible, however, varies from allergy sufferer to allergy sufferer. Since all cats shed skin and spread saliva around their environment, there is no such thing as a cat incapable of provoking allergic reactions, although it is common for a given cat to cause an allergic reaction in some—but not all—people who are allergic to cats.

 Which one of the following statements is **most strongly supported** by the information above?

 (A) Any particular individual will be allergic to some breeds of cat but not to others.

 (B) No cat is capable of causing an allergic reaction in all types of allergy sufferers.

(C) Not all cats are identical with respect to the proteins contained in their skin secretions and saliva.

 (D) The allergic reactions of some people who are allergic to cats are more intense than the allergic reactions of other allergy sufferers.

 (E) There is no way to predict whether a given cat will produce an allergic reaction in a particular allergy sufferer.

Type: Inference
Tag: Conditionals

Stem – "Most strongly supported" tells you that this is an Inference problem.

Stimulus – 1) Read the stimulus carefully. There are some complex ideas here. People are allergic to proteins in cats' skin and saliva although which proteins trigger allergies varies from person to person. All cats cause allergic reactions, but which people are affected varies.

2) Look for an Obvious Inference. With a stimulus this dense and hard to follow, it is difficult to see a link.

Choices – 1) Eliminate incorrect choices. (E) – The stimulus doesn't talk at all about *predicting* whether a cat could cause an allergy, so this choice is unproven. The variance in causing allergies doesn't mean that prediction is impossible. (D) – The stimulus never talks about the intensity of allergic reactions, either. (C) – We know that a given cat will cause an allergic reaction in only some allergy sufferers (final sentence). We also know that the allergy comes from the proteins. Linking these two, we see that cats must differ in their proteins. Otherwise, if cats all had the same proteins, then every allergy sufferer would be allergic to all cats. (C) looks good, but let's keep analyzing choices to be safe. (B) – We are told that it is common for a cat to cause an allergic reaction in some people but not all people. That leaves open the possibility that there is a cat out there that has all the allergic proteins and can cause an allergic reaction in all people. Epically-allergic cat! (A) – We know that people allergic to cats will be allergic to some breeds but not others, but we can't say that about any individual. Some people are not allergic to cats after all and the stimulus doesn't ever talk about them.

2) Confirm. (C) is the best choice.

8. In order to save money, many consumers redeem coupons that are distributed by retail stores. However, in general, retail stores that distribute and accept store coupons as a way of discounting the prices on certain products charge more for their products, on average, than other retail stores charge for the same products—even after lower prices available on coupon-discounted products are factored in. This is because producing and distributing coupons usually costs a great deal. To compensate for this expense without reducing profits, retail stores must pass it on to consumers.

Which one of the following can be properly inferred from the information above?

(A) Many consumers who redeem coupons save little if any money, overall, by doing so.

(B) Retail stores that distribute coupons generally compensate for the expense of producing and distributing coupons by charging higher prices for certain products.

(C) The profits of retail stores that use coupons are not significantly lower, on average, than the profits of similar stores that do not use coupons.

(D) At least some retail stores that do not use coupons do not have expenses that they pass on to consumers.

(E) The undiscounted price charged for a good for which a retail store offers a coupon will be higher than the price charged for that same good by a retail store that does not offer a coupon for it.

Techniques Summary

- Core Focus: Start with (E) and use Prove and Move.

- Stimulus: Understand the facts and look for an Obvious Inference.

- Choices:

    o Start with (E).

    o Eliminate unproven choices.

    o If you find a proven choice, Prove and Move.

8. In order to save money, many consumers redeem coupons that are distributed by retail stores. However, in general, retail stores that distribute and accept store coupons as a way of discounting the prices on certain products charge more for their products, on average, than other retail stores charge for the same products—even after lower prices available on coupon-discounted products are factored in. This is because producing and distributing coupons usually costs a great deal. To compensate for this expense without reducing profits, retail stores must pass it on to consumers.

Which one of the following can be **properly inferred** from the information above?

(A) Many consumers who redeem coupons save little if any money, overall, by doing so.

(B) Retail stores that distribute coupons generally compensate for the expense of producing and distributing coupons by charging higher prices for certain products.

(C) The profits of retail stores that use coupons are not significantly lower, on average, than the profits of similar stores that do not use coupons.

(D) At least some retail stores that do not use coupons do not have expenses that they pass on to consumers.

(E) The undiscounted price charged for a good for which a retail store offers a coupon will be higher than the price charged for that same good by a retail store that does not offer a coupon for it.

Type: Inference
Tag: Prove and Move

Stem – "Properly inferred" tells you that this is an Inference problem. Get ready to understand a set of facts in the stimulus.

Stimulus – 1) Read the stimulus carefully. We learn all about coupons. Stores that have coupons charge more on average for their products. Also, stores that use coupons have to deal with the costs of producing and distributing coupons, and they pass those costs onto consumers.

2) Look for an Obvious Inference. Nothing stands out.

Choices – 1) Eliminate incorrect choices. (E) – The stimulus only compares *average prices* at coupon and non-coupon stores, so this statement about the price for a specific good is unproven. (D) – The stimulus doesn't talk about non-coupon-related expenses at stores that could be passed on to consumers. It is possible that all retail stores that do use coupons have expenses that they pass on to consumers, such as higher advertising expenses. (C) – The stimulus never talks specifically about profits. We know that the costs of the coupons are passed on to consumers, meaning the store does not deal with those costs. But, we don't know how the overall profits between these two types of stores compare. (B) is a simple inference, and it's almost a restatement of the final sentence. Passing the cost of coupons onto consumers means charging higher prices, which is what the beginning of the stimulus discusses. (B) is proven. Prove and Move here.

Let's analyze (A) for teaching purposes. We know that coupons save people money on items purchased using them. If consumers only buy coupon items, then they could save money overall even though they are shopping at a store that has on average higher prices for all of its goods. So, (A) is not proven. Again, it is crucial to understand that non-coupon stores have lower prices than coupon stores only on average.

END OF SET

Logically Completes Subtype

Inference problems have a subtype that accounts for 20% of Inference problems. The <u>Logically Completes</u> subtype stems look like this:

> | Which one of the following most **logically completes** the argument?

The Logically Completes subtype sometimes features a <u>Parallel Situation</u>, a unique type of stimulus. Normal Inference problems do not have Parallel Situation stimuli.

A <u>Parallel Situation</u> is when the stimulus features an analogy—it compares one situation to another—and the stem asks you to use the stimulus as a comparison to describe how the second situation will play out. These stimuli end in a *blank* that you will fill in by extending the analogy to the new situation. Here is an example of a Parallel Situation stimulus:

> Roxanne promised Luke that she would finish their report while he was on vacation; however, the deadline for that report was postponed. Clearly, if you promised a friend that you would meet them for lunch but just before lunch you felt ill, it would not be wrong for you to miss the lunch; your friend would not expect you to be there if you felt ill. Similarly, _____.

The analogy drawn is between these two situations:

- Canceling a meeting with a friend for lunch because of feeling ill
- Finishing a report late because the deadline was postponed

What is at the heart of the analogy? In both situations, there are external circumstances that help the person with whom the commitment was made *understand* why the commitment can be canceled. Here is the correct choice for this stimulus:

> (D)   if Luke would not expect Roxanne to finish the report under the circumstances, then it would not be wrong for Roxanne to fail to finish it

(D) is an inference, but you can see how it is hard to *prove* that this choice is correct. The choice correctly extends the analogy, but (D) is not an inference that links two pieces of information in the stimulus. It isn't easy to say for sure that (D) is correct just by analyzing it. Instead, you need to compare it to the other choices to confirm it is the best.

As a consequence, there's a strategy shift for problems with Parallel Situations. During the eliminate step, read every choice to make sure you find the best one. Do not use the Prove and Move technique on problems with Parallel Situation stimuli. Use the typical method of working the choices. First, eliminate incorrect choices, starting with (E) and moving to (A). After the elimination step, confirm the remaining choice.

On Logically Completes problems that do not feature a Parallel Situation, you can use the Prove and Move technique.

Logically Completes Technique Set

Directions

- Technique Summary: For each problem, after you read the stem and stamp it, pause working the problem and read the Technique Summary. As you complete the rest of the problem, actively apply the techniques.

- Time Limit: There is no time limit for completing the problems, so do your best to answer each correctly.

- Review: For each problem, read the explanation intently to check that you used the techniques properly. Also, use the explanation to improve your understanding of how the problem works.

- Milk every drop of learning out of a problem and its explanation before moving on so that your skills build steadily during this set.

1. A salesperson who makes a sale does not change the desires of the customer. Rather, the salesperson finds out what these desires are and then convinces the customer that a particular product will satisfy them. Persuading people to vote for a politician to whom they are initially indifferent is not significantly different. After discovering what policies the prospective voter would like to see in place, one tries to _____.

    Which one of the following most logically completes the argument?

    (A) show that the opponents of the politician in question do not favor all of those policies

    (B) disguise any difference between the policies the politician supports and the policies supported by other candidates

    (C) convince the voter that the policies favored by the politician in question are preferable to those favored by the voter

    (D) demonstrate that the politician is a person of outstanding character and is interested in some of the same issues as the voter

    (E) persuade the voter that voting for the politician in question is the best way to get these policies adopted

Techniques Summary

- Core Focus: Fact group proves correct choice.

- Logically Completes are like regular Inference problems, but the correct choice isn't necessarily 100% proven, though it is supported

- Look for Parallel Situations in the stimulus

1. A salesperson who makes a sale does not change the desires of the customer. Rather, the salesperson finds out what these desires are and then convinces the customer that a particular product will satisfy them. Persuading people to vote for a politician to whom they are initially indifferent is not significantly different. After discovering what policies the prospective voter would like to see in place, one tries to _____.

    Which one of the following most **logically completes** the argument?

     (A) show that the opponents of the politician in question do not favor all of those policies

     (B) disguise any difference between the policies the politician supports and the policies supported by other candidates

     (C) convince the voter that the policies favored by the politician in question are preferable to those favored by the voter

     (D) demonstrate that the politician is a person of outstanding character and is interested in some of the same issues as the voter

    (E) persuade the voter that voting for the politician in question is the best way to get these policies adopted

Type: Inference
Tag: Logically Completes, Parallel Situation

Stem – "Logically completes" in the stem and the blank at the end of the stimulus signal that this is a Logically Completes subtype. This means that you likely cannot use the Prove and Move technique.

Stimulus – 1) Read the stimulus carefully. It features an analogy between persuading someone to buy something and persuading someone to vote for a politician. The key for the salesperson is to learn the customer's desires and work with them to convince the customer that a certain product will satisfy those desires. This is a Parallel Situation, and you are asked to draw an inference on how to persuade someone to vote for a politician based on the description of how to persuade someone to buy something.

2) Look for an Obvious Inference. Any time you are given a Parallel Situation like this, you can envision a solid answer. Using the guidance from the salesperson, once we learn the policies of the voter, we need to convince her that the candidate will help those policies get enacted. This is just like convincing her that a product will fulfill her desires.

Choices – 1) Eliminate incorrect choices, starting with (E). Because this is a Logically Completes subtype, you cannot use the Prove and Move technique. The correct answer is not always provable logically. Sometimes, it is just the best answer because it fits the situation the best

(E) is a good match because it touches on concept of fulfilling a voter's desires (enacting the policies she supports). Nevertheless, we can't tell that this choice is 100% proven, so let's analyze the rest of the choices to see if we can find a better fit than (E). (D) – The concept of outstanding character is not matched in the analogy, and "interested in the same issues" doesn't mean those policies will get enacted and the voter will have her desires. (C) goes against the analogy by trying to change the person's policy requirements. The first line of the stimulus says that the salesperson does not change the desires of the customer. (B) – The idea of disguising differences and tricking the voter goes against the analogy. (A) talks about a comparison with other politicians, and that is outside the nature of the analogy. The salesperson never says that different products do not meet the customer's needs to make the sale.

2) Confirm. (E) is the best answer because it talks about working with the voter's policies. (E) is correct.

2. Editorial: Painting involves a sequential application of layers, each of which adheres satisfactorily only if the underlying layer has been properly applied. Education is, in this respect, like the craft of painting. Since the most important steps in painting are preparation of the surface to be painted and application of the primer coat, it makes sense to suppose that _____.

Which one of the following most logically completes the editorial's argument?

(A) in the educator's initial contact with a student, the educator should be as undemanding as possible

(B) students who have a secure grasp of the fundamentals of a subject are likely to make progress in that subject

(C) educators who are not achieving the goals they intended should revise their teaching methods

(D) teaching new students is rewarding but much more difficult than teaching more advanced students

(E) the success of a student's overall educational experience depends above all upon that student's initial educational experience

Techniques Summary

- <u>Core Focus</u>: Fact group proves correct choice.

- Logically Completes are like regular Inference problems, but the correct choice isn't necessarily 100% proven, though it is supported

- Look for Parallel Situations in the stimulus

2. Editorial: Painting involves a sequential application of layers, each of which adheres satisfactorily only if the underlying layer has been properly applied. Education is, in this respect, like the craft of painting. Since the most important steps in painting are preparation of the surface to be painted and application of the primer coat, it makes sense to suppose that _____.

 Which one of the following most **logically completes** the editorial's argument?

 (A)   in the educator's initial contact with a student, the educator should be as undemanding as possible

(B)   students who have a secure grasp of the fundamentals of a subject are likely to make progress in that subject

 (C)   educators who are not achieving the goals they intended should revise their teaching methods

 (D)   teaching new students is rewarding but much more difficult than teaching more advanced students

(E)   the success of a student's overall educational experience depends above all upon that student's initial educational experience

Type: Inference
Tag: Logically Completes, Parallel Situation

Stem – "Logically Completes" tells you that this is an Inference problem, and it is a Logically Completes subtype.

Stimulus – 1) Read the stimulus carefully. Painting requires applying many layers sequentially, and the most important steps are the preparation and the first layer of paint. Education is like painting in this regard. This is a Parallel Situation.

2) Look for an Obvious Inference. We hear that the setup, the very beginning of painting, is the most important part, so we would assume the same to be true of education.

Choices – 1) Eliminate choices, starting with (E). (E) says that the initial education experience is very important in terms of the entire education. (E) sounds very good, but it is not fully proven by the stimulus. The answer to a Parallel Situation problem is more subjective and less firmly logical than the answer to a typical Inference problem, so we need to analyze the rest of the choices to see if one is a better fit than (E). (D) talks about rewards and difficulties in teaching, which the stimulus never talks about. (C) talks about revision of methods, which is also not a concept discussed as the stimulus describes painting. (B) talks about fundamentals and making progress, but those concepts aren't a precise match to the concept of the first layer of a painting being the most important. (A) is an Opposite Choice because the educator needs to make sure that the first interaction with a student goes well and the student is challenged.

2) Confirm. (E) is the best choice here, and it is correct.

END OF SET

Logically Completes Review

Stem

- "Logically completes" = the <u>Logically Completes</u> subtype. These often feature a Parallel Situation.

Choices

- <u>Parallel Situation</u>: Some Logically Completes problems ask you to use an analogy to draw a conclusion about a situation.

  - The correct choice is not 100% proven as most correct answers typically will be on Inference problems.

  - Eliminate all the incorrect choices before you select an answer. Do not use Prove and Move.

Techniques Summary

- <u>Core Focus</u>: Fact group proves correct choice.

- These are like regular Inference problems, but the correct choice isn't necessarily 100% proven, though it is supported.

- Look for Parallel Situations in the stimulus.

Inference Challenge Sets

Now that you have completed both Technique Sets, you will deeply practice your skills on difficult Inference problems with the Challenge Sets. Here is an overview:

- 20 problems divided into four Sets.

- Read the Techniques Summary before you start each Set.

- Take your time on each Set.

- Review only incorrect and marked problems. First, self-review the problem, then read its explanation.

The Challenge Sets are on average much more difficult than normal Inference problems. They will push you to answer challenging problems correctly using the techniques. The problems in the Sets increase in difficulty, so the final Sets are *very* difficult.

Directions

- Attempt each Set and then review your work for those problems before moving onto the next Set.

- <u>Technique Summary:</u> Before you attempt a Set, read the Technique Summary to further engrain the techniques.

- <u>Time Limit:</u> There is no time limit for each Set, so work every problem carefully. Aim for 100% accuracy on each Set, even on the most difficult ones. Expect the final Sets to take longer to attempt per problem than the problems in the Technique Set because of their greater difficulty.

- <u>Review:</u> In the Sets, you will only review the problems you missed and those you *marked to review*. Mark any problems that you find difficult or confusing as you attempt a Set so you know to review them later even if you answer them correctly.

- Unlike in the Technique Set, you don't need to review every problem after you attempt a Set. If you answered a problem correctly, you're confident you approached it efficiently, and you understood it fully, then you do not need to analyze it.

- To review a problem, first *self-review* it. After completing the Technique Set, you now have a solid understanding of Inference problems, so self-review can be valuable. Insights from self-review are often more memorable than those gained from reading an explanation. To self-review, analyze the correct choice and consider why it's correct. Refer to the stimulus for help. Next, analyze any incorrect choices that were tempting. Figure out why they are incorrect using the stimulus.

- After you self-review the problem, carefully read the problem explanation. As you read the explanation, analyze how well you used the techniques and look for aspects of the problem you overlooked during your self-review.

Challenge Set 1

Techniques Summary

- <u>Core Focus</u>: Start with (E) and use Prove and Move.

- Stimulus: Understand the facts and look for an Obvious Inference.

- Choices:

    o Start with (E).

    o Eliminate unproven choices.

    o If you find a proven choice, Prove and Move.

1. Failure to rotate crops depletes the soil's nutrients gradually unless other preventive measures are taken. If the soil's nutrients are completely depleted, additional crops cannot be grown unless fertilizer is applied to the soil. All other things being equal, if vegetables are grown in soil that has had fertilizer applied rather than being grown in non-fertilized soil, they are more vulnerable to pests and, as a consequence, must be treated with larger amounts of pesticides. The more pesticides used on vegetables, the greater the health risks to humans from eating those vegetables.

    Suppose there were some vegetables that were grown in soil to which fertilizer had never been applied. On the basis of the passage, which one of the following would have to be true regarding those vegetables?

    (A) The soil in which the vegetables were grown may have been completely depleted of nutrients because of an earlier failure to rotate crops.

    (B) It is not possible that the vegetables were grown in soil in which crops had been rotated.

    (C) The vegetables were grown in soil that had not been completely depleted of nutrients but not necessarily soil in which crops had been rotated.

    (D) Whatever the health risks to humans from eating the vegetables, these risks would not be attributable to the use of pesticides on them.

    (E) The health risks to humans from eating the vegetables were no less than the health risks to humans from eating the same kinds of vegetables treated with pesticides.

2. Every delegate to the convention is a party member. Some delegates to the convention are government officials, and each government official who is at the convention is a speaker at the convention, as well.

    If the statements above are true, then which one of the following statements must be true?

    (A) Every party member at the convention is a delegate to the convention.

    (B) At least some speakers at the convention are neither delegates nor party members.

    (C) At least some speakers at the convention are delegates to the convention.

    (D) All speakers at the convention are government officials.

    (E) Every government official at the convention is a party member.

3. Birds and mammals can be infected with West Nile virus only through mosquito bites. Mosquitoes, in turn, become infected with the virus when they bite certain infected birds or mammals. The virus was originally detected in northern Africa and spread to North America in the 1990s. Humans sometimes catch West Nile virus, but the virus never becomes abundant enough in human blood to infect a mosquito.

    The statements above, if true, most strongly support which one of the following?

    (A) West Nile virus will never be a common disease among humans.

    (B) West Nile virus is most common in those parts of North America with the highest density of mosquitoes.

    (C) Some people who become infected with West Nile virus never show symptoms of illness.

    (D) West Nile virus infects more people in northern Africa than it does in North America.

    (E) West Nile virus was not carried to North America via an infected person.

4. Although instinct enables organisms to make complex responses to stimuli, instinctual behavior involves no reasoning and requires far fewer nerve cells than does noninstinctual (also called flexible) behavior. A brain mechanism capable of flexible behavior must have a large number of neurons, and no insect brain has yet reached a size capable of providing a sufficiently large number of neurons.

Which one of the following can be properly inferred from the statements above?

(A)   The behavior of organisms with elaborate brain mechanisms is usually not instinctual.

(B)   Insect behavior is exclusively instinctual.

(C)   All organisms with brains larger than insects' brains are capable of some measure of flexible behavior.

(D)   All organisms with large brains are biologically equipped for flexible behavior.

(E)   Only organisms with brains of insect size or smaller engage in purely instinctual behavior.

5. Political scientist: One of the most interesting dilemmas in contemporary democratic politics concerns the regulation of political campaign spending. People certainly should be free, within broad limits, to spend their money as they choose. On the other hand, candidates who can vastly outspend all rivals have an unfair advantage in publicizing their platforms. Democratic governments have a strong obligation to ensure that all voices have an equal chance to be heard, but governments should not subsidize expensive campaigns for each candidate. The resolution of the dilemma, therefore, is clear: _____.

Which one of the following most logically completes the political scientist's argument?

(A)   only candidates with significant campaign resources should be permitted to run for public office

(B)   an upper limit on the political campaign spending of each candidate is warranted

(C)   government subsidization of all political campaigns at a low percentage of their total cost is warranted

(D)   all wealthy persons should be prohibited from spending their own money on political campaigns

(E)   each candidate should be allowed to spend as much money on a political campaign as any other candidate chooses to spend

END OF SET

Set 1 Key & Explanations

1. C

2. C

3. E

4. B

5. B

1. Failure to rotate crops depletes the soil's nutrients gradually unless other preventive measures are taken. If the soil's nutrients are completely depleted, additional crops cannot be grown unless fertilizer is applied to the soil. All other things being equal, if vegetables are grown in soil that has had fertilizer applied rather than being grown in non-fertilized soil, they are more vulnerable to pests and, as a consequence, must be treated with larger amounts of pesticides. The more pesticides used on vegetables, the greater the health risks to humans from eating those vegetables.

   Suppose there were some vegetables that were grown in soil to which fertilizer had never been applied. On the basis of the passage, which one of the following would **have to be true** regarding those vegetables?

   (A) The soil in which the vegetables were grown may have been completely depleted of nutrients because of an earlier failure to rotate crops.

   (B) It is not possible that the vegetables were grown in soil in which crops had been rotated.

   (C) The vegetables were grown in soil that had not been completely depleted of nutrients but not necessarily soil in which crops had been rotated.

   (D) Whatever the health risks to humans from eating the vegetables, these risks would not be attributable to the use of pesticides on them.

   (E) The health risks to humans from eating the vegetables were no less than the health risks to humans from eating the same kinds of vegetables treated with pesticides.

Type: Inference
Tag: Prove & Move

Stem – "Would have to be true" tells us this is an Inference problem, but this stem looks different from everything we've seen so far. It gives us a small hint: we know we need to consider what happens to vegetables grown in soil without fertilizer.

Stimulus – 1) Read the stimulus carefully. This Stimulus looks pretty complicated, but it's actually just four conditionals that form one long Logic Chain. It's an exhausting logic chain, but it's relatively simple when you break it down. Failure to rotate crops → depleted nutrients → fertilizer → more pesticides → greater health risks.

2) Look for an Obvious Inference. There is no Obvious Inference from the Stimulus itself, but we know that we need to pay attention to what happens to vegetables grown in soil without fertilizer (because we read the Stem first!). If fertilizer has never been added to the soil, then we know the nutrients were not depleted because obviously crops were grown. We also know that our farmer did not need to use larger amounts of pesticides because the use of fertilizer did not make these crops more vulnerable to pests. With that in mind, we can also infer that the health risks to people who ate these vegetables were not as bad.

Choices – 1) Eliminate choices, starting with (E). We can eliminate (E) quickly. The Stimulus told us that vegetables grown with more pesticides would have greater health risks. Because our farmer didn't use fertilizer, she did not need larger amounts of pesticides, so our vegetables would have *lower* health risks. By that same logic, (D) looks a little tempting. A smaller amount of pesticides means lower health risk, but nothing in the Stimulus tells us our farmer wouldn't use *some* pesticides, even on plants grown in nutrient-rich, non-fertilized soil. There could still be health risks from the pesticides our farmer did use. (D) looks like a New Concept. Eliminate it. (C) fits our line of thinking from the Stimulus. If fertilizer was never used on the soil, then the soil's nutrients were never depleted in the first place. Got it. But, what do we know about rotating crops? We learned that failure to rotate crops depletes the nutrients in the soil, but the stimulus emphasizes that this is a gradual process. It is possible that our farmer hasn't needed to rotate crops because there are still plenty of nutrients in the soil. By that logic, (C) is proven.

If you feel confident in (C), then you might Prove and Move here. For teaching purposes, let's look at the other choices. We can eliminate (B) quickly. We inferred that our vegetables were grown in soil that was not depleted of nutrients, so the farmer did not fail to rotate her crops. These vegetables could easily have been grown in perfectly rotated soil. We can eliminate (A) quickly, too. If fertilizer was never applied to the soil in which our farmer grew these vegetables, then all of the nutrients in the soil were never depleted of nutrients. That means our farmer never failed to rotate crops and depleted the nutrients as a consequence.

2. Every delegate to the convention is a party member. Some delegates to the convention are government officials, and each government official who is at the convention is a speaker at the convention, as well.

l If the statements above are true, then which one of the following statements **must be true**?

(A) Every party member at the convention is a delegate to the convention.

(B) At least some speakers at the convention are neither delegates nor party members.

(C) At least some speakers at the convention are delegates to the convention.

(D) All speakers at the convention are government officials.

(E) Every government official at the convention is a party member.

Type: Inference
Tags: Prove & Move, Obvious Inference, Quantifier Combination

Stem – "Must be true" tells us this is an Inference problem.

Stimulus – 1) Read the Stimulus carefully. The stimulus is relatively simple. It is full of Quantifiers, which could indicate some conditional relationships when we combine them.

2) Look for an Obvious Inference. When we consider the Quantifier Combinations in the Stimulus, we can infer a few things that might show up in the Choices. *All* delegates are party members, and *some* delegates are government officials. So, we can infer that *some* (not necessarily all) government officials at the convention are party members. Also, we learn that *each* government official is a speaker at the convention. If *some* delegates at the convention are government officials, then we can infer that *some* delegates are also speakers at the convention.

Choices - 1) Eliminate Choices, starting with (E). (E) is not proven because we inferred that only some government officials at the convention are party members. There could be plenty of government officials attending the convention who are not delegates and therefore not necessarily party members. Because we know that every government official at the convention is a speaker, (D) might look Plausible at first, but it's actually a New Concept. Even though every government official is a speaker, every speaker is not necessarily a government official. We only know that *some* speakers are government officials. There could be plenty of speakers at the convention who are not government officials. (C) matches our Obvious Inference. *All* government officials at the convention are speakers, and *some* delegates are government officials. When we combine these Quantifiers, we find that *some* speakers are delegates. Prove and Move.

3. Birds and mammals can be infected with West Nile virus only through mosquito bites. Mosquitoes, in turn, become infected with the virus when they bite certain infected birds or mammals. The virus was originally detected in northern Africa and spread to North America in the 1990s. Humans sometimes catch West Nile virus, but the virus never becomes abundant enough in human blood to infect a mosquito.

l The statements above, if true, **most strongly support** which one of the following?

(A) West Nile virus will never be a common disease among humans.

(B) West Nile virus is most common in those parts of North America with the highest density of mosquitoes.

(C) Some people who become infected with West Nile virus never show symptoms of illness.

(D) West Nile virus infects more people in northern Africa than it does in North America.

(E) West Nile virus was not carried to North America via an infected person.

Type: Inference
Tags: Obvious Inference, Prove & Move

Stem – "Most strongly support" – this is an Inference problem.

Stimulus – 1) Read the Stimulus carefully. Everything you wanted to know about West Nile virus. There are a few important pieces of information that should stick out. The West Nile virus is only spread to birds and mammals through mosquito bites, and mosquitoes can only pick up the virus when they bite certain infected birds or mammals. Humans can catch West Nile virus, but mosquitoes cannot pick up the virus from biting an infected human.

2) Look for an Obvious Inference. The last sentence of the Stimulus sets you up to make a slick conclusion: humans cannot spread the West Nile virus. They can be infected, but a mosquito will not catch the virus if it bites an infected human. As a consequence, a mosquito cannot spread the virus from a human to another bird or mammal.

Choices – 1) Eliminate choices, starting with (E). (E) seems to follow our line of thinking from the Stimulus. Based on the Fact Group, we were able to infer that humans cannot spread the West Nile virus, so an infected human could not be responsible for the spread of the virus to North America. Even if an infected person traveled from northern Africa to North America, the virus could not be spread to other birds or mammals because the virus is spread only through mosquito bites and mosquitoes will not catch it from biting an infected human. (E) is proven. Prove and move.

4. Although instinct enables organisms to make complex responses to stimuli, instinctual behavior involves no reasoning and requires far fewer nerve cells than does noninstinctual (also called flexible) behavior. A brain mechanism capable of flexible behavior must have a large number of neurons, and no insect brain has yet reached a size capable of providing a sufficiently large number of neurons.

Which one of the following can be **properly inferred** from the statements above?

(A) The behavior of organisms with elaborate brain mechanisms is usually not instinctual.

(B) Insect behavior is exclusively instinctual.

(C) All organisms with brains larger than insects' brains are capable of some measure of flexible behavior.

(D) All organisms with large brains are biologically equipped for flexible behavior.

(E) Only organisms with brains of insect size or smaller engage in purely instinctual behavior.

Type: Inference
Tags: Obvious Inference, Prove & Move

Stem – "Properly inferred" tells us this an Inference problem.

Stimulus – 1) Read the Stimulus carefully. Although the Stimulus seems to be chock full of complex information about instinctual behavior, neurons, different brains, etc., it's actually pretty simple. It seems overly complicated because it uses different terms to identify the same ideas. For example, "noninstinctual behavior" means the same thing as "flexible behavior," and "nerve cells" means the same thing as "neurons." Synonymous terms like these can trip you up when a Fact Group presents a topic that is probably unfamiliar to you.

2) Look for an Obvious Inference. Following the logic in the stimulus, it seems pretty clear that insects are not capable of noninstinctual (or "flexible") behavior. If flexible behavior requires more neurons than any known insect brain has, then insects must not be capable of flexible behavior. Let's see if this comes up in the choices.

Choices – 1) Eliminate unproven choices, starting with (E). (E) almost matches our thinking on the stimulus. Because insect brains don't have enough neurons to handle flexible behavior, then all insect behavior must be instinctual. But, the stimulus didn't tell us how much bigger a brain must be to process flexible behavior (or how small it must be to be incapable of it). An organism could have a brain with twice as many neurons as an insect brain but still be incapable of flexible behavior. We just don't know enough to prove (E). (D) might look plausible at first, but it stretches us beyond what we learned in the stimulus toward a New Concept. We only learned that a brain must have a sufficiently large number of neurons to process flexible behavior. That is the only requirement we know. What determines a large brain? Just because a brain is "large" doesn't mean it has a sufficient number of neurons to process flexible behavior. (C) is similar to both (D) and (E). We don't know the specific requirement for flexible behavior. We just know that an insect brain does not have the sufficient number of neurons for it, so we don't have enough information to prove (C). By contrast, (B) matches our Obvious Inference. Because insect brains don't have enough neurons, they are not capable of flexible behavior. As a consequence, all insect behavior must be instinctual. Prove and Move.

5. Political scientist: One of the most interesting dilemmas in contemporary democratic politics concerns the regulation of political campaign spending. People certainly should be free, within broad limits, to spend their money as they choose. On the other hand, candidates who can vastly outspend all rivals have an unfair advantage in publicizing their platforms. Democratic governments have a strong obligation to ensure that all voices have an equal chance to be heard, but governments should not subsidize expensive campaigns for each candidate. The resolution of the dilemma, therefore, is clear: _____.

/ Which one of the following most logically completes the political scientist's argument?

(A) only candidates with significant campaign resources should be permitted to run for public office

(B) an upper limit on the political campaign spending of each candidate is warranted

(C) government subsidization of all political campaigns at a low percentage of their total cost is warranted

(D) all wealthy persons should be prohibited from spending their own money on political campaigns

(E) each candidate should be allowed to spend as much money on a political campaign as any other candidate chooses to spend

Type: Inference
Tags: Logically Completes

Stem – "Logically Completes" tells you this is an Inference problem, and it is a Logically Completes Subtype. We probably won't be able to use Prove and Move on this problem.

Stimulus – 1) Read the Stimulus carefully. The stimulus gives us a lot of information about political campaign spending. It emphasizes a clear dilemma about campaign spending: people should be free to spend their money as they see fit, but political candidates who can outspend their opponent have an unfair advantage in advancing their platform.

2) Look for an Obvious Inference. Nothing sticks out, but we know we need to find a resolution to our dilemma in the choices. The stimulus tells us that governments should not subsidize expensive campaigns, but they need to ensure all political voices have an equal chance to be heard. As we go through the choices, we want to look for a resolution that levels the playing field in political campaign spending – something that might add an element of fairness to our dilemma.

Choices – 1) Eliminate incorrect choices, starting with (E). Remember, this is a Logically Completes subtype, so we probably cannot use the Prove and Move technique.

(E) ties into the element of fairness we need in our resolution, but it wouldn't effectively level the playing field. Just because every candidate is allowed to spend as much money as their opponent doesn't mean they have as much to spend. With this requirement, a wealthy candidate can still vastly outspend their opponent, so our dilemma isn't resolved. (D) directly overlooks one of the key points to the stimulus. A crucial component to the dilemma is that people should be free to spend their money as they choose, so prohibiting a wealthy person from spending their own money on the campaign prevents that person from exercising this basic right. Also, it wouldn't necessarily solve our dilemma. (C) also overlooks an important part of the dilemma: governments should not subsidize expensive campaigns. Also, (C) doesn't offer a clear resolution, either. Even if the government subsidizes every candidate's campaign, a wealthy candidate can still outspend an opponent just as easily. By contrast, (B) provides a nice resolution to the dilemma. If each candidate can only spend up to a certain amount on her campaign, then the wealthy candidate's advantage is not as severe. The wealthy candidate might still outspend opponents with fewer resources, but an upper limit would close the gap in spending, leveling the playing field as a consequence. Even though we like (B), this is a Logically Completes subtype, so we need to consider (A). While (A) might close the gap in campaign spending, it would create another dilemma altogether. The stimulus emphasizes the government's responsibility to ensure that all voices have an equal chance to be heard. If only certain candidates are able to run for office, then all voices wouldn't have that equal chance.

2) Confirm. (B) is the best choice here, and it is correct.

Challenge Set 2

Techniques Summary

- <u>Core Focus</u>: Start with (E) and use Prove and Move.

- Stimulus: Understand the facts and look for an Obvious Inference.

- Choices:

    o Start with (E).

    o Eliminate unproven choices.

    o If you find a proven choice, Prove and Move.

1. When uncontrollable factors such as lack of rain cause farmers' wheat crops to fail, fertilizer and seed dealers, as well as truckers and mechanics, lose business, and fuel suppliers are unable to sell enough diesel fuel to make a profit.

    Which one of the following claims follows logically from the information above?

    (A) If several of the businesses that sell to farmers do not prosper, it is because farming itself is not prospering.

    (B) If rainfall is below average, those businesses that profit from farmers' purchases tend to lose money.

    (C) Farmers are not responsible for the consequences of a wheat crop's failing if wheat growth has been affected by lack of rain.

    (D) A country's dependence on agriculture can lead to major economic crises.

    (E) The consequences of a drought are not restricted to the drought's impact on farm productivity.

2. Trust, which cannot be sustained in the absence of mutual respect, is essential to any long-lasting relationship, personal or professional. However, personal relationships, such as marriage or friendship, additionally require natural affinity. If a personal relationship is to endure, it must be supported by the twin pillars of mutual respect and affinity.

    If the statements above are true, then which one of the following must also be true?

    (A) A friendship supported solely by trust and mutual respect will not be long-lasting.

    (B) In the context of any professional relationship, mutual respect presupposes trust.

    (C) If a personal relationship is supported by mutual respect and affinity, it will last a long time.

    (D) Personal relationships, such as marriage or friendship, are longer-lasting than professional relationships.

    (E) Basing a marriage on a natural affinity will ensure that it will endure.

3. Insurgent political parties that are profoundly dissatisfied with the dominant party's reign and justificatory ideology always produce factions whose views and aims differ as greatly from each other's as they do from the dominant party's. Although these factions ignore their own disagreements for the sake of defeating the dominant party, their disagreements inevitably come forward upon victory. Therefore, _____.

    Which one of the following is the most logical completion of the argument?

    (A) no victorious insurgent party ever manages to stay in power for as long as the party it displaces did

    (B) a victorious insurgent party must address the disagreements between its factions if it is to stay in power

    (C) the heretofore insurgent party will not always promulgate a new ideology to justify its own policies, once it is victorious

    (D) a victorious insurgent party always faces opposition from the party it recently ousted

    (E) it is impossible for the different factions of a victorious insurgent party to effect the compromises necessary to keep the new party in power

4. Any good garden compost may appropriately be used for soil drainage and fertility. The best compost is 40 to 60 percent organic matter and is dark brown in color. However, compost that emits a strong ammonia smell should not be used for drainage and fertility, for that smell means that the organic matter has not sufficiently decomposed.

Which one of the following is most strongly supported by the information above?

(A) Compost that is 80 percent organic matter has probably not decomposed sufficiently.

(B) If compost is less than 40 percent organic matter and is not dark brown in color, then it will make soil less fertile and will worsen soil drainage.

(C) If compost is 50 percent organic matter and that organic matter is sufficiently decomposed, then the compost is good.

(D) In the best garden compost, the organic matter is completely decomposed.

(E) Compost that is dark brown in color and emits a strong ammonia smell is not good garden compost.

5. Archaeologists are currently analyzing plant remains found at a site that was last occupied more than 10,000 years ago. If the plants were cultivated, then the people who occupied the site discovered agriculture thousands of years before any other people are known to have done so. On the other hand, if the plants were wild— that is, uncultivated—then the people who occupied the site ate a wider variety of wild plants than did any other people at the time.

The statements above, if true, most strongly support which one of the following?

(A) The archaeologists analyzing the plant remains at the site will be able to determine whether the plants were cultivated or were wild.

(B) The people who occupied the site used some plants in ways that no other people did at that time.

(C) If the people who occupied the site had reached a more advanced stage in the use of wild plants than any other people at the time, then the plants found at the site were uncultivated.

(D) If the people who occupied the site discovered agriculture thousands of years before people anywhere else are known to have done so, then there are remains of cultivated plants at the site.

(E) It is more likely that the people who occupied the site discovered agriculture thousands of years before people anywhere else did than it is that they ate a wider variety of wild plants than any other people at the time.

END OF SET

Set 2 Key & Explanations

1. E
2. A
3. B
4. E
5. B

1. When uncontrollable factors such as lack of rain cause farmers' wheat crops to fail, fertilizer and seed dealers, as well as truckers and mechanics, lose business, and fuel suppliers are unable to sell enough diesel fuel to make a profit.

   Which one of the following claims **follows logically** from the information above?

   (A)   If several of the businesses that sell to farmers do not prosper, it is because farming itself is not prospering.

   (B)   If rainfall is below average, those businesses that profit from farmers' purchases tend to lose money.

   (C)   Farmers are not responsible for the consequences of a wheat crop's failing if wheat growth has been affected by lack of rain.

   (D)   A country's dependence on agriculture can lead to major economic crises.

   (E)   The consequences of a drought are not restricted to the drought's impact on farm productivity.

Type: Inference
Tags: Obvious Inference, Prove & Move

Stem – "Follows logically" tells you this is an Inference problem. Don't confuse this as a Logically Completes subtype because of the similar language.

Stimulus – 1) Read the Stimulus carefully. The stimulus is one long sentence about agriculture. It gives us a list of things that are negatively affected when uncontrollable factors – in this case, lack of rain – cause farmers' wheat crops to fail.

2) Look for an Obvious Inference. The stimulus gives us a very simple conclusion: uncontrollable factors such as a drought can cause many problems beyond failing crops. When farmers' crops fail, here's a laundry list of related, interconnected businesses that will feel that burden.

Choices – 1) Eliminate incorrect choices, starting with (E). (E) matches our thinking perfectly. The stimulus tells us all about the various consequences when uncontrollable factors cause crops to fail. If the fertilizer and seed dealers, truckers, mechanics, and fuel suppliers lose business, then clearly the negative impacts of a drought extend much further than failing crops. Prove and Move.

For teaching purposes, let's look at some of the other choices that you may have found tempting. (D) might seem plausible, but it introduces the New Concept of major economic crises, which isn't a component of the stimulus. Because a drought can have so many different consequences, it's definitely possible that it could lead to a serious economic burden. Nevertheless, there's a clear difference between losing business and a major economic crisis. Just because the drought's impact on farmers is wearing other businesses thin doesn't mean there will be sincere economic ramifications. (B) looks tempting, but we're talking about the greater consequences of *uncontrollable factors* that cause crops to *fail*. Below average rainfall may not necessarily cause crops to fail, so we can't assume that businesses profiting from farmers' purchases will lose money. Below average rainfall and a severe drought that causes crops to fail are very different concepts.

2. Trust, which cannot be sustained in the absence of mutual respect, is essential to any long-lasting relationship, personal or professional. However, personal relationships, such as marriage or friendship, additionally require natural affinity. If a personal relationship is to endure, it must be supported by the twin pillars of mutual respect and affinity.

 If the statements above are true, then which one of the following must also be true?

 (A) A friendship supported solely by trust and mutual respect will not be long-lasting.

 (B) In the context of any professional relationship, mutual respect presupposes trust.

 (C) If a personal relationship is supported by mutual respect and affinity, it will last a long time.

(D) Personal relationships, such as marriage or friendship, are longer-lasting than professional relationships.

 (E) Basing a marriage on a natural affinity will ensure that it will endure.

Type: Inference
Tags: Conditionals

Stem – "Must also be true." Got it. This is an Inference problem.

Stimulus – 1) Read the Stimulus carefully. The stimulus gives us a lot of information about what it takes for a relationship to last a long time. There are a few important pieces of information that should stick out. Any long-lasting relationship – personal or professional – requires trust, which cannot be sustained without mutual respect. We also learn that there is an important distinction between personal relationships and professional relationships; personal relationships require natural affinity to last a long time. Thus, all relationships require trust and mutual respect, but personal relationships also require natural affinity in order to last a long time.

2) Look for an Obvious Inference. Nothing sticks out in particular.

Choices – 1) Eliminate choices, starting with (E). We can eliminate (E) quickly because we know that natural affinity is only one component of a successful, long-lasting personal relationship – in this case, marriage. In order for a marriage to endure, it will require mutual respect and trust in addition to natural affinity. (D) proposes a New Concept. In the stimulus, we didn't learn anything about which type of relationship will last longer than the other. (C) is a very tempting choice because it almost restates the last sentence of the stimulus. Nevertheless, we need to refer back to Conditionals 101 to dissect this choice. Remember, a conditional has two components: a *sufficient* condition and a *necessary* condition. The sufficient condition is *enough* to *require* the necessary condition. In the last sentence of the stimulus, the personal relationship enduring is the sufficient condition, and that it is supported by mutual respect and affinity is the necessary condition. So, that a relationship endures is *enough* to *require* that it is supported by mutual respect and affinity. With that in mind, (C) confuses the sufficient and necessary conditions. Just because a relationship is supported by mutual respect and affinity is not *enough* to *require* that it will last a long time. (B) may also look tempting, but it's the reverse of what we learned in the stimulus. In order for trust to be sustained, there must be mutual respect, so mutual respect is a precondition for trust. (B) means the opposite: in order for mutual respect to be sustained, there must be trust. That isn't what we learned in the stimulus. (A) – the last choice remaining – is proven by the stimulus. A friendship is a type of personal relationship, so we know a long-lasting friendship will require trust, mutual respect, and affinity. If the friendship is supported *solely* by trust and mutual respect, then it will not be long lasting because there is no natural affinity.

2) Confirm. There's no opportunity for Prove and Move here because we had to work through all of the choices., but (A) is proven. It is also correct.

3. Insurgent political parties that are profoundly dissatisfied with the dominant party's reign and justificatory ideology always produce factions whose views and aims differ as greatly from each other's as they do from the dominant party's. Although these factions ignore their own disagreements for the sake of defeating the dominant party, their disagreements inevitably come forward upon victory. Therefore, _____.

    Which one of the following is the most **logical completion** of the argument?

    (A) no victorious insurgent party ever manages to stay in power for as long as the party it displaces did

    (B) a victorious insurgent party must address the disagreements between its factions if it is to stay in power

    (C) the heretofore insurgent party will not always promulgate a new ideology to justify its own policies, once it is victorious

    (D) a victorious insurgent party always faces opposition from the party it recently ousted

    (E) it is impossible for the different factions of a victorious insurgent party to effect the compromises necessary to keep the new party in power

Type: Inference
Tags: Logically Completes Subtype, Prove and Move

Stem – "Logical completion" tells us this is an Inference problem, and it is specifically a Logically Completes Subtype. If there is a Parallel Situation, we probably can't use the Prove and Move technique.

Stimulus – 1) Read the Stimulus carefully. We learn all about the intricacies of insurgent political parties. There doesn't appear to be a Parallel Situation, so we might be able to Prove and Move in the choices. Through rather complicated language, we're given three relatively simple interconnected pieces of information: insurgent political parties dissatisfied with the dominant party always produce factions with different ideology; these factions ignore their differences for the sake of defeating the dominant party; and, these disagreements always come forward after the dominant party is defeated.

2) Look for an Obvious Inference. There doesn't appear to be an obvious conclusion to the logic in the stimulus. However, we can make a simple link: if an insurgent party is victorious against a dominant party, the disagreements between factions within the party will likely be a problem. That may not seem like much, but a simple link like this might help us through the choices.

Choices – 1) Eliminate incorrect choices, starting with (E). Based on our simple link, (E) might be tempting, but it proposes a New Concept. Even though we know an insurgent party will have different factions with different views and aims, we don't know anything about compromising and addressing those differences. We don't have enough information to say that compromise is impossible. (D) is tricky because we can comfortably assume that there will be some backlash if an insurgent party takes power. However, (D) is not a logical extension or conclusion of the stimulus, and we're looking for a choice that *logically completes* the stimulus. On the other hand, (D) jumps to an idea that could be true, but it is not directly proven by the stimulus. (C) goes against the basic foundation of the stimulus. If an insurgent party is dissatisfied with the dominant party's ideology and policies, then it *intends* to promulgate a new ideology to promote its own policies if victorious over the dominant party. (C) defies the purpose of the insurgent party's taking power in the first place. (B) ties into our line of thinking from the stimulus. If an insurgent party is victorious against a dominant party, the disagreements between factions within the party will likely be a problem, so a victorious insurgent party will need to address those disagreements to stay in power. Otherwise, the factions within the party that has just taken power might form other insurgent parties seeking to take power. (B) is a nice conclusion of the stimulus, so you might Prove and Move here.

For teaching purposes, let's review (A) in case you were uncomfortable with the Prove and Move technique on a Logically Completes Subtype. (A) is a New Concept; we don't know anything about how long a party might stay in power. In the stimulus, we inferred that the differences within an insurgent party will likely be a problem if that party is victorious against the dominant party, but that doesn't tell us anything about how long that insurgent party can stay in power. If they're able to compromise and resolve their differences, an insurgent party could lead a successful regime. We don't have enough information to prove otherwise.

4. Any good garden compost may appropriately be used for soil drainage and fertility. The best compost is 40 to 60 percent organic matter and is dark brown in color. However, compost that emits a strong ammonia smell should not be used for drainage and fertility, for that smell means that the organic matter has not sufficiently decomposed.

Which one of the following is **most strongly supported** by the information above?

(A)   Compost that is 80 percent organic matter has probably not decomposed sufficiently.

(B)   If compost is less than 40 percent organic matter and is not dark brown in color, then it will make soil less fertile and will worsen soil drainage.

(C)   If compost is 50 percent organic matter and that organic matter is sufficiently decomposed, then the compost is good.

(D)   In the best garden compost, the organic matter is completely decomposed.

(E)   Compost that is dark brown in color and emits a strong ammonia smell is not good garden compost.

Type: Inference
Tag: Prove & Move

Stem – "Most strongly supported" tells you that this is an Inference problem.

Stimulus – 1) Read the stimulus carefully. We learn that good garden compost can be used for soil drainage and fertility. The stimulus tells us traits of the best compost. Then, we hear that compost that has not decomposed sufficiently to be used for drainage and fertility smells like ammonia!.

2) Look for an Obvious Inference. Nothing jumps out as a key link the facts add up to.

Choices – 1) Analyze each choice, starting with (E). (E) – The final sentence of the stimulus tells us that compost dark brown in color that smells of ammonia should not be used for drainage and fertility. But what is good garden compost? "Any good garden compost can be used for soil drainage and fertility." The ability to use compost for drainage and fertility is a *requirement* to be good compost. Because the dark brown, ammonia-smelling compost cannot be used for drainage and fertility (because it does not meet the requirement), it is not good garden compost. (E) is logically proven, and you can Prove and Move!

For shits and giggles, let's analyze (C). (C) says that compost that is 50 percent organic matter and sufficiently decomposed is good compost. The stimulus says compost that can be used for drainage and fertility is good compost, but the choice doesn't say that this compost can be used for those purposes. We also know that the *best* compost is 40 to 60 percent organic matter *and* is dark brown. This compost is the right amount of organic matter to be the best, but alas, we don't know the compost's color, so we cannot say it is the best compost either. (C) is unproven; the information about being sufficiently decomposed doesn't prove anything.

5. Archaeologists are currently analyzing plant remains found at a site that was last occupied more than 10,000 years ago. If the plants were cultivated, then the people who occupied the site discovered agriculture thousands of years before any other people are known to have done so. On the other hand, if the plants were wild—that is, uncultivated—then the people who occupied the site ate a wider variety of wild plants than did any other people at the time.

The statements above, if true, **most strongly support** which one of the following?

(A) The archaeologists analyzing the plant remains at the site will be able to determine whether the plants were cultivated or were wild.

(B) The people who occupied the site used some plants in ways that no other people did at that time.

(C) If the people who occupied the site had reached a more advanced stage in the use of wild plants than any other people at the time, then the plants found at the site were uncultivated.

(D) If the people who occupied the site discovered agriculture thousands of years before people anywhere else are known to have done so, then there are remains of cultivated plants at the site.

(E) It is more likely that the people who occupied the site discovered agriculture thousands of years before people anywhere else did than it is that they ate a wider variety of wild plants than any other people at the time.

Type: Inference
Tags: Conditionals, Prove and Move

Stem – "Most strongly support" tells you that this is an Inference problem.

Stimulus – 1) Read the stimulus carefully. The plant remains give two possibilities. One: the plants were cultivated and the people of the site developed agriculture far before anyone else. Two: the plants were wild and the people ate a wider variety of plants than did other people at the time.

2) Look for an Obvious Inference. Either scenario—and it must be one or the other because the plants are either cultivated or uncultivated—implies that the people who occupied the area were doing something unique with plants. Either they started agriculture much earlier than normal or they were eating a wider variety of plants than other people at that time. These people were innovators.

Choices – 1) Eliminate incorrect choices, starting with (E). (E) – The stimulus never gives any indication about which possibility is more likely, so this idea is unproven. (D) – The stimulus tells us:

Cultivated plants → Agriculture

(D) says:

Agriculture → Cultivated plants

(D) is a conditional error; it confuses a necessary condition for being sufficient one. The people could have discovered agriculture and left no evidence of that discovery at the site in the form of remains of cultivated plants. (C) talks about an advanced use of wild plants, which is not discussed in the stimulus. Eating a wide variety of plants is not the same as using them in advanced ways. (B) is a match for the inference we spotted after working the stimulus. Regardless of whether the plant remains were cultivated or uncultivated, the people used plants in unique ways for their time. (B) is proven, and you can Prove and Move.

For instructional purposes, let's take a gander at (A), which is a tempting incorrect answer. The stimulus says that the archaeologists are analyzing the plants, and we learn about the implications of the two possible results of their analysis. However, there is no evidence that the archaeologists will be able to analyze the remains successfully. Based on the stimulus, the archaeologists could try and fail to analyze the plants.

Challenge Set 3

This is a difficult Set, so take your time on each problem and be careful with the choice you select.

Techniques Summary

- Core Focus: Start with (E) and use Prove and Move.

- Stimulus: Understand the facts and look for an Obvious Inference.

- Choices:

  o   Start with (E).

  o   Eliminate unproven choices.

  o   If you find a proven choice, Prove and Move.

1. If the city starts requiring residents to sort the materials that they put out for recycling, then many residents will put more recyclables in with their regular garbage. This will result in more recyclables being buried in the city's landfill. However, because of the cost of having city workers do the sorting, the sanitation department will not stay within its budget unless the sorting requirement for residents is implemented.

    Which one of the following statements logically follows from the information above?

    (A)   Most of the city's residents will continue to recycle even if a sorting requirement is implemented.

    (B)   If the city starts requiring residents to sort their recyclables, then all of the residents who continue to recycle will sort their recyclables.

    (C)   Implementing the sorting requirement would not cause the city's annual cost of sending garbage to its landfill to exceed its current annual cost of sorting recyclables.

    (D)   The amount of recyclables going to the city's landfill will increase if the sanitation department stays within its budget.

    (E)   If the city implements the sorting requirement, the sanitation department will stay within its budget.

2. False chicory's taproot is always one half as long as the plant is tall. Furthermore, the more rain false chicory receives, the taller it tends to grow. In fact, false chicory plants that receive greater than twice the average rainfall of the species' usual habitat always reach above-average heights for false chicory.

    If the statements above are true, then which one of the following must also be true?

    (A)   If two false chicory plants differ in height, then it is likely that the one with the shorter taproot has received less than twice the average rainfall of the species' usual habitat.

    (B)   If a false chicory plant has a longer than average taproot, then it is likely to have received more than twice the average rainfall of the species' usual habitat.

    (C)   It is not possible for a false chicory plant to receive only the average amount of rainfall of the species' usual habitat and be of above average height.

    (D)   If the plants in one group of false chicory are not taller than those in another group of false chicory, then the two groups must have received the same amount of rainfall.

    (E)   If a false chicory plant receives greater than twice the average rainfall of the species' usual habitat, then it will have a longer taproot than that of an average-sized false chicory plant.

3. Interior decorator: All coffeehouses and restaurants are public places. Most well-designed public places feature artwork. But if a public place is uncomfortable it is not well designed, and all comfortable public places have spacious interiors.

    If all of the interior decorator's statements are true, then which one of the following must be true?

    (A)   Any restaurant that has a spacious interior is comfortable.

    (B)   Most public places that feature artwork are well designed.

    (C)   Most coffeehouses that are well designed feature artwork.

    (D)   Any well-designed coffeehouse or restaurant has a spacious interior.

    (E)   Any coffeehouse that has a spacious interior is a well-designed public place.

4. Decentralization enables divisions of a large institution to function autonomously. This always permits more realistic planning and strongly encourages innovation, since the people responsible for decision making are directly involved in implementing the policies they design. Decentralization also permits the central administration to focus on institution-wide issues without being overwhelmed by the details of daily operations.

The statements above most strongly support which one of the following?

(A) In large institutions whose divisions do not function autonomously, planning is not maximally realistic.

(B) Innovation is not always encouraged in large centralized institutions.

(C) For large institutions the advantages of decentralization outweigh its disadvantages.

(D) The central administrations of large institutions are usually partially responsible for most of the details of daily operations.

(E) The people directly involved in implementing policies are always able to make innovative and realistic policy decisions.

5. Human resources director: While only some recent university graduates consider work environment an important factor in choosing a job, they all consider salary an important factor. Further, whereas the only workers who consider stress level an important factor in choosing a job are a few veteran employees, every recent university graduate considers vacation policy an important factor.

If all of the statements of the human resources director are true, then which one of the following must be true?

(A) All people who consider work environment an important factor in choosing a job also consider salary an important factor.

(B) At least some people who consider work environment an important factor in choosing a job consider vacation policy an important factor as well.

(C) At least some veteran employees do not consider work environment an important factor in choosing a job.

(D) All people who consider vacation policy an important factor in choosing a job also consider salary an important factor.

(E) No one for whom salary is an important factor in choosing a job also considers stress level an important factor.

END OF SET

Set 3 Key & Explanations

These are difficult problems so do a careful review of each one to rapidly improve your Inference skills. Milk every drop of learning from these problems.

1. D

2. E

3. D

4. A

5. B

1. If the city starts requiring residents to sort the materials that they put out for recycling, then many residents will put more recyclables in with their regular garbage. This will result in more recyclables being buried in the city's landfill. However, because of the cost of having city workers do the sorting, the sanitation department will not stay within its budget unless the sorting requirement for residents is implemented.

     Which one of the following statements **logically follows** from the information above?

    (A)   Most of the city's residents will continue to recycle even if a sorting requirement is implemented.

    (B)   If the city starts requiring residents to sort their recyclables, then all of the residents who continue to recycle will sort their recyclables.

    (C)   Implementing the sorting requirement would not cause the city's annual cost of sending garbage to its landfill to exceed its current annual cost of sorting recyclables.

     (D)   The amount of recyclables going to the city's landfill will increase if the sanitation department stays within its budget.

    (E)   If the city implements the sorting requirement, the sanitation department will stay within its budget.

Type: Inference
Tags: Conditionals, Logic Chain, Prove & Move

Stem – "Logically follows" tells you that this is an Inference problem. This is a unique stem for an Inference problem, but you are used to a wide variety in stems.

Stimulus – 1) Read the stimulus carefully. There are a few conditionals related to requiring citizens to sort the materials they put out for recycling. One is that requiring residents to sort their recyclables will cause them to put more recyclables in their garbage, which will then end up in the landfill.

Here is the diagram, although you probably shouldn't draw it out when reading the stimulus:

Sort → Recyclables in Landfill

This makes sense because some people are lazy and don't want to take the extra time to sort their recyclables.

The second conditional says the sanitation department needs the sorting requirement to be enacted to stay within budget. Here's the diagram:

Within budget → Sort

2) Look for an Obvious Inference. We've got two related conditionals, so let's link them. The concept they have in common is requiring the sorting, so let's line that up:

Within budget → Sort

+   Sort → Recyclables in Garbage
_____

Within budget → Recyclables in Garbage

If the sanitation department stays within budget, then more recycling will go into the garbage and end up in the landfill.

Choices – 1) Eliminate unproven choices, starting with (E). (E) – Enacting the sorting measure is *required* for the sanitation department to stay within their budget; it is not sufficient to ensure that, so (E) has a conditional error. (D) is our envisioned inference. It uses both of the conditionals. If the sanitation department stays within budget, then that means the sorting requirement has been enacted. The first conditional tells us that when the sorting requirement is enacted, more residents will put recyclables in their regular garbage, leading to more recyclables going to the landfill. (D) is proven. Prove and Move!

Let's analyze (C) because it is a popular incorrect choice. We don't know the city's costs for sending garbage and sorting recyclables. These costs only make up part of the budget, so we can't extrapolate on them. This choice is trying to infer based on the final conditional about the sanitation department budget, but it makes the same conditional error as (E): assuming that the sorting requirement will be sufficient to keep the sanitation department within its budget. It implies that because (C) says that, with the sorting requirement, the cost of sending garbage to the landfill will not exceed its current cost of sorting recyclables. Simply put, it says the added cost of sending more garbage to the landfill will not put the department over budget. We don't know that to be true.

2. False chicory's taproot is always one half as long as the plant is tall. Furthermore, the more rain false chicory receives, the taller it tends to grow. In fact, false chicory plants that receive greater than twice the average rainfall of the species' usual habitat always reach above-average heights for false chicory.

   If the statements above are true, then which one of the following **must also be true**?

   (A) If two false chicory plants differ in height, then it is likely that the one with the shorter taproot has received less than twice the average rainfall of the species' usual habitat.

   (B) If a false chicory plant has a longer-than average taproot, then it is likely to have received more than twice the average rainfall of the species' usual habitat.

   (C) It is not possible for a false chicory plant to receive only the average amount of rainfall of the species' usual habitat and be of above average height.

   (D) If the plants in one group of false chicory are not taller than those in another group of false chicory, then the two groups must have received the same amount of rainfall.

   (E) If a false chicory plant receives greater than twice the average rainfall of the species' usual habitat, then it will have a longer taproot than that of an average-sized false chicory plant.

Type: Inference

Tags: Prove & Move, Obvious Inference, Conditionals

Stem – "Must also be true" tells us this is an Inference problem.

Stimulus – 1) Read Stimulus carefully. We learn all about false chicory – a plant you probably know nothing about. Don't let the unfamiliarity trip you up. The Fact Group tells us that the false chicory's taproot is directly proportional to the height of the plant. We also learn that the plant grows taller with more rainfall. The stimulus closes with an important conditional: if false chicory receives more than twice the average rainfall of its usual habitat, it will always reach above-average heights.

2) Look for an Obvious Inference. The stimulus gives us essentially two pieces of information: the relationship between the length of false chicory's taproot and its height and the effect of increased rainfall on the height of the plant. Although the stimulus seems complicated because it's an unfamiliar topic, there's only one way we can link these two pieces of information. Because we know that the length of the taproot is directly proportional to the plant's height, we know that any above-average false chicory will have an extra-long taproot. So if the plant receives more than twice its average rainfall, it will have a longer-than-average taproot. Of course, we don't know anything about what determines "average" (in both plant size and rainfall), but that doesn't matter. We can still make a link between the two interconnected pieces of information.

Choices – Eliminate incorrect choices, starting with (E). (E) matches our line of thinking from the stimulus. It is the only link we can comfortably make from the fact group. The length of the taproot depends on the height of the plant. False chicory plants that receive greater than twice the average rainfall always reach above-average heights, so their taproots must also reach above-average lengths. Prove and Move.

For teaching purposes, let's review some popular choices. (D) introduces the New Concept of comparing the heights of plants that received the same amount of rainfall. We learn that the plant will grow taller the more rain it receives, and twice the average amount of rainfall will always lead to above-average size plants. We don't know anything about how the heights of plants grown under the same conditions will compare. (C) follows a similar idea. We only know one condition that requires above-average height: twice the average amount of rainfall. That doesn't mean there aren't other conditions that require the outcome of above-average height. It is absolutely possible for a plant that receives the average amount of rainfall to reach an above-average height. We don't have enough information to prove (C). To examine (B), we have to refer back to Conditionals 101 and the relationship between necessary and sufficient conditions. In our stimulus, the *necessary* condition of twice the average rainfall is enough to require the *sufficient* condition of above-average plant height. Because we know that taproot length is directly proportional to plant height, we can substitute above-average taproot length as our sufficient condition, but (B) confuses the necessary and sufficient conditions. Above-average taproot length is not *enough* to *require* twice the average amount of rainfall. However, twice the average amount of rainfall is *enough* to *require* longer-than-average taproots as we proved with (E).

3. Interior decorator: All coffeehouses and restaurants are public places. Most well-designed public places feature artwork. But if a public place is uncomfortable it is not well designed, and all comfortable public places have spacious interiors.

    If all of the interior decorator's statements are true, then which one of the following **must be true**?

    (A) Any restaurant that has a spacious interior is comfortable.

    (B) Most public places that feature artwork are well designed.

    (C) Most coffeehouses that are well designed feature artwork.

    (D) Any well-designed coffeehouse or restaurant has a spacious interior.

    (E) Any coffeehouse that has a spacious interior is a well-designed public place.

Type: Inference
Tags: Prove and Move, Logic Chain, Quantifiers

Stem – "Must be true" tells us this is an Inference problem.

Stimulus – 1) Read the Stimulus carefully. The interior decorator tells us all about the design of public places. The first sentence is important because it defines coffeehouses and restaurants as public places. The last sentence is tricky because it includes two important conditionals: if a public place is uncomfortable, then it is not well designed; and, if a public place is comfortable, then it has a spacious interior. When we consider the contrapositive of the first conditional, the final sentence actually gives us a neat Logic Chain. If a public place is well designed (the opposite of not well designed), then it must be comfortable (the opposite of uncomfortable). Since we know that all comfortable public places have spacious interiors, our Logic Chain looks like this: well-designed → comfortable → spacious interior.

2) Look for an Obvious Inference. Nothing sticks out in particular, but let's see if our Logic Chain shows up in the choices.

Choices – 1) Eliminate incorrect choices, starting with (E). We're lucky we uncovered the Logic Chain in the last sentence of the stimulus because (E) defies it. If a coffeehouse is well designed, then it must be comfortable. If it is comfortable, then it has a spacious interior. Therefore, if a coffeehouse is well designed, then it has a spacious interior. (E) confuses the necessary and sufficient conditions of that conditional. (E) tells us that, if a coffeehouse has a spacious interior, then it is well designed. That a public place is well designed is *enough* to *require* that it has a spacious interior, but the spacious interior itself is not *enough* to *require* that it is well designed. By contrast, (D) matches the thinking of Logic Chain perfectly. We know that all coffeehouses and restaurants are public places, so we can conclude that, if a coffeehouse or restaurant is well designed, then it must have a spacious interior. Prove and Move.

For teaching purposes, let's review (C) – a popular choice that might have caused you some trouble. We'll need to refer back to what we know about Quantifiers. The stimulus tells us that *all* coffeehouses and restaurants are public places, and *most* well-designed public places feature artwork. Even though *every* coffeehouse is defined as a public place, coffeehouses only make up *some* public places. We can't make the assumption that *most* public places are coffeehouses. Just because most well-designed public places hang paintings doesn't mean most coffeehouses do. Most public places is a very different group from most coffeehouses.

4. Decentralization enables divisions of a large institution to function autonomously. This always permits more realistic planning and strongly encourages innovation, since the people responsible for decision making are directly involved in implementing the policies they design. Decentralization also permits the central administration to focus on institution-wide issues without being overwhelmed by the details of daily operations.

The statements above **most strongly support** which one of the following?

   (A)   In large institutions whose divisions do not function autonomously, planning is not maximally realistic.

   (B)   Innovation is not always encouraged in large centralized institutions.

   (C)   For large institutions the advantages of decentralization outweigh its disadvantages.

   (D)   The central administrations of large institutions are usually partially responsible for most of the details of daily operations.

   (E)   The people directly involved in implementing policies are always able to make innovative and realistic policy decisions.

Type: Inference

Stem – "Most strongly support" tells you this is an Inference problem.

Stimulus – 1) Read the Stimulus carefully. The stimulus tells us about some advantages of decentralization in a large institution. There are two key advantages discussed: decentralization enables divisions to function autonomously; and, decentralization allows central administration to focus on bigger issues without worrying about details of daily operations. Those are the two advantages to decentralization, but we're also given some advantages to autonomous functioning of divisions – we'll want to be careful that we don't confuse those. Although decentralization might bring those about, their sufficient condition is autonomous functioning, not decentralization.

2) Look for an Obvious Inference. The stimulus doesn't seem to guide us in any particular direction.

Choices – 1) Eliminate incorrect Choices, starting with (E). (E) might look tempting at first. We know that autonomous functioning of divisions *always* permits more realistic planning and encourages innovation because the people responsible are directly involved in implementing policies. Without autonomous functioning, though, these people might not be able to make innovative and realistic policy decisions. Without autonomous functioning, we can't say that they're *always* capable of that. (D) gives us a New Concept. One of the key advantages of decentralization is that central administration can focus on bigger issues without being overwhelmed by the details of daily operations, and that's all we know about the details of daily operations. If separating central administrations from daily operations is an advantage, then it's very possible that most central administrations have little to no influence over the details of daily operations. We don't have enough information to prove either way. (C) is also a New Concept because we don't know anything about the disadvantages of decentralization. The stimulus only told us about some of its advantages. Decentralization could have debilitating disadvantages, but we just don't know. (B) also stretches us beyond what we learned in the stimulus. We learned that autonomous functioning of divisions through decentralization *strongly* encourages innovation. The word "strongly" implies a difference in degree. Essentially, we have one condition that *strongly* encourages innovation: autonomous functioning of divisions. That's not enough to say that innovation is not always encouraged in a centralized setting. It could be encouraged consistently, just not as *strongly* as when divisions can operate independently. By contrast, (A) is an extension of similar logic. We know that autonomous functioning of divisions permits more realistic planning. That doesn't mean that planning is not realistic without autonomous functioning; it just means planning can be *more* realistic under a certain condition. As a consequence, a large institution without autonomous functioning can improve its planning, so their planning is not as realistic as it can be. (A) is proven.

2) Confirm Choices. We worked through all of the choices, and we were able to prove (A).

5. Human resources director: While only some recent university graduates consider work environment an important factor in choosing a job, they all consider salary an important factor. Further, whereas the only workers who consider stress level an important factor in choosing a job are a few veteran employees, every recent university graduate considers vacation policy an important factor.

If all of the statements of the human resources director are true, then which one of the following **must be true**?

(A) All people who consider work environment an important factor in choosing a job also consider salary an important factor.

(B) At least some people who consider work environment an important factor in choosing a job consider vacation policy an important factor as well.

(C) At least some veteran employees do not consider work environment an important factor in choosing a job.

(D) All people who consider vacation policy an important factor in choosing a job also consider salary an important factor.

(E) No one for whom salary is an important factor in choosing a job also considers stress level an important factor.

Type: Inference
Tags: Prove & Move, Quantifiers

Stem – "Must be true" – this is an Inference problem.

Stimulus – 1) Read the Stimulus carefully. The human resources director gives a lot of quantifiers and four factors that help people choose a job: salary, vacation policy, job environment, and stress level. Even though the language makes this Fact Group seem complicated, it's actually very simple. All recent college graduates consider salary and vacation policy when choosing a job. *Some* recent college graduates consider job environment. No recent college graduates – just a few veteran employees – consider stress level.

2) Look for an Obvious Inference. Nothing sticks out. Let's work through the choices and see what we find.

Choices – 1) Eliminate incorrect choices, starting with (E). Because we know that just a few veteran employees consider stress level an important factor when choosing a job, we know that the individuals in (E) are veteran employees. We know that all recent college graduates consider salary an important factor, but do we know how veteran employees feel about salary? We don't have enough information to prove (E). (D) presents an interesting Quantifier Combination. We know that all recent college graduates consider vacation policy and salary an important factor, but all recent college graduates are only *some* people who value their vacation time. *All* people is a huge leap from all recent college graduates, which is fairly specific. (C) is another choice that pushes us beyond what we know. We learned one fact about veteran employees: at least some veteran employees consider stress level an important factor in choosing a job. We don't know anything about how veteran employees feel about work environment, so we don't have enough information to prove (C). (B) gives us another Quantifier Combination, but this one looks plausible. Because some recent college graduates consider work environment an important factor, that group represents *at least some* of the greater group of people who care about their work environment. Since we know that *all* recent college graduates want their vacation days, then we can conclude that *at least some* people who care about work environment consider vacation policy an important factor. (B) is proven. Prove and Move.

Challenge Set 4

This is a very difficult Set, so take your time on each problem and be careful with the choice you select.

Techniques Summary

- Core Focus: Start with (E) and use Prove and Move.

- Stimulus: Understand the facts and look for an Obvious Inference.

- Choices:

  - Start with (E).

  - Eliminate unproven choices.

  - If you find a proven choice, Prove and Move.

1. Each of the many people who participated in the town's annual spring cleanup received a community recognition certificate. Because the spring cleanup took place at the same time as the downtown arts fair, we know that there are at least some spring cleanup participants who are not active in the town's artistic circles.

   If the statements above are true, which one of the following must be true?

   (A) Some of the persons who are active in the town's artistic circles received community recognition certificates.

   (B) Not all of those who received community recognition certificates are active in the town's artistic circles.

   (C) No participants in the downtown arts fair received community recognition certificates.

   (D) No person who received a community recognition certificate has not participated in the spring cleanup.

   (E) Persons who are active in the town's artistic circles are not concerned with the town's environment.

2. Most lecturers who are effective teachers are eccentric, but some noneccentric lecturers are very effective teachers. In addition, every effective teacher is a good communicator.

   Which one of the following statements follows logically from the statements above?

   (A) Some good communicators are eccentric.

   (B) All good communicators are effective teachers.

   (C) Some lecturers who are not effective teachers are not eccentric.

   (D) Most lecturers who are good communicators are eccentric.

   (E) Some noneccentric lecturers are effective teachers but are not good communicators.

3. No small countries and no countries in the southern hemisphere have permanent seats on the United Nations Security Council. Each of the five countries with a permanent seat on the Security Council is in favor of increased international peacekeeping efforts and a greater role for the United Nations in moderating regional disputes. However, some countries that are in favor of increased international peacekeeping efforts are firmly against increased spending on refugees by the United Nations.

   If the statements above are true, which one of the following must also be true?

   (A) Some small countries do not want the United Nations to increase its spending on refugees.

   (B) Some countries in the southern hemisphere are not in favor of increased international peacekeeping efforts.

   (C) Some countries that have permanent seats on the United Nations Security Council are against increased spending on refugees by the United Nations.

   (D) Some small countries are in favor of a greater role for the United Nations in moderating regional disputes.

   (E) Some countries that are in favor of a greater role for the United Nations in moderating regional disputes are not located in the southern hemisphere.

4. Essayist: Winners of a Nobel prize for science, who are typically professional scientists, have all made significant contributions to science. But amateur scientists have also provided many significant contributions. And unlike professional scientists, who are often motivated by economic necessity or a desire for fame, amateur scientists are motivated by the love of discovery alone.

If the essayist's statements are true, then which one of the following must also be true?

(A) Some amateur scientists who did not win a Nobel prize for science nevertheless made significant contributions to science.

(B) Typically, winners of a Nobel prize for science are not motivated at all by the love of discovery.

(C) The love of discovery is the motive behind many significant contributions to science.

(D) Professional scientists have made a greater overall contribution to science than have amateur scientists.

(E) A professional scientist is more likely to make a significant contribution to science if he or she is motivated by the love of discovery.

5. Unusually large and intense forest fires swept the tropics in 1997. The tropics were quite susceptible to fire at that time because of the widespread drought caused by an unusually strong El Niño, an occasional global weather phenomenon. Many scientists believe the strength of the El Niño was enhanced by the global warming caused by air pollution.

Which one of the following can be properly inferred from the information above?

(A) Air pollution was largely responsible for the size and intensity of the forest fires that swept the tropics in 1997.

(B) If the El Niño in 1997 had not been unusually strong, few if any large and intense forest fires would have swept the tropics in that year.

(C) Forest fires in the tropics are generally larger and more intense than usual during a strong El Niño.

(D) At least some scientists believe that air pollution was responsible for the size and intensity of the forest fires that swept the tropics in 1997.

(E) If air pollution enhanced the strength of the El Niño in 1997, then it also contributed to the widespread drought in that year.

END OF SET

Set 4 Key & Explanations

Review these problems thoroughly. Out of all of the Challenge Sets, you'll learn the most from reviewing and mastering these super-difficult problems.

1. B

2. A

3. E

4. C

5. E

1. Each of the many people who participated in the town's annual spring cleanup received a community recognition certificate. Because the spring cleanup took place at the same time as the downtown arts fair, we know that there are at least some spring cleanup participants who are not active in the town's artistic circles.

 If the statements above are true, which one of the following **must be true**?

(A) Some of the persons who are active in the town's artistic circles received community recognition certificates.

(B) Not all of those who received community recognition certificates are active in the town's artistic circles.

(C) No participants in the downtown arts fair received community recognition certificates.

(D) No person who received a community recognition certificate has not participated in the spring cleanup.

(E) Persons who are active in the town's artistic circles are not concerned with the town's environment.

Type: Inference
Tags: Obvious Inference, Prove & Move, Quantifiers

Stem – "Must be true" tells us this is an Inference problem.

Stimulus – 1) Read the Stimulus carefully. This stimulus is fairly simple. It gives us three facts: everyone who participated in the spring cleanup received a community recognition certificate; the spring cleanup took place at the same time as the downtown arts fair; and, some spring cleanup participants are not active in the town's artistic circles.

2) Look for an Obvious Inference. There's a very simple link we can make if we combine some of the quantifiers in the stimulus. *Every* spring cleanup participant received a community recognition certificate, and *some* spring cleanup participants are not active in the town's artistic circles. So, *at least some* people who received a community recognition certificate are not active in the town's artistic circles. Let's see if that pops up in the choices.

Choices – 1) Eliminate incorrect choices, starting with (E). (E) introduces a New Concept. We don't know anything about how people active in the town's artistic circles feel about the town's environment. We know that the spring cleanup was scheduled at the same time as the downtown arts fair, but that isn't enough to prove that people active in the arts don't care about the town's environment. (D) might look plausible initially. We know that every participant in the spring cleanup received a community recognition certificate. However, we don't know that *every* community recognition certificate was given to a spring cleanup participant. The town could give community recognition certificates for a lot of different reasons, so (D) is a bit of a stretch. (C) follows a similar logic. We know that there was a scheduling conflict between the spring cleanup and the downtown arts fair, but we don't know enough about community recognition certificates. The town could also give community recognition certificates to those who contribute to the town's artistic community. We don't know enough about these community recognition certificates to prove (C). On the other hand, (B) matches up with our Obvious Inference. We inferred that *at least some* people who received a community recognition certificate are not active in the town's artistic circles. In this case, the quantifier "some" means any number of people greater than zero, but it also means any number of people less than the total possible ("not all"). If *some* people who received a certificate are not active in the arts, then *not all* people who received certificates are active in the town's artistic circles. Prove and Move.

2.   Most lecturers who are effective teachers are eccentric, but some noneccentric lecturers are very effective teachers. In addition, every effective teacher is a good communicator.

Which one of the following statements **follows logically** from the statements above?

   (A)   Some good communicators are eccentric.

   (B)   All good communicators are effective teachers.

   (C)   Some lecturers who are not effective teachers are not eccentric.

   (D)   Most lecturers who are good communicators are eccentric.

(E)   Some noneccentric lecturers are effective teachers but are not good communicators.

Type: Inference
Tags: Quantifier Combination, Obvious Inference

Stem – "Follows logically" tells us this is an Inference problem.

Stimulus – 1) Read the Stimulus carefully. This stimulus is packed full of quantifiers about what makes an effective teacher. The most valuable piece of information is the last sentence because it gives a condition that applies to *all* effective teachers. If *all* effective teachers are good communicators, then we have an edge that could help us eliminate choices.

2) Look for an Obvious Inference. With this stimulus, it's hard to pin down anything in particular. Nevertheless, because *most* effective teachers are eccentric and *some* are noneccentric, we can conclude that *some* good communicators are eccentric and *some* are not. That doesn't give us much, but it's the only connection we can make.

Choices – 1) Eliminate incorrect choices, starting with (E). We can eliminate (E) quickly because we know that every effective teacher is a good communicator. Regardless of whether or not they are eccentric, the lecturers are good communicators if they are effective teachers. (D) might look plausible because we know that *all* effective teachers are good communicators. However, that doesn't mean that *all* good communicators are effective teachers. The group of effective teachers only represents *some* of the great group of good communicators. Even though most lecturers who are effective teachers are eccentric, we can't prove that most lecturers who are good communicators are eccentric. (C) is a complicated choice, and it sort of pushes us toward a New Concept. In the stimulus, we're given information about lecturers who are effective teachers, so we know very little about teachers who are not effective. In fact, the only thing we know for certain is that, if the teacher is not a good communicator, than they are not an effective teacher (the contrapositive of the conditional we found). Some lecturers who are not effective teachers could be eccentric, but they could all be eccentric. We only know that most lecturers who are effective teachers are eccentric, and some non-eccentric lecturers are effective teachers. That doesn't tell us anything about whether or not a lecturer who is not an effective teacher will be eccentric. We can't prove (C). We can eliminate (B) quickly because we know that effective teachers represent only *some* good communicators. (A) matches our thinking from the stimulus perfectly. If *all* effective teachers are good communicators and *some* effective teachers are eccentric, then *some* good communicators are eccentric. It's a very simple Quantifier Combination, and it's the correct choice.

2) Confirm. We worked through all the choices, so we couldn't really Prove and Move here. We're left with (A), which we can prove comfortably.

3. No small countries and no countries in the southern hemisphere have permanent seats on the United Nations Security Council. Each of the five countries with a permanent seat on the Security Council is in favor of increased international peacekeeping efforts and a greater role for the United Nations in moderating regional disputes. However, some countries that are in favor of increased international peacekeeping efforts are firmly against increased spending on refugees by the United Nations.

If the statements above are true, which one of the following **must also be true**?

(A) Some small countries do not want the United Nations to increase its spending on refugees.

(B) Some countries in the southern hemisphere are not in favor of increased international peacekeeping efforts.

(C) Some countries that have permanent seats on the United Nations Security Council are against increased spending on refugees by the United Nations.

(D) Some small countries are in favor of a greater role for the United Nations in moderating regional disputes.

(E) Some countries that are in favor of a greater role for the United Nations in moderating regional disputes are not located in the southern hemisphere.

Type: Inference
Tags: Obvious Inference, Prove & Move, Quantifier Combination

Stem – "Must also be true" – This is an Inference problem.

Stimulus – 1) Read the Stimulus carefully. Through a lot of different quantifiers, we learn about the UN Security Council.

2) Look for an Obvious Inference. When we consider a few quantifier combinations, we can make some simple links. We know that every country with a permanent seat on the Security Council is in favor of increased international peacekeeping efforts and a greater role in moderating regional disputes. Also, we know that no small countries and no countries in the southern hemisphere have permanent seats. When we combine these two, it looks like this: *some* countries in favor of increased international peacekeeping and a greater role in moderating regional disputes are not small countries and are not located in the southern hemisphere. That may not seem like much, but it's the only link we can comfortably make from the Fact Group.

Choices – 1) Eliminate incorrect choices, starting with (E). (E) matches up with our link pretty nicely. No countries located outside of the southern hemisphere have permanent seats on the council, and every country with a permanent seat is in favor of a greater role in moderating regional disputes. So, *some* countries pushing for more influence in regional disputes are not located in the southern hemisphere. It's important to understand why we must use "some" in this case. *Every* country with a permanent seat on the council represent *some* of the greater group of countries who support expanded peacekeeping and moderating of regional disputes. There could be plenty of countries without permanent seats that promote these aims also. Because none of those five are located in the southern hemisphere, *some* of that greater group of countries are not located in the southern hemisphere. Prove and Move.

For teaching purposes, let's review (C), which may have looked tempting if you weren't comfortable with (E). The last sentence of the stimulus tells us that some countries that support expanded peacekeeping are against increased spending on refugees. We know that all the countries with permanent seats represent *some* countries that support expanded peacekeeping, but the last sentence of the stimulus doesn't give us enough information to prove (C). Every country with a permanent seat could be pushing for increased spending on refugees, and that sentence could still be true.

4. Essayist: Winners of a Nobel prize for science, who are typically professional scientists, have all made significant contributions to science. But amateur scientists have also provided many significant contributions. And unlike professional scientists, who are often motivated by economic necessity or a desire for fame, amateur scientists are motivated by the love of discovery alone.

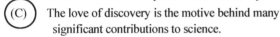

If the essayist's statements are true, then which one of the following **must also be true**?

(A) Some amateur scientists who did not win a Nobel prize for science nevertheless made significant contributions to science.

(B) Typically, winners of a Nobel prize for science are not motivated at all by the love of discovery.

(C) The love of discovery is the motive behind many significant contributions to science.

(D) Professional scientists have made a greater overall contribution to science than have amateur scientists.

(E) A professional scientist is more likely to make a significant contribution to science if he or she is motivated by the love of discovery.

Type: Inference
Tag: Prove & Move

Stem – "Must also be true" tells you that this is an Inference problem.

Stimulus – 1) Read the stimulus carefully. It talks about those who make contributions to science. Here are some highlights: Nobel Prize winners have made significant contributions to science. So have amateur scientists, and they are motivated by the love of discovery alone when making their discoveries.

2) Look for an Obvious Inference. Nothing jumps out from all of this information.

Choices – 1) Eliminate incorrect choices, starting with (E). (E) – The stimulus never says that motivation by the love of discovery is more powerful than the motivation for economic necessity or fame. We have no reason to believe that a professional scientist would be more likely to make a significant discovery with that motivation. (D) – Nobel Prize winners (mostly pro scientists) have made significant contributions, and amateur scientists have also made many significant contributions. Based on those descriptions of contributions, we can't say that pro scientists have made a greater overall contribution. (C) – We know that amateur scientists are motivated by the love of discovery, and we know that these scientists have provided many significant contributions. Linking these two pieces of information about amateur scientists shows that (C) is a valid inference. Select it and move on.

(A) is a tempting choice. We know that most Nobel Prize winners are professional scientists, but the rest therefore could be amateurs for all we know. We don't know if any amateur scientists who didn't win a Nobel Prize made significant contributions to science. The passage doesn't address how many amateurs did or did not win the Nobel Prize, so (A) is unproven.

5. Unusually large and intense forest fires swept the tropics in 1997. The tropics were quite susceptible to fire at that time because of the widespread drought caused by an unusually strong El Niño, an occasional global weather phenomenon. Many scientists believe the strength of the El Niño was enhanced by the global warming caused by air pollution.

Which one of the following can be **properly inferred** from the information above?

(A) Air pollution was largely responsible for the size and intensity of the forest fires that swept the tropics in 1997.

(B) If the El Niño in 1997 had not been unusually strong, few if any large and intense forest fires would have swept the tropics in that year.

(C) Forest fires in the tropics are generally larger and more intense than usual during a strong El Niño.

(D) At least some scientists believe that air pollution was responsible for the size and intensity of the forest fires that swept the tropics in 1997.

(E) If air pollution enhanced the strength of the El Niño in 1997, then it also contributed to the widespread drought in that year.

Type: Inference
Tag: Logic Chain Stimulus, Prove & Move

Stem – "Properly inferred" tells you that this is an Inference problem.

Stimulus – 1) Read the Stimulus carefully. We learn about the large forest fires that swept the tropics and their contributing factors. A Logic Chain is created here: The drought made the fires worse, the strong El Nino caused the drought, and many scientists believe that global warming caused by air pollution made the El Nino so strong.

2) Look for an Obvious Inference. With a Logic Chain this long and with some links that are fairly weak, nothing really stands out.

Choices – 1) Eliminate incorrect choices, starting with (E). (E) – This choice is a conditional. We know that the unusually strong El Nino caused the widespread drought, so yes, air pollution indirectly contributed to the widespread drought if it enhanced the strength of El Nino that year. Although it's a smaller point, this choice is certainly proven. (E) is correct, and you can Prove and Move here.

Let's lay bare a couple of tempting choices. (D) – We know that many scientists believe that the strength of the El Nino was *enhanced* by the air pollution. The stimulus says that the strength of the El Nino caused the drought, which made the tropics *susceptible* to fire. But, (D) is too strong; concluding that air pollution was *responsible* for the size and intensity of the fires is too big of a stretch based on the evidence. We don't know that *any* scientists believe that. (C) – All the information we have is about the year 1997. We can't say that a strong El Nino in other years causes more intense forest fires. Maybe in other years there weren't droughts associated with the intensity of El Ninos.

Inference Test Set

Use the Test Set to practice your Inference skills under time pressure. Set overview:

- 11 problems with a 14-minute time limit.

- Complete the full set in one go.

- Only review problems that you missed or were unsure on. For each, self-review, and then read the explanation.

This set matches the difficulty of the average Inference problem, so it is a good test of your Inference skills. The time limit coupled with the fact that you're working the set straight through will approximate the time pressure of a real test. It's a chance to work on your pacing, so try to get as many of the 11 problems correct as you can in the allotted time.

Directions

- Time Limit: There is a 14-minute time limit for this set. Pace with your watch and set a timer. If you're tight on time, guess on any problems you do not reach, just as you will on the official LSAT.

- Mark any problems you are unsure of as you attempt the set.

- Bubble Sheet: Like all timed sets, fill in your answers in the bubble sheet for this Test Set. This is important practice because bubbling answers takes some time, and it's something you need to get used to for full LR sections.

- Review: Review problems that you answer incorrectly and those that you mark as unsure. First self-review the problem, then carefully read the explanation.

1. Literary historian: William Shakespeare, a humble actor, could have written the love poetry attributed to him. But the dramas attributed to him evince such insight into the minds of powerful rulers that they could only have been written by one who had spent much time among them; Francis Bacon associated with rulers, but Shakespeare did not.

   Which one of the following logically follows from the literary historian's claims?

   (A) Bacon wrote the dramas attributed to Shakespeare, but could not have written the love poetry.

   (B) Bacon wrote both the love poetry and the dramas attributed to Shakespeare.

   (C) Shakespeare wrote neither the love poetry nor the dramas attributed to him.

   (D) One person could not have written both the love poetry and the dramas attributed to Shakespeare.

   (E) Shakespeare may have written the love poetry but did not write the dramas attributed to him.

2. Economic growth accelerates business demand for the development of new technologies. Businesses supplying these new technologies are relatively few, while those wishing to buy them are many. Yet an acceleration of technological change can cause suppliers as well as buyers of new technologies to fail.

   Which one of the following is most strongly supported by the information above?

   (A) Businesses supplying new technologies are more likely to prosper in times of accelerated technological change than other businesses.

   (B) Businesses that supply new technologies may not always benefit from economic growth.

   (C) The development of new technologies may accelerate economic growth in general.

   (D) Businesses that adopt new technologies are most likely to prosper in a period of general economic growth.

   (E) Economic growth increases business failures.

3. People are not happy unless they feel that they are needed by others. Most people in modern society, however, can achieve a feeling of indispensability only within the sphere of family and friendship, because almost everyone knows that his or her job could be done by any one of thousands of others.

   The statements above most strongly support which one of the following?

   (A) People who realize that others could fill their occupational roles as ably as they do themselves cannot achieve any happiness in their lives.

   (B) The nature of modern society actually undermines the importance of family life to an individual's happiness.

   (C) Most people in modern society are happy in their private lives even if they are not happy in their jobs.

   (D) A majority of people in modern society do not appreciate having the jobs that they do have.

   (E) Fewer than a majority of people in modern society can find happiness outside the sphere of private interpersonal relationships.

4. Like a genetic profile, a functional magnetic-resonance image (fMRI) of the brain can contain information that a patient wishes to keep private. An fMRI of a brain also contains enough information about a patient's skull to create a recognizable image of that patient's face. A genetic profile can be linked to a patient only by referring to labels or records.

   The statements above, if true, most strongly support which one of the following?

   (A) It is not important that medical providers apply labels to fMRIs of patients' brains.

   (B) An fMRI has the potential to compromise patient privacy in circumstances in which a genetic profile would not.

   (C) In most cases patients cannot be reasonably sure that the information in a genetic profile will be kept private.

   (D) Most of the information contained in an fMRI of a person's brain is also contained in that person's genetic profile.

   (E) Patients are more concerned about threats to privacy posed by fMRIs than they are about those posed by genetic profiles.

5. Antibiotics are standard ingredients in animal feed because they keep animals healthy and increase meat yields. However, scientists have recommended phasing out this practice, believing it may make antibiotics less effective in humans. If meat yields are reduced, however, some farmers will go out of business.

Which one of the following is most strongly supported by the information above?

(A) If scientists are correct that antibiotic use in animal feed makes antibiotics less effective in humans, then some farmers will go out of business.

(B) If antibiotic use in animal feed is not phased out, some antibiotics will become ineffective in humans.

(C) If the scientists' recommendation is not heeded, no farmers will go out of business due to reduced meat yields.

(D) If the health of their animals declines, most farmers will not be able to stay in business.

(E) If antibiotic use in animal feed is phased out, some farmers will go out of business unless they use other means of increasing meat yields.

6. Why are violins made by Stradivarius in the early 1700s far superior to most other violins? Some experts suggest secret varnishes, but there is no evidence for this. However, climatologists have found that in the 1600s and early 1700s weather patterns in the region of Italy where Stradivarius worked affected tree growth to produce wood with special acoustic properties. Therefore, it is likely that

_____.

Which one of the following most logically completes the argument?

(A) some other Italian violin makers in the early 1700s produced violins that equaled the quality of Stradivarius violins

(B) Stradivarius was the only violin maker in the early 1700s to use the wood produced in that part of Italy

(C) no violin made from present-day materials could rival a Stradivarius violin for sound quality

(D) the special qualities of Stradivarius violins are due in part to the wood used to make them

(E) Stradivarius did not employ any secret techniques in making his violins

7. Copyright was originally the grant of a temporary government-supported monopoly on copying a work. Its sole purpose was to encourage the circulation of ideas by giving authors the opportunity to derive a reasonable financial reward from their works. However, copyright sometimes goes beyond its original purpose since sometimes _____.

The conclusion of the argument is most strongly supported if which one of the following completes the passage?

(A) publication of copyrighted works is not the only way to circulate ideas

(B) authors are willing to circulate their works even without any financial reward

(C) authors are unable to find a publisher for their copyrighted work

(D) there is no practical way to enforce copyrights

(E) copyrights hold for many years after an author's death

8. Philosopher: Effective tests have recently been developed to predict fatal diseases having a largely genetic basis. Now, for the first time, a person can be warned well in advance of the possibility of such life-threatening conditions. However, medicine is not yet able to prevent most such conditions. Simply being informed that one will get a disease that is both fatal and incurable can itself be quite harmful to some people. This raises the question of whether such "early warning" tests should be made available at all.

Which one of the following statements is best illustrated by the state of affairs described by the philosopher?

(A) The advance of medicine fails to provide solutions to every problem.

(B) The advance of medicine creates new contexts in which ethical dilemmas can arise.

(C) Medical technologies continue to advance, increasing our knowledge and understanding of disease.

(D) The more we come to learn, the more we realize how little we know.

(E) The advance of technology is of questionable value.

9. Coffee and tea contain methylxanthines, which cause temporary increases in the natural production of vasopressin, a hormone produced by the pituitary gland. Vasopressin causes clumping of blood cells, and the clumping is more pronounced in women than in men. This is probably the explanation of the fact that women face as much as a tenfold higher risk than men do of complications following angioplasty, a technique used to clear clogged arteries.

Which one of the following statements is most strongly supported by the information above?

(A) Men, but not women, should be given methylxanthines prior to undergoing angioplasty.

(B) In spite of the risks, angioplasty is the only effective treatment for clogged arteries.

(C) Women probably drink more coffee and tea, on average, than do men.

(D) Prior to undergoing angioplasty, women should avoid coffee and tea.

(E) Angioplasty should not be used to treat clogged arteries.

10. Editorial: When legislators discover that some public service is not being adequately provided, their most common response is to boost the funding for that public service. Because of this, the least efficiently run government bureaucracies are the ones that most commonly receive an increase in funds.

The statements in the editorial, if true, most strongly support which one of the following?

(A) The least efficiently run government bureaucracies are the bureaucracies that legislators most commonly discover to be failing to provide some public service adequately.

(B) When legislators discover that a public service is not being adequately provided, they never respond to the problem by reducing the funding of the government bureaucracy providing that service.

(C) Throughout the time a government bureaucracy is run inefficiently, legislators repeatedly boost the funding for the public service that this bureaucracy provides.

(D) If legislators boost funding for a public service, the government bureaucracy providing that service will commonly become less efficient as a result.

(E) The most inefficiently run government bureaucracy receives the most funding of any government bureaucracy.

11. Philosopher: The rational pursuit of happiness is quite different from always doing what one most strongly desires to do. This is because the rational pursuit of happiness must include consideration of long-term consequences, whereas our desires are usually focused on the short term. Moreover, desires are sometimes compulsions, and while ordinary desires result in at least momentary happiness when their goals are attained, compulsions strongly drive a person to pursue goals that offer no happiness even when reached.

If all of the philosopher's statements are true, each of the following could be true EXCEPT:

(A) The majority of people do not have compulsions.

(B) Attaining the goal of any desire results in momentary happiness.

(C) Most people do not pursue happiness rationally.

(D) Most people want more than their own personal happiness.

(E) All actions have long-term consequences.

END OF SET

Test Set Answer Key

Great job completing this Set. Correct your work with the answer key below. For each problem you answered incorrectly or marked to review, first self-review it. Then, read its explanation carefully.

1. E
2. B
3. E
4. B
5. E
6. D
7. E
8. B
9. D
10. A
11. B

Test Set Explanations

1. Literary historian: William Shakespeare, a humble actor, could have written the love poetry attributed to him. But the dramas attributed to him evince such insight into the minds of powerful rulers that they could only have been written by one who had spent much time among them; Francis Bacon associated with rulers, but Shakespeare did not.

   Which one of the following **logically follows** from the literary historian's claims?

   (A)   Bacon wrote the dramas attributed to Shakespeare, but could not have written the love poetry.

   (B)   Bacon wrote both the love poetry and the dramas attributed to Shakespeare.

   (C)   Shakespeare wrote neither the love poetry nor the dramas attributed to him.

   (D)   One person could not have written both the love poetry and the dramas attributed to Shakespeare.

   (E)   Shakespeare may have written the love poetry but did not write the dramas attributed to him.

Type: Inference
Tags: Obvious Inference, Prove & Move

Stem – "Logically follows" indicates that this is an Inference problem. Understand the facts in the stimulus and then look for an Obvious Inference.

Stimulus – 1) Read the stimulus carefully. The stimulus discusses the idea that Shakespeare may have written the love poetry attributed to him, but in order to write the dramas that bear his name he would have had to spend a great amount of time among rulers. Another famous author of the time, Francis Bacon, associated with rulers, while Shakespeare did not.

2) Look for an Obvious Inference. The stimulus implies that Shakespeare didn't write the dramas attributed to him, and that Bacon was the actual author.

Choices – The correct answer will reflect the idea that Shakespeare could very well have written the love poetry that bears his name, but he didn't have the requisite experience in order to write the dramas attributed to him. Because you're able to spot an Obvious Inference, let's use the Prove and Move method of elimination.

1) Eliminate incorrect choices, starting with (E).. (E) looks exactly like the Obvious Inference; Shakespeare could have written the love poetry attributed to him, but he didn't write the dramas. (E) links the fact that one must spend time with powerful rulers in order to write a drama about them and the fact that Francis Bacon spent a lot of time among rulers, while Shakespeare did not. (E) is proven correct. Note that in using the Prove and Move technique, the Confirm step is built into the "Prove" part of analyzing the choice.

Let's briefly analyze (A) for practice. (A) focuses on Bacon instead of Shakespeare, claiming that he could've written the plays attributed to Shakespeare but not the love poetry. But, that inference is unsupported by the stimulus because the stimulus only tells you that Bacon spent time with rulers. His spending time with rulers by no means implies Bacon didn't have a soft side to him; based on the info in the stimulus, he totally could have written Shakespeare's love poetry, too. (A) is unsupported, and thus incorrect.

2. Economic growth accelerates business demand for the development of new technologies. Businesses supplying these new technologies are relatively few, while those wishing to buy them are many. Yet an acceleration of technological change can cause suppliers as well as buyers of new technologies to fail.

    Which one of the following is **most strongly supported** by the information above?

    (A) Businesses supplying new technologies are more likely to prosper in times of accelerated technological change than other businesses.

    (B) Businesses that supply new technologies may not always benefit from economic growth.

    (C) The development of new technologies may accelerate economic growth in general.

    (D) Businesses that adopt new technologies are most likely to prosper in a period of general economic growth.

    (E) Economic growth increases business failures.

Type: Inference
Tags: Obvious Inference, Prove & Move

Stem – "Most strongly supported" is an Inference problem stem.

Stimulus – 1) Read the stimulus carefully. Economic growth stimulates and speeds up business demand for the development of new technologies. The suppliers of those technologies are few in number, while those businesses that use the technologies are many in number. However, it's not all good for the suppliers. Accelerated technological change sometimes means the suppliers can't keep up, and both the suppliers and buyers fail in that instance.

2) Look for an Obvious Inference. You'd think that the suppliers would be in a great position; there's a lot of demand for their product, and there are few competitors in the industry to take fight for profits. But, the same accelerated growth that drives their profits can also drive them to failure. Thus, one Obvious Inference is that accelerated demand for tech isn't always a good thing for the supplier.

Choices – 1) Eliminate incorrect choices, starting with (E). (E) infers that economic growth increases business failures, but that isn't necessarily the case. You just know that businesses can fail under the pressure of accelerated growth, but businesses always fail—there's no reason to believe that economic growth "increases" the number of those failures. (D) infers that businesses that adopt new tech are likely to prosper during a period of economic growth, but the stimulus doesn't talk about which businesses prosper and at what times. It just talks about the suppliers and buyers of tech in the present-day business world. (C) infers that developing new tech may accelerate economic growth, but that's not a supported inference. You know that accelerating *economic growth* leads to the development of new technologies (so, accelerated economic growth is the "cause" and the development of new tech is an "effect"), but to assume that means the "effect" is also the "cause" is not logical. (B) infers that suppliers may not always benefit from economic growth. Economic growth is the catalyst for accelerated technological advancement, which you know can cause suppliers and buyers of new tech to fail. (B) fits the Obvious Inference in this way, so you can Prove and Move. (B) is correct.

3.   People are not happy unless they feel that they are needed by others. Most people in modern society, however, can achieve a feeling of indispensability only within the sphere of family and friendship, because almost everyone knows that his or her job could be done by any one of thousands of others.

The statements above **most strongly support** which one of the following?

(A)   People who realize that others could fill their occupational roles as ably as they do themselves cannot achieve any happiness in their lives.

(B)   The nature of modern society actually undermines the importance of family life to an individual's happiness.

(C)   Most people in modern society are happy in their private lives even if they are not happy in their jobs.

(D)   A majority of people in modern society do not appreciate having the jobs that they do have.

(E)   Fewer than a majority of people in modern society can find happiness outside the sphere of private interpersonal relationships.

Type: Inference
Tags: Obvious Inference, Prove & Move

Stem – "Most strongly support" is an Inference problem stem, so first seek to understand the facts and then look for an Obvious Inference.

Stimulus – 1) Read the Stimulus carefully. People aren't happy if they don't feel like others need them, but most people in society can only get that sense of worth from their family or friends.

2) Look for an Obvious Inference. The quantifier "most" is helpful because it allows you to make an inference of amounts. Combining the first sentence with the second, one potential Obvious Inference is that most people in society can't feel happy outside of their personal relationships.

Choices – 1) Eliminate incorrect choices, starting with (E). (E) says that "fewer than a majority" of people in modern society are able to find happiness outside of their private personal relationships. That is the same statement as the Obvious Inference except it switches the quantifier "most" for "fewer than a majority" and also changes the verb from "can't" to "can." That is supported by the stimulus, which tells you that in order to find happiness one must first feel needed by others. The stimulus also says most people only get that sensation from their families. "Most" indicates the majority, so those people who can find happiness outside their friends family, as (E) talks about, is in the minority This is indicated by the phrase, "fewer than a majority." (E) is correct.

Let's analyze (A) for demonstration's sake. (A) tells you that people who realize that others could do their jobs just as well as they can cannot achieve happiness in their lives. That's not supported by the stimulus, though, because the stimulus just says they need to feel needed by someone, which could include family or friends. Jobs are brought into the stimulus to show that, outside of the friend or family groups, it's difficult for most people to feel needed.

4. Like a genetic profile, a functional magnetic-resonance image (fMRI) of the brain can contain information that a patient wishes to keep private. An fMRI of a brain also contains enough information about a patient's skull to create a recognizable image of that patient's face. A genetic profile can be linked to a patient only by referring to labels or records.

The statements above, if true, **most strongly support** which one of the following?

(A) It is not important that medical providers apply labels to fMRIs of patients' brains.

(B) An fMRI has the potential to compromise patient privacy in circumstances in which a genetic profile would not.

(C) In most cases patients cannot be reasonably sure that the information in a genetic profile will be kept private.

(D) Most of the information contained in an fMRI of a person's brain is also contained in that person's genetic profile.

(E) Patients are more concerned about threats to privacy posed by fMRIs than they are about those posed by genetic profiles.

Type: Inference

Stem – "Most strongly support" tells you that this is an Inference problem stem.

Stimulus – 1) Read the stimulus carefully. A fMRI is compared to a genetic profile. Both can contain information that a patient would like to keep private. The stimulus finishes with the idea that a genetic profile is only linked to a patient by referring to labels or records. This implies that genetic profiles are a little more secure, or secure in a different way, than fMRIs in terms of privacy.

2) Look for an Obvious Inference. Nothing jumps out, so get ready to work the choices carefully.

Choices – 1) Eliminate incorrect choices, starting with (E). (E) talks about patients' concerns, which is beyond the scope of the stimulus. We never learn anything about what the patients might be concerned about. (D) – We have no reason to believe that the information contained in an image of the brain is also in the genetic profile. These are two totally different information stores for a patient. (C) –All we know about genetic profiles is that to be linked to a patient someone needs to refer to labels or records. We don't know whether that information is kept securely or not. (B) seems supported because both fMRIs and genetic profiles contain private information, and we know that a genetic profile has to be linked to the patient by referring to records, while a fMRI could create a recognizable image of a patient's face. That means that an fMRI doesn't need to be referred to records to give up private information; it can do it just by itself through the face thing. Keep (B) although it is not quite strong enough for Prove and Move. (A) talks about labeling fMRIs, which is a subject not directly discussed in the stimulus.

2) – Confirm. (B) is the best choice here, the only one that is supported.

5. Antibiotics are standard ingredients in animal feed because they keep animals healthy and increase meat yields. However, scientists have recommended phasing out this practice, believing it may make antibiotics less effective in humans. If meat yields are reduced, however, some farmers will go out of business.

Which one of the following is **most strongly supported** by the information above?

(A) If scientists are correct that antibiotic use in animal feed makes antibiotics less effective in humans, then some farmers will go out of business.

(B) If antibiotic use in animal feed is not phased out, some antibiotics will become ineffective in humans.

(C) If the scientists' recommendation is not heeded, no farmers will go out of business due to reduced meat yields.

(D) If the health of their animals declines, most farmers will not be able to stay in business.

(E) If antibiotic use in animal feed is phased out, some farmers will go out of business unless they use other means of increasing meat yields.

Type: Inference
Tags: Prove & Move

Stem – "Most strongly supported" tells us this is an Inference problem.

Stimulus – 1) Read the Stimulus carefully. Antibiotics keep animals healthy and increase meat yields, but the use of antibiotics in farming may make antibiotics less effective in humans. But, some farmers will go out of business if meat yields are reduced.

2) Look for an Obvious Inference. Nothing sticks out in particular. Nevertheless, we can make a simple link: phasing out antibiotics will reduce meat yields, which could hurt some farmers.

Choices – 1) Eliminate incorrect choices, starting with (E). (E) is a nice extension of the link that we made from the stimulus. Phasing out antibiotics in animal feed will decrease meat yields because one of the key advantages of antibiotics is increasing meat yields. Reduced meat yields will put some farmers out of business. Nevertheless, the use of antibiotics is only one means to increase meat yields, so farmers will not necessarily go out of business because of phasing out antibiotics. If they phase out antibiotics and don't compensate for the subsequent decrease in meat yield, some farmers will go out of business. (E) takes that important distinction into account nicely. Prove and Move.

6. Why are violins made by Stradivarius in the early 1700s far superior to most other violins? Some experts suggest secret varnishes, but there is no evidence for this. However, climatologists have found that in the 1600s and early 1700s weather patterns in the region of Italy where Stradivarius worked affected tree growth to produce wood with special acoustic properties. Therefore, it is likely that

    _____.

    Which one of the following most **logically completes** the argument?

    (A) some other Italian violin makers in the early 1700s produced violins that equaled the quality of Stradivarius violins

    (B) Stradivarius was the only violin maker in the early 1700s to use the wood produced in that part of Italy

    (C) no violin made from present-day materials could rival a Stradivarius violin for sound quality

    (D) the special qualities of Stradivarius violins are due in part to the wood used to make them

    (E) Stradivarius did not employ any secret techniques in making his violins

Type: Inference
Tags: Logically Completes Subtype, Obvious Inference, Prove & Move

Stem – "Logically completes" and the blank at the end of the Stimulus are clear indicators that this is an Inference problem and specifically a Logically Completes Subtype.

Stimulus – 1) Read the Stimulus carefully. This Logically Completes Subtype does not include a Parallel Situation. Instead, we are given a Fact Group about fine Stradivarius violins. In general, the stimulus tries to explain why Stradivarius violins are far superior to other violins. We learn that secret varnishes are probably not a factor because there is no evidence that he used them. However, weather patterns affected tree growth in Italy, producing wood with special acoustic properties.

2) Look for an Obvious Inference. Even though it will be hard to see an Obvious Inference in most Logically Completes problems, this stimulus seems to be headed in a particular direction. If weather patterns affected tree growth in a way that improved the wood's acoustic properties, then the weather patterns and the wood they produced probably had an impact on the superior qualities of these violins. Let's see if this idea comes up in the choices.

Choices – 1) Eliminate unproven choices, starting with (E). Even though there is no evidence of secret varnishes, we don't have enough information to prove that Stradivarius didn't use secret techniques in building his violins. Stradivarius could have used a lot of different secret techniques even if he didn't use secret varnishes. Eliminate (E). (D) matches our thinking from the stimulus. If weather patterns created conditions that produced wood with special acoustic properties, then those special acoustic properties help explain why his violins are superior. So, we can conclude that the wood is at least partially responsible for the superior qualities of Stradivarius violins. There could be a litany of other factors involved, but wood with special acoustic properties will help produce a special violin. Unlike most Logically Completes problems, you can Prove and Move here because there is no Parallel Situation, and we found a choice that matches our Obvious Inference.

7. Copyright was originally the grant of a temporary government-supported monopoly on copying a work. Its sole purpose was to encourage the circulation of ideas by giving authors the opportunity to derive a reasonable financial reward from their works. However, copyright sometimes goes beyond its original purpose since sometimes _____.

The conclusion of the argument is most strongly supported if which one of the following **completes the passage**?

(A) publication of copyrighted works is not the only way to circulate ideas

(B) authors are willing to circulate their works even without any financial reward

(C) authors are unable to find a publisher for their copyrighted work

(D) there is no practical way to enforce copyrights

(E) copyrights hold for many years after an author's death

Type: Inference
Tags: Logically Completes Subtype

Stem – "Completes the passage" and the blank at the end of the stimulus signal that this is an Inference problem and specifically a Logically Completes subtype.

Stimulus – 1) Read the Stimulus carefully. There doesn't appear to be a Parallel Situation in this stimulus, so we know we need to follow the logic and find a reasonable conclusion in the choices. We learn that the original purpose of copyrighting was to encourage the spread of ideas by giving authors an opportunity to earn money from their works. In the choices, we will need to look for a conclusion that shows an example of how copyrights could go beyond that original purpose.

2) Look for an Obvious Inference. Like most Logically Completes problems, the stimulus doesn't give us enough to make an Obvious Inference.

Choices – 1) Eliminate incorrect choices, starting with (E). (E) looks pretty nice. Part of the original purpose of copyrights was to give authors a chance to earn money from their writing. If an author dies and the copyrights hold for years after her death, then obviously she is no longer able to derive a financial reward through the copyright, so the copyright isn't serving that crucial part of the original purpose. (E) sounds alright, but we'll need to consider the other choices and confirm that it is the best conclusion of the stimulus. (D) doesn't seem like a good extension of the logic in the Stimulus. We need a conclusion that shows how copyrights go further than the original purpose, but (D) gives us a scenario in which copyrights could never serve that original purpose in the first place. If there is no practical way to enforce copyrights, how could copyrights go beyond encouraging the spread of ideas and allowing authors to profit from their writings? If copyrights don't work in the first place, they can't serve any purpose. (C) also stretches us beyond what we learn in the stimulus. If authors are unable to find a publisher, that is a different problem altogether. The original purpose of the copyright is to encourage authors to publish their ideas because they know they will be compensated fairly for the spread of their writings. If the ideas are not published, then there would be no reason to protect them. In that sense, (C) proposes a scenario that eliminates the need for copyrights' original purpose. That's not the type of conclusion we need. (B) is similar in that it presents us with a scenario that eliminates the need for copyrights. If authors are willing to spread their ideas without financial gain, then why would we need something that protects their work so they can earn money? If that were the case, then copyrights are unnecessary, and we're not looking for a conclusion that shows why copyrights are unnecessary. (A) is somewhat similar, but it also introduces a New Concept. It's very possible that there are a lot of different ways to circulate ideas. We need a conclusion that shows how or why copyrights go beyond the original purpose, and (A) doesn't come close.

2) Confirm. (E) is the best answer because it is the only one that effectively shows how copyrights go beyond the original purpose, and it is correct.

8. Philosopher: Effective tests have recently been developed to predict fatal diseases having a largely genetic basis. Now, for the first time, a person can be warned well in advance of the possibility of such life-threatening conditions. However, medicine is not yet able to prevent most such conditions. Simply being informed that one will get a disease that is both fatal and incurable can itself be quite harmful to some people. This raises the question of whether such "early warning" tests should be made available at all.

Which one of the following statements is **best illustrated** by the state of affairs described by the philosopher?

 (A) The advance of medicine fails to provide solutions to every problem.

(B) The advance of medicine creates new contexts in which ethical dilemmas can arise.

 (C) Medical technologies continue to advance, increasing our knowledge and understanding of disease.

 (D) The more we come to learn, the more we realize how little we know.

 (E) The advance of technology is of questionable value.

Type: Inference

Stem – "Best illustrated" is a little different from the stems we've seen so far, but it tells you this is an Inference problem.

Stimulus – 1) Read the Stimulus carefully. This stimulus is lengthy and full of facts, but it's actually pretty simple. Essentially, modern medical tests can predict the possibility of genetic fatal diseases, but most of such diseases are unpreventable and incurable. Consequently, these "early warning" tests may not be helpful at all. We're presented with an interesting scenario in which medicine has clearly advanced but in a direction that could be harmful to patients. It's a perplexing predicament. It's important to note that the Philosopher portrays the complexity of the debate; he doesn't choose sides. In light of that, we want to avoid choices that push us toward a particular side.

2) Look for an Obvious Inference. Nothing sticks out on this one.

Choices – 1) Eliminate incorrect choices, starting with (E). (E) takes a big leap from our scenario. According to the stimulus, "early warning" medical tests are of questionable value. Clearly, these tests represent some sincere advance in medical technology. Although these tests are of questionable value, that's not enough to say that the advance of technology in general is of questionable value. (D) also overgeneralizes the stimulus. If medical professionals are able to conduct these tests, then we as a society have come to learn more, but the dilemma described isn't really about how little we know. The predicament is much more specific. A person can be warned well in advance of the possibility of a life-threatening condition, but often medicine may not be able to prevent or cure such conditions. So, there may be little value in conducting these tests. (D) jumps pretty far beyond that. (C) is pretty tempting. In the stimulus, we are definitely given the impression that advancing medical technology increases our knowledge and understanding of disease. Nevertheless, the predicament we have described illustrates a scenario when our knowledge and understanding of disease is inefficient. We're able to identify the possibility of a fatal condition, but doctors might not be able to do anything about it. That doesn't prove (C). If anything, it makes (C) look pretty thin. On the other hand, (B) is pretty nice summation of our predicament. The advance of medicine has a created an ethical dilemma: is it more harmful to patients to know that they might develop a fatal disease that is unpreventable and incurable? For medical professionals, this is certainly a question of ethics. Their job is to help patients improve their medical condition, and these tests might cause unnecessary concern and stress. Keep (B), but let's look at (A) because we don't quite have enough to Prove and Move. (A) overgeneralizes the scenario from the stimulus. In this case, the advance of medicine has failed to provide a solution to a problem. We are able to predict the possibility of a fatal condition, but we might not be able to do anything to prevent it. In that sense, (A) is plausible, but it ignores the crux of the stimulus: the questionable value of "early warning" tests.

2) Confirm. (B) is the best choice because it addresses the predicament the Philosopher describes. Some of the other choices might be tempting, but none are as specific to the stimulus as (B). Ultimately, (B) is best illustrated by the state of affairs the Philosopher describes.

9. Coffee and tea contain methylxanthines, which cause
    temporary increases in the natural production of
    vasopressin, a hormone produced by the pituitary gland.
    Vasopressin causes clumping of blood cells, and the
    clumping is more pronounced in women than in men. This
    is probably the explanation of the fact that women face as
    much as a tenfold higher risk than men do of
    complications following angioplasty, a technique used to
    clear clogged arteries.

Which one of the following statements is **most strongly
supported** by the information above?

(A)   Men, but not women, should be given
        methylxanthines prior to undergoing angioplasty.

(B)   In spite of the risks, angioplasty is the only
        effective treatment for clogged arteries.

(C)   Women probably drink more coffee and tea, on
        average, than do men.

(D)   Prior to undergoing angioplasty, women should
        avoid coffee and tea.

(E)   Angioplasty should not be used to treat clogged
        arteries.

Type: Inference
Tags: Obvious Inference, Prove & Move, Logic Chain

Stem – "Most strongly supported" tells you this is an Inference
problem.

Stimulus – 1) Read the Stimulus carefully. The Stimulus is full of
technical terminology that might trip you up, but we don't need
to know the specifics of methylxanthines, vasopressin, and
angioplasty to find the correct choice. We just need to understand
how they relate logically. In this case, we have a big Logic Chain:
coffee and tea → methylxanthines → increased vasopressin →
clumping of blood cells. According to the stimulus, clumping of
the blood cells is more pronounced in women. We also learn that
angioplasty is a technique to clear clogged arteries, and that
women have a much higher risk of complications following
angioplasty than men.

2) Look for an Obvious Inference. We can make a very simple link
from the Logic Chain to the last fact about angioplasty: women
should avoid coffee and tea if they are having angioplasty.
Through the Logic Chain, we know that coffee and tea ultimately
lead to clumping of blood cells. Because women have such a high
risk of complications during angioplasty, they will need to avoid
anything that could cause complications during the procedure.

Choices – 1) Eliminate incorrect choices, starting with (E). We can
eliminate (E) quickly because the only clear fact we know about
angioplasty is that it is a technique used to clear clogged arteries.
Although we do know that there can be complications from the
procedure, we don't have nearly enough information to prove
that it should not be used. On the other hand, (D) aligns with the
inference we made from the stimulus. Because coffee and tea lead
to clumping blood cells, women should avoid coffee and tea prior
to angioplasty to avoid complications from the procedure. Prove
and Move.

10. Editorial: When legislators discover that some public service is not being adequately provided, their most common response is to boost the funding for that public service. Because of this, the least efficiently run government bureaucracies are the ones that most commonly receive an increase in funds.

 The statements in the editorial, if true, **most strongly support** which one of the following?

(A) The least efficiently run government bureaucracies are the bureaucracies that legislators most commonly discover to be failing to provide some public service adequately.

(B) When legislators discover that a public service is not being adequately provided, they never respond to the problem by reducing the funding of the government bureaucracy providing that service.

(C) Throughout the time a government bureaucracy is run inefficiently, legislators repeatedly boost the funding for the public service that this bureaucracy provides.

(D) If legislators boost funding for a public service, the government bureaucracy providing that service will commonly become less efficient as a result.

(E) The most inefficiently run government bureaucracy receives the most funding of any government bureaucracy.

Type: Inference
Tags: Quantifiers

Stem – "Most strongly support" – This is an Inference problem.

Stimulus – 1) Read the Stimulus carefully. This stimulus is laden with some tricky quantifiers. When a public service is not adequately provided, the *most common* response is to boost funding. As a consequence, the least efficiently run bureaucracies – which probably do not adequately provide a public service – *most commonly* receive increased funding. It's a pretty simple stimulus, but we can be certain that those two quantifiers will be extremely important as we work through the choices.

2) Look for an Obvious Inference. Nothing sticks out in particular. Let's move on to the choices.

Choices – 1) Eliminate incorrect Choices, starting with (E). We don't have enough information to prove (E). In the Stimulus, we learned that the least efficient bureaucracies are most likely to receive increased funding, but that doesn't mean that the most inefficient bureaucracy receives the most funding. It's highly likely that that particular bureaucracy would receive increased funding, but there could be an extremely efficient bureaucracy that receives the most funding overall because of the nature of the service it provides. We only have information about increases in funding; we know nothing about the greatest or the least amounts of funding. We also don't have enough information to prove (D). We don't know anything about the effect of a boost in funding on the bureaucracy's performance. An inefficient bureaucracy will be more likely to receive more funds, but that doesn't mean it will become less efficient as a consequence. Furthermore, why would increased funding be the most common response if it will only make the bureaucracy less efficient at providing its service? (C) is a tempting choice because it seems to echo the logic of the stimulus. However, those two very important quantifiers we picked out are not taken into consideration. If a bureaucracy is inefficient, the *most common* response will be to boost the funding, but more funding will not necessarily be the response in every situation. In some cases, legislators may choose from any number of different responses even though most of the time they'll increase funding. (B) is similar to (C). Look out for the quantifier "never." There could be a situation where reducing the funding is the appropriate response. We know the most common response is boosting funding, but that doesn't have to be the response every time. On the other hand, (A) does a good job of combining the two key facts. We know that the least efficiently run bureaucracies most commonly receive an increase in funds. If legislators find out a public service is not adequately, their most common response is to boost the funding. If inefficient bureaucracies are more likely to receive more funding, then legislators have probably found that they are not providing their service adequately.

2) Confirm. We weren't able to Prove and Move because we worked through all the choices, but we were left with (A) – the only choice proven by the stimulus.

11. Philosopher: The rational pursuit of happiness is quite different from always doing what one most strongly desires to do. This is because the rational pursuit of happiness must include consideration of long-term consequences, whereas our desires are usually focused on the short term. Moreover, desires are sometimes compulsions, and while ordinary desires result in at least momentary happiness when their goals are attained, compulsions strongly drive a person to pursue goals that offer no happiness even when reached.

If all of the philosopher's statements are true, each of the following **could be true EXCEPT**:

 (A) The majority of people do not have compulsions.

(B) Attaining the goal of any desire results in momentary happiness.

 (C) Most people do not pursue happiness rationally.

 (D) Most people want more than their own personal happiness.

(E) All actions have long-term consequences.

Type: Inference EXCEPT

Stem – "Could be true EXCEPT" is a little different from Inference problems we've seen so far. Instead of looking for a choice that is proven by the stimulus, we'll need to find one that is *proven false* by the stimulus, a choice that cannot be true based on the information in the stimulus. All of the incorrect choices could be true based on the stimulus.

Stimulus – 1) Read the Stimulus carefully. The Philosopher tells us about the distinction between the rational pursuit of happiness and simply following any desire. Most desires are focused on the short term, but the rational pursuit of happiness must include consideration of long-term consequences. Some desires are just compulsions, and these strongly drive people to pursue goals that might not result in happiness. On the other hand, ordinary desires result in at least momentary happiness.

2) Due to the unique nature of this problem (we are looking for a choice that is not possible), don't look for an Obvious Inference.

Choices – 1) As we work through the choices, keep in mind that we need to eliminate choices that "could be true." We don't have to prove them absolutely. (E) is a perfect example of a Plausible Choice. In the stimulus, we learn that considering long-term consequences is critical for the rational pursuit of happiness. This implies that at least some actions have long-term consequences. In general, the Philosopher's statements seem to imply that there may be long-term consequences connected to every action. We don't have enough information to prove this choice, but we also don't enough information to disprove it. (D) is similar. The Philosopher seems to imply that many people want to improve their happiness, often through pursuing desires. We can't prove this one without a doubt, but we don't have any information that would disprove it. (C) also looks pretty plausible. Because the Philosopher is taking the time to draw the distinction between the rational pursuit of happiness and chasing after momentary desires and compulsions, he seems to imply that many people do not pursue happiness rationally. "Many" is very different from "most," but it's good enough to eliminate this choice because we can't disprove this one either. On the other hand, (B) goes against some of the facts in the stimulus. We learned that some desires are compulsions, which strongly drive a person to pursue goals that offer no happiness. So, attaining the goals of *some* desires does not result in any happiness even when reached. We learned that ordinary desires result in at least momentary happiness, but ordinary desires and compulsions are two very specific types of desires. As a consequence, we can definitely disprove (B) because we know that attaining the goal of some desires – compulsions – offers no momentary happiness. Keep (B), but let's consider (A) just in case. (A) might look like a tempting choice, but we don't have any definitive information to disprove it. The Philosopher seems to imply that everyone has desires, and, since some desires are compulsions, it makes logical sense to think that most people have compulsions. However, (A) can be true, and nothing in our stimulus would need to change. That's a Plausible Choice, so we can eliminate it.

2) Confirm. We're left with (B) – the only answer we can definitely disprove.

Argument Parts

Inference problems have fact group stimuli, but most LR problems have argument stimuli. This chapter will teach you to identify the conclusion, support, and other parts of an argument. Understanding argument parts is a fundamental LR Skill, and you will get to put it into action on the upcoming Justify chapter.

Chapter Contents
Argument Parts
Conclusion and Support Indicators
Scope
Bracket the Conclusion
Conclusion Types
Opposing Views and Setups

Skill Tags
Single Sentence Conclusion
Soft Conclusion
Sub-conclusion
Referential Conclusion
Opposing View
Setup

Argument Parts

Identifying Argument Parts is a skill that you'll use on 80% of the questions in the Logical Reasoning section because 80% of LR stimuli are arguments. This skill will also come in handy on the Reading Comprehension section.

The word "argument" most likely carries some anecdotal meaning in your mind. Maybe you hear "argument" and think of having a heated discussion with a sibling at the dinner table. These are real world arguments. Arguments in the LSAT world, a magical place where logic rules are very strict, are less intense as long as they're properly approached and understood.

As briefly described in the 'stimulus' introduction section, an argument on the LSAT contains *support,* (or premises*),* that lead to a *conclusion.* Check out this abstract argument:

A is B, and B is C. So, A is C.

This argument makes a conclusion about the relationship between A and C based on two supporting relationships between A and B and B and C. Let's break down the argument into its parts, the premises and the conclusion.

- Premise 1: A is B.
- Premise 2: B is C.
- Conclusion: So, A is C.

This structure is the foundation of sound logical reasoning, both in the LSAT world and in the real world. However, logical arguments don't always appear in such a straightforward premise-premise-conclusion order on the LSAT. For instance, the conclusion might come in the middle of the stimulus, or perhaps it is stated outright at the beginning of the argument.

LSAT writers try to make conclusions and support difficult to identify, but they aren't *that* hard to spot. They're actually somewhat simple to find once you know the patterns. After you identify the conclusion and support, your task will typically ask you to do specific things with them. For this reason, identifying argument parts correctly is *vital* to securing a good LSAT score. It's the first key step to solving most Logical Reasoning problems.

Conclusion and Support Indicators

An <u>indicator</u> is a word that signals that a specific kind of information is about to follow. For instance, "because" is a support indicator as it comes *right before* the key supporting evidence for a given conclusion. There are indicators for a number of different topics on the LSAT. For instance, words like 'most,' 'all,' and 'some' indicate that you're dealing with quantifiers, which refer to very specific quantities in the LSAT world.

It's helpful to recognize indicators, also referred to as buzzwords, because they will trigger your LSAT-specific understanding of these concepts. We'll introduce these indicators and other indicators throughout the curriculum. There aren't many, though—the conclusion and support indicators are by far the most important. Let's look at them now.

Conclusion Indicators

Common conclusion indicators include "therefore" and "so." Other conclusion indicators are terms that express obviousness like "surely" and "clearly." This argument features the conclusion indicator "so:"

> A reason Larson cannot do the assignment is that she has an unavoidable scheduling conflict. On the other hand, a reason Franks cannot do the assignment is that he does not quite have the assertiveness the task requires. **So**, the task must be assigned to Parker, the only supervisor in the shipping department other than Larson and Franks.

"So" comes right before the conclusion that the task must be assigned to Parker.

Support Indicators

As for support indicators, you can expect to see "for," "for instance," "since," and "because." Here's an example stimulus that uses the support indicator "because:"

> Commentator: Many people argue that the release of chlorofluorocarbons into the atmosphere is harming humans by damaging the ozone layer, thus allowing increased amounts of ultraviolet radiation to reach Earth. But 300,000 years ago a supernova greatly damaged the ozone layer with no significant effect on our earliest ancestors. **Because** the supernova's disruption was much greater than the estimated effect of chlorofluorocarbons today, there is no reason to think that these chemicals in the atmosphere harm humans in this way.

The supernova's disruption supports the conclusion that there's no reason to believe that the chlorofluorocarbons harm humans, at least in the argument's eyes.

We will **bold** indicator words in the Problem Set Explanations in the same style as the argument above. This bolding highlights the indicator word so you notice it during your review. When you are completing LR problems, you don't need to annotate (mark) indicator words. The indicator points to the conclusion or support, so once you see what the indicator is pointing to, the actual indicator word has done its job.

Scope

Understanding <u>scope</u>, whether a statement is broad or specific, is a very helpful way to find the conclusion when there are no indicators. Support is *more specific* while the conclusion is *broad* or *general*.

A difference in scope occurs because the support tends to contain specific evidence while conclusions make larger final statements. To draw an analogy, support is like evidence at a trial—specific and distinct—while the conclusion is like a final verdict: broad and encompassing in scope. Let's look at an example to see scope in action.

> Eating broccoli is good for you. It's a source of calcium and fiber, and it contains other healthy nutrients.

This argument has no indicators. We can still easily find the conclusion by focusing on scope. The first sentence is broader than the second sentence, so the first sentence is the conclusion. Calcium, fiber, and nutrient content are all *specific factors* that support the broader statement "broccoli is good for you."

Relativity

It's important to note that all scope is relative to the other information around it. For instance, in the example above the conclusion is "eating broccoli is good for you" because the scope is broader than the second sentence. However, consider the scope of the sentences in this example:

> Eating broccoli is good for you. Paul should eat more broccoli.

Here, we have a specific fact about broccoli and then a more general statement about Paul's diet. Notice how the role of the first sentence changes in relation to a new second sentence. In the earlier example, it is the argument's main point, and the rest is just supporting the idea that broccoli is good for you. In the second example, the statement about broccoli becomes a specific fact that supports the more general claim, "Paul should eat more broccoli."

Bracket the Conclusion

There are different ways to mark the parts of an argument. The simplest and best method is to put *brackets* (parenthesis) around the conclusion. This bracket system ensures that you identify the conclusion, the most important part of any argument. Here's an example of an argument marked with brackets:

> 3. A reason Larson cannot do the assignment is that she has an unavoidable scheduling conflict. On the other hand, a reason Franks cannot do the assignment is that he does not quite have the assertiveness the task requires. (**So, the task must be assigned to Parker,**) the only supervisor in the shipping department other than Larson and Franks.

With the conclusion identified, the support is easier to find. This is by far the most important annotation you will make on an LR stimulus. We will cover the few other possible annotations as they arise on specific problem types.

Try it Out

Below are three simple arguments. Use scope to determine which statement is the conclusion and which is the support. Bracket the sentence that has the conclusion.

1. Steve thinks every single pen writes smoother than pencils. Steve is a serious idiot.

2. My doctor said I should run more often. He told me that it will make me tired but the increase in overall health will make it worth the effort.

3. Mary knows how to tag seals. She must know a lot about aquatic wildlife.

Try it Out – Answers

The conclusions are marked below:

1. Steve thinks every single pen writes smoother than pencils.(Steve is a serious idiot.)

2.(My doctor said I should run more often.)He told me that it will make me tired but the increase in overall health will make it worth the effort.

3. Mary knows how to tag seals.(She must know a lot about aquatic wildlife.)

Conclusion Types

There are several different types of conclusions you might come across in an LSAT argument. Again, these sections are meant to expose you to these types, so don't worry about memorizing the concepts at this point. We will use tags and explanations to point out when these concepts show up in problems.

Referential Conclusions

When they are used to refer to an entire supporting clause, words like 'this' and 'that' can make the conclusion harder to pinpoint. These words are essentially substitutes used to refer to an earlier concept. For example, you may see a conclusion that says:

(Tomorrow we go to Disneyland.)People love Disneyland, but I have to say:(**this** is unacceptable.)

Put brackets around each part of the conclusion, the concluding statement and the statement that the referential word substitutes.

Technically, the conclusion is "this is unacceptable," but obviously there's more to it—the 'this' refers to the sentence, "Tomorrow we go to Disneyland." So, this grump's full conclusion is "it's unacceptable that tomorrow we go to Disneyland."

The stimuli that use referential words in conclusions are by nature longer and more complex than the example above. As you can imagine, a strong mental understanding of the conclusion and how to mark it are important for dealing with these separated thoughts.

Soft Conclusions

A <u>soft conclusion</u> is one that is very cautious. Unlike most LSAT conclusions, it's wary of being disproven. As such, it says something to the effect of "IF the claim is correct, THEN we can draw this conclusion." Implicit in this if-then structure is the idea that the initial claim – the claim from which the argument draws its conclusion – might be false.

Consider this example:

Some people think cats have nine lives.(**If this claim is correct**, then it follows that cats are closer to immortality than humans)because humans have but one life.

The argument concludes that cats are more immortal than humans, but it qualifies that conclusion with the phrase in bold: "If this claim is correct…" The conclusion is based on the idea that cats have nine lives, but the conclusion doesn't fully buy into that claim. If it did, it wouldn't need to say, "If this claim is correct." Instead, the conclusion would use the claim as a fact.

The conclusion preceded by "if this claim is correct" is "soft" because it is not as absolute as if the argument were to say, "Cats are more immortal than humans because cats have nine lives." Yet, it is not so concrete; it says that the conclusion is true *provided that* this piece of support is also true. In so doing, the argument safeguards itself against critique. You could say, "It's not true that cats have nine lives," and then the argument still is technically not wrong because it acknowledged that possibility.

This just means that the structure of a soft conclusion is a bit longer and more complex. Instead of being a straightforward conclusion, a soft conclusion inherently contains the safeguarding clause "if the support is true," and that clause must be considered *part* of the conclusion.

Sub-Conclusions

Some complex arguments contain more than one conclusion. These arguments have a <u>sub-conclusion</u>, an intermediary conclusion used as support for the main conclusion of the argument. In this case, it's necessary to understand which is the *main conclusion* as opposed to the sub-conclusion.

A sub-conclusion is a supported statement that is drawn in order to reach a final conclusion. Identifying a sub-conclusion can be tricky because of conclusion placement. You'll see some main conclusions in the middle of a stimulus, followed by a sub-conclusion, which can be confusing from an ordering perspective.

If a main conclusion is mid-stimulus followed by a sub-conclusion, you might write the main conclusion off as just a piece of support. We will develop your ability to see which conclusion is the final one in situations such as the stimulus below:

> Chefs at a local restaurant will soon release a plate made from lab-created meat. While this is a new horizon in agricultural technology (people will not buy it.) People don't buy food that they don't understand, and **people don't understand lab-created meat.**

The sub-conclusion here is in bold. This claim supports the conclusion that people won't buy the dish from this local restaurant, so you know it's not the main conclusion. If you ask yourself what the point of this argument is, you'll be able to spot the true conclusion. The only "main point" is that people won't buy the restaurant's meat, and the rest of the information just supports that point.

Single-Sentence Arguments

Some stimuli contain the entire argument in one sentence. That doesn't mean the whole stimulus is a single sentence. In some cases, there will be multiple sentences, but one contains everything you need to know: both the support and the conclusion. These often take the following form:

> Hot dogs taste good, but they probably aren't very healthy. **So, since** they might be bad for me (I have vowed never to eat a hot dog again.)

"Since" indicates support, and it shows up directly before the argument's support. The second part of the sentence is the conclusion in this example.

The final sentence contains both the conclusion and the support, so you know that you don't have to spend any energy or attention on the first sentence. That's the beauty of Single-Sentence Arguments. Once you notice that it's a Single-Sentence Argument, you can focus on the relevant information.

Opposing Views & Setups

In this section, we discuss two other argument elements that often show up in LR arguments.

Opposing Views

Arguments sometimes contain statements that introduce an <u>Opposing View</u>, a viewpoint that the argument ultimately argues against. For instance:

> Sometimes it's hard to know whether or not to eat peanut butter. **Scientists say we shouldn't eat peanut butter**, but peanut butter is very, very tasty. So, we should eat peanut butter.

The conclusion is "we should eat peanut butter." The argument could stand without the opposing view that "scientists say we shouldn't eat peanut butter," but it adds another dimension to the stimulus. The argument only includes opposing view statements to argue against it or to say that the people who believe it to be true are wrong.

Setups

LSAT writers will often include <u>Setup</u> information in a stimulus at the beginning of a stimulus. This information may appear to be relevant support, but in it's actually included only to set the scene and to orient you to the argument about to unfold. Setup familiarizes you with the situation at hand, but it has no major impact on the argument from a logical perspective. Read and understand the background information, but don't put too much importance on it. Consider the example argument about peanut butter:

> **Sometimes it's hard to know whether or not to eat peanut butter.** Scientists say we shouldn't eat peanut butter, but peanut butter is very, very tasty. So, we should eat peanut butter.

The first sentence has no major impact on the conclusion that "we should eat peanut butter." The argument would be the same if it were just the last two sentences alone, so the first sentence is just background information—it sets the scene for the argument about to unfold.

Argument Parts Review

Argument Parts

- Learning how to identify the conclusion and support in an argument is a crucial LSAT skill.

- The support backs the conclusion.

Conclusion and Support Indicators

- An indicator is a word that signals that a specific kind of information is about to follow. Conclusion and support indicators are two of the most important kinds of indicators.

- Common conclusion indicators include "therefore," "so," and "clearly."

- Common support indicators are "for," "since," and "because."

Scope

- Scope refers to how broad or specific a statement is. The scope of a sentence is relative to those sentences around it.

- Watching the scope of different statements can help you determine which is the conclusion in an argument.

- The conclusion tends to have a broader scope than the support because the support needs to be specific to back the conclusion.

Bracket the Conclusion

- Put parentheses around the conclusion when you identify it in an argument.

- This focuses your thinking and ensures that you locate the conclusion, a crucial step when working with any LR argument.

Conclusion Types

- Referential Conclusion – 'This,' 'that,' 'she,' and 'their' are examples of words that are used in place of concepts to refer to the original idea, e.g. "The bank is corrupt. *They* told me so."

- Soft Conclusions – The argument is wary to make absolute conclusion, e.g.. "If the testimony is indeed true, then we should act accordingly."

- Sub-Conclusions – The argument bases its final conclusion on an intermediate conclusion, e.g. "Because he often tells the truth, I believe him [intermediate conclusion]. Because I believe him, we should support his mayoral campaign [final conclusion]."

- Single-Sentence Arguments – The argument (support and conclusion) is contained in one sentence.

Opposing Views & Setups

- Opposing View Statement – The argument introduces information, and then it shows how that info is incorrect.

- Background Information – This sets the scene for the argument. It is not necessary for the conclusion, but it can still be informative.

Argument Parts Drill

This drill will develop your ability to identify the parts of an argument, reinforcing everything you have learned in this chapter.

Directions

For each stimulus:

1. Circle the conclusion and support indicators. This step is practice for this drill; don't circle indicators when working other LR stimuli.

2. Bracket the conclusion.

3. Underline the support. This step is also practice; don't underline the support in other LR problems.

1. Scientists recently unearthed 500 feet of the Sonoran Desert floor in Arizona. Previously, researchers had only reached depths of 100 feet, where they found shards of clay pottery next to mammal bones. The recent excavation revealed a much greater variety of mammal remains and no trace of manmade pottery. Clearly, the arrival of humans must have severely reduced the mammalian biodiversity of the Sonoran Desert.

2. Studying mathematics enlarges the hippocampus, especially if one studies applied mathematics. Mathematicians on average tend to have a much larger hippocampus, a region of the brain, than that of regular people. This difference is even more pronounced when the mathematician is an expert in the field of applied mathematics.

3. When blueberries fall off their bush, they land in the soil and the blueberry flesh begins to rot. This decomposition process provides an excellent environment for new growth, which is why blueberry seeds are found in the center of this fruity flesh. These pods of nutrient-dense flesh act as natural fertilizers because they hasten seed growth. It must be the case that any inorganic fertilizer used to hasten seed growth does not endanger humans in any serious way. People eat the natural fertilizer of blueberries all the time and suffer no ill effects. In fact, blueberries and other similar fruits form a huge part of the global agricultural market.

4. In order to reverse global starvation, people must be willing to donate some of their resources to those who are less fortunate than they are. But people will only donate their surplus resources if they see benefit for themselves. Because few people are able to see any direct benefit from giving away their extra resources, no serious progress will soon be made towards reversing starvation around the world.

5. Psychologist: Because of a perceived social stigma against psychotherapy, and because of age discrimination on the part of some professionals, some elderly people feel discouraged about trying psychotherapy. They should not be, however, for many younger people have greatly benefited from it, and people in later life have certain advantages over the young—such as breadth of knowledge, emotional maturity, and interpersonal skills—that contribute to the likelihood of a positive outcome.

6. Mayor McKinney's policies have often been criticized on the grounds that they benefit only wealthy city residents, but that is not a fair evaluation. Some of McKinney's policies have clearly benefited the city's less affluent residents. McKinney actively supported last year's proposal to lower the city's high property taxes. Because of this tax decrease, more development is taking place in the city, helping to end the housing shortage and stabilize the rents in the city.

END OF SET

Drill Explanations

1. Scientists recently unearthed 500 feet of the Sonoran Desert floor in Arizona. Previously, researchers had only reached depths of <u>100 feet, where they found shards</u> of clay pottery next to mammal bones. The recent excavation revealed a much <u>greater variety of mammal remains and no trace of manmade pottery.</u> (Clearly, the arrival of humans must have severely reduced the mammalian biodiversity of the Sonoran Desert.)

1) Conclusion: The conclusion here comes after the indicator "clearly," tipping you off that the argument is reaching its climax. The conclusion is about how humans have reduced biodiversity of a desert.

2) Support: There are two main support pieces here, and both discuss the correlation between human pottery and diversity of animal bones.

2. (Studying mathematics enlarges the hippocampus,) especially if one studies applied mathematics. <u>Mathematicians on average tend to have a much larger</u> hippocampus, a region of the brain, than that of regular people. This difference is even more pronounced when the mathematician is an expert in the field of applied mathematics.

1) Conclusion: This conclusion comes right away in the first line. Studying math makes a part of the brain bigger.

2) Support: The rest of the stimulus is support. The main supporting idea is that mathematicians tend to have a larger hippocampus than non-mathematicians. Of course, if this were a Find Flaw Task, you might point out that just because a large hippocampus correlates to someone who's good at math does not mean math is causing the enlarged brain—maybe the large hippocampus is a prerequisite for being good at math. Correlation does not show causation.

3. When blueberries fall off their bush, they land in the soil and the blueberry flesh begins to rot. This decomposition process provides an excellent environment for new growth, which is why blueberry seeds are found in the center of this fruity flesh. These pods of nutrient-dense flesh can be thought of as natural fertilizers, as they hasten seed growth. (It must be the case that any inorganic fertilizer used to hasten seed growth does not endanger humans in any serious way.) <u>People eat the natural fertilizer of blueberries all the time and suffer no ill effects.</u> In fact, blueberries and other similar fruits form a huge part of the global agricultural market.

1) Conclusion: "It must be the case that any inorganic fertilizer used to hasten seed growth does not endanger humans in any serious way." Note the indicator "must be," which indicates a deduction (i.e. if A does B and B is good for C, then A *must be* good for C).

2) Support: The main support is the parallel between natural and synthetic blueberries. It's okay for humans to eat one, so, the argument reasons it must be okay for humans to eat the other. Of course, synthetic pesticides are different from natural pesticides that are more defense mechanisms than pesticides. That's not necessarily a strong comparison there…

4. In order to reverse global starvation, people must be willing to donate some of their resources to those who are less fortunate than they are. But <u>people will only donate their surplus resources if they see benefit for themselves.</u> (Because few people are able to see any direct benefit from giving away their extra resources (no serious progress will soon be made towards reversing starvation around the world.)

1) Conclusion: The argument comes to the main conclusion that no significant progress will be made towards reversing global starvation.

2) Support: The support is marked by the indicator "because." Because few people see direct benefit from giving away their extra resources and people will only donate surplus if there's benefit in it for themselves, the argument sees this as grounds for its conclusion.

5. Psychologist: Because of a perceived social stigma against psychotherapy, and because of age discrimination on the part of some professionals (some elderly people feel discouraged about trying psychotherapy. They should not be) however, for many younger people have greatly benefited from it, and people in later life have certain advantages over the young—such as breadth of knowledge, emotional maturity, and interpersonal skills—that contribute to the likelihood of a positive outcome.

1) Conclusion: The main conclusion here is "they should not be" although we must take into account the information the conclusion refers to in order to fully understand it. To mark a Referential Conclusion like this, bracket the main conclusion and the other piece of information that most helps you to understand the main conclusion. In this argument, the conclusion is that the elderly people who feel discouraged about trying psychotherapy because of age discrimination should not be discouraged.

2) Support: The indicator "for" precedes the support. "Many younger people have greatly benefited from it," and older people have different life experiences that make them more aptly suited to reap the benefits of psychotherapy.

6. (Mayor McKinney's policies have often been criticized on the grounds that they benefit only wealthy city residents, but that is not a fair evaluation.) Some of McKinney's policies have clearly benefited the city's less affluent residents. McKinney actively supported last year's proposal to lower the city's high property taxes. Because of this tax decrease, more development is taking place in the city, helping to end the housing shortage and stabilize the rents in the city.

1) Conclusion: It is not fair to say that the Mayor's policies only benefit wealthy city residents. Note the word "clearly" in the second sentence; this is a trick indicator as it doesn't actually indicate the conclusion. When "clearly" is used as a conclusion indicator, it tends to open the sentence. When in doubt, rely on scope over indicators.

2) Support: As support for this statement, the argument gives an example of some of the Mayor's policies that benefit the city's less affluent population.

 **Justify**

Each Justify problem has an argument as its stimulus. That argument has a gap in its logic, and the correct choice provides the link needed to make the argument valid. This type helps you practice identifying argument parts and working with conditional reasoning.

Chapter Contents
Stem
Stimulus
Choices
Unlinked Concepts Drill
Technique Set
Challenge Set
Test Set

Problem Type Information
Stimulus type: Argument
Stimulus skills: Identify argument parts, find the unlinked concepts
Can Envision Correct Answer: Often
Choice skills: Eliminate choices that don't contain both concepts

Problem Type Tags
Missing Link Flaw
Unlinked Concepts
Logic Chain
Justify the Application Stimuli

Introduction

Justify problem stems feature variety, but they always ask you to do the same essential task: make the argument in the stimulus valid. The argument will have a gap, so your job is to make the argument whole by linking the two concepts on either side of that gap. Difficulty in Justify problems comes almost entirely in locating the two unlinked concepts on either side of the argument's gap.

Justify problems are common. You will see around seven on any given two LR sections.

Stem

For all the variety in Justify problem stems, they boil down to two main phrasings: "the *conclusion follows logically* if which one of the following is assumed" and "which one of the following *principles* most helps to *justify* the argument?"

The primary indicators are noted in italics: "conclusion follows logically" and "principles… justify." Both ask you to do the same thing: link the gap. Let's look at each.

Conclusion Follows Logically

The first variety of stem proposes the idea of the *making the conclusion valid*. It is often worded as "follows logically" or "properly inferred." Notice the "J" stem stamps next to each example stem.

> *J*   The business ethicist's **conclusion follows logically** if which one of the following is assumed?

> *J*   The main **conclusion** of the literary critic's argument can be **properly inferred** if which one of the following is assumed?

The main identifying characteristic is that the stem talks about finding a choice that fully supports or justifies the argument's conclusion. To identify the type correctly with this stem variety, mentally connect the concept of making a conclusion logical with justifying (conclusion follows logically = justify).

Justify

The other variety of stem explicitly uses the word "justify" and will have you fix the gap with a "principle."

> *J*   Which one of the following principles, if valid, most helps to **justify** the government agency's decision?

> *J*   Which one of the following principles most helps in **justifying** the application of the guideline?

These stems are easy to spot. Notice that these stems also introduce the idea of a *principle* justifying a conclusion. Do not let that trip you up; a principle is a general rule – nothing too special. These stems require the exact same solving process as the "conclusion follows logically" variety of stem.

Justify problems have more variety in their stems than most problems, but that shouldn't cause any issues. You'll come to group all these slightly different stems into the category of Justify.

Stimulus

Almost all of the arguments in the Logical Reasoning section are flawed. The next two Modules of the curriculum teach the Understand Flaw Skill Group, which is large and almost exclusively problem types with flawed arguments. Similarly, all Justify stimuli are flawed arguments. Unlike the problem types in the Understand Flaw section, however, all Justify problems have the same flaw: a <u>Missing Link</u>. This flaw is gap or missing piece in the reasoning.

Missing Link flaws are characterized by a jump in the logic, which is essentially a gap in the reasoning. This makes sense because Justify problems ask you to make the argument valid, so these arguments have *one* small, specific gap in their logic that you will link up to make the argument valid using the correct choice. The gap comes between two <u>Unlinked Concepts</u>: ideas or subjects in the conclusion or the support that the argument assumes match up even though they aren't inherently linked. Essentially, the argument fails to state that these concepts are linked, which is what causes the gap in the reasoning.

These unlinked concepts border the gap in logic. In other words, the argument jumps from one concept to the other without mentioning the connection that *should* be in the middle in order to make such a leap in logic valid. There are two core concepts that the argument fails to properly link: one in the conclusion and one in a part of the support.

Before we dive into the specific characteristics of the gap and the techniques to find the unlinked concepts, let's talk a bit about how to make an argument valid.

Creating Validity

To make an argument fully valid, you must connect its support directly to its conclusion. Because of the gap that shows up in all Justify problems and because your mission for Justify problems is to make the arguments *valid*, you'll always seek to add a second piece of support that, when combined with the argument's support piece, makes the argument 100% logically airtight.

Let's look at a super-simple example of a how you'll validate a Justify stimulus' argument. First, take a look at this argument, looking for the gap:

> Dogs love treats. Thus, Jimmy will love a treat.

The conclusion is that Jimmy will love a treat, and why will he love that treat? Because dogs love treats. There is a gap here; we have no connection between "Jimmy" and "dogs." Jimmy is just a name and not a particularly doggy-sounding name, so we need a second support piece, one that connects "Jimmy" with "dogs." Here's the piece we need to make the argument valid:

> Jimmy is a dog.

With that added piece in place, we now have this argument structure:

> Dogs love treats.
>
> Jimmy is a dog.
>
> _____
>
> Jimmy will love a treat.

Thanks to our added support piece that directly *links* "Jimmy" to "dogs," we have a valid argument. Note how important seeing the gap is to make the argument valid. If you see that the conclusion about Jimmy loving treats doesn't match up with the concept that all dogs love treats, then you can begin to link the argument's gap and make it valid. That's exactly what we've done here. The conclusion is nicely backed up by the two support pieces, and there are no flaws because the pieces are so simple and direct. If all dogs love treats and Jimmy is a dog, then it must be the case that Jimmy would love a treat.

Now that you have a good feel for how to make a Justify conclusion valid through linking pieces, let's walk through the specific steps of working a Justify stimulus in detail.

Step 1 - Identify the Conclusion

As with all arguments, begin your analysis by locating the conclusion and then the support. You need to grasp the reasoning of the argument first so you can then find the gap's unlinked concepts. Usually, identifying the argument parts is easy on this type. However, the test writers try to make the unlinked concepts difficult to spot, so it is crucial to understand the argument clearly.

Justify arguments are often simple. The Justify problems of easy and medium difficulty are generally two sentences: one is the support, and one is the conclusion. The arguments rarely have setup information. To find the conclusion, look for the statement that the rest of the stimulus supports. The conclusions often have indicators, so don't be afraid of relying on words like "therefore," "thus," and "so" to help spot a conclusion.

Step 2 – Identify the Support

Once you locate the conclusion, find the support. This is usually straightforward; just locate the information that most directly backs up the conclusion.

The support in Justify problems usually follows the same pattern. The stimulus gives you the *key* support piece, and then the argument expands on that support concept. This is basically support *for the support*. You can generally disregard that expansion and just focus on the core of the support. Take a look at this example of a stimulus with a statement that supports the support:

> Anyone who knows Ellsworth knows that **he is bursting with self-righteousness**, touting the idealism of his generation over the greed of the previous generation (So no one who knows him will be surprised that Ellsworth is offended by the suggestions in the media that he has engaged in unethical business practices.)

We've made bold the primary support that Ellsworth is bursting with self-righteousness. Notice the expansion of the support that follows the piece, further explaining that he is self-righteous because he thinks his generation has a better philosophy than the previous generation. In all arguments, focus on the primary support piece. On Justify problems, it is much easier to identify the unlinked concept in the support, the support side of the gap, when you are focused on the *primary* support and not distracted by its expansion.

For some of the more difficult Justify problems, the stimulus will be a three- or four-link <u>Logic Chain</u> with the conclusion as the final link. In those cases, find the *most direct* support piece for the conclusion. This can be challenging if the stimulus is particularly dense.

Here's an example of a stimulus with multiple support links:

> University president: We will be forced to reduce spending next year if we do not increase our enrollment(So, if we are to maintain the quality of the education we provide, we must market our programs more aggressively) Without such marketing we will be unable to increase our enrollment.

We've bracketed the conclusion to make the stimulus easier to analyze. The argument talks about the need to reduce spending if enrollment isn't increased. Then, it states that, in order to maintain the current quality of education, the school must market their programs more effectively because that's the only way they'll be able to increase enrollment.

Amid all these links, there's one spot that doesn't quite match up. Can you spot it? If not, don't worry—this is a tough argument. It talks about reducing spending, and then out of nowhere it states that increasing enrollment is also a matter of maintaining the school's quality of education. Apparently, the school cannot maintain their quality of education if they have to reduce their spending next year. That is the gap, and the unlinked concepts on either side are "forced to reduce spending" and "maintain the quality of the education we provide."

Step 3 – Find the Gap

Once you have clearly identified the conclusion and support, look for a gap in how they match up. There will always be two key concepts between them that do not link.

The gap will sometimes present itself as a <u>Concept Jump</u>, where you'll read the stimulus and think to yourself, "When did we start talking about that concept?" Typically, Concept Jumps occur between two important concepts that are both mentioned only once in the argument. You will often notice Concept Jumps as you identify and analyze the conclusion and support. Concept Jumps point you towards the two concepts that are unlinked and thus to the gap in the logic. When you can spot the gap as a clear Concept Jump, it may be helpful to underline the two concepts—we'll practice this in a bit.

Other times, the gap will be more abstract and you won't be able to state two clear and distinct concepts that fail to match up. Instead, you'll spot a hole in the argument and know what's wrong, but you won't be able to put your finger on two key words that fail to match up. These abstract cases are in fact concept jumps where the concept is just stated in long form as its own clause or sentence as opposed to just a word or two. Let's look at some easy Justify gaps first and then come back to the more abstract ones.

The easier Justify gaps are characterized by two concepts that stand out as distinct, perhaps even jarring in their different-ness. Because the stimulus is not terribly complex, the gap is easy to spot.

Here is an example of a stimulus with distinct, unlinked concepts. Please take a moment to identify the gap in the stimulus. Start by finding the conclusion and its support, and then underline the two concepts on either side of the gap in logic for the sake of the exercise.

> When Teresa runs out of gas driving home she is late for dinner. So, because she ran out of gas driving home yesterday, she was unhappy yesterday.

Let's break this argument down into its parts. First, as always, identify the conclusion: Teresa was unhappy yesterday. What supports that idea? She ran out of gas driving home, and she was late for dinner as a consequence. "Running out of gas" is linked in the support and conclusion; it appears in both. Nevertheless, there is no link between "being late for dinner" and "being unhappy," so we know that those are the two unlinked concepts.

In identifying the concepts on either side of the gap, here is what you should underline:

> When Teresa runs out of gas driving home she is <u>late for dinner</u>. So, because she ran out of gas driving home yesterday, she was <u>unhappy</u> yesterday.

From a logical perspective, "being late for dinner" and "being unhappy" are distinct concepts even though in real life we might see an automatic connection between them. We can imagine many people getting upset because they are late for dinner, but on the LSAT—and therefore in this argument—those concepts are not so inherently linked.

On challenging Justify problems, the two concepts may be *similar* in meaning but ever so slightly—and significantly—distinct. This can make it harder to spot the concepts when you first read the stimulus. Here is an example of a stimulus with two unlinked concepts that sound similar. Identify the two concepts that are unconnected.

> Tomorrow is the running of the bulls in Pamplona and the runner turnout is expected to be large. Running with the bulls is quite dangerous, due to the possibility of getting trampled or gored. Yet, people come from all over the world regardless of this fact. So, people from all over the world will be frightened tomorrow as they run with the bulls.

The argument says that running with the bulls is dangerous, and the conclusion is that many of the people who run with the bulls will be frightened. But those concepts are not the same. Perhaps everyone who runs with the bulls is a daredevil with an extremely high fear tolerance, so they wouldn't be frightened even though it's so dangerous. We can't logically connect *danger* to *fear* on the LSAT. Underlining the unlinked concepts to make the gap even more obvious, here is how you would mark that stimulus:

> Tomorrow is the running of the bulls in Pamplona and the runner turnout is expected to be large. Running with the bulls is quite <u>dangerous,</u> due to the possibility of getting trampled or gored. Yet, people come from all over the world regardless of this fact. So, people from all over the world will be <u>frightened</u> tomorrow as they run with the bulls.

Another way Justify problems become more difficult is when the concepts are abstract, when they are not clearly defined single-word concepts. This is evidenced in the example from earlier, which features a gap that's bookended by two rather lengthy clauses as unlinked concepts.

> University president: We will be forced to reduce spending next year if we do not increase our enrollment(So, if we are to maintain the quality of the education we provide, we must market our programs more aggressively) Without such marketing we will be unable to increase our enrollment.

Instead of the easily definable concepts in the previous examples, the gap here is between reducing spending and the quality of education. If you were to put pencil to paper and underline the unlinked concepts in this stimulus, you'd have to cover the clause "reduce spending next year" first and "maintain the quality of the education" on the other side of the gap. Taken together, these underlined phrases are somewhat unwieldy. For these more abstract or long-winded gaps, don't feel the pressure to underline them (it's an optional technique for every Justify, anyway). The important skill with all Justify problems is being able to spot the gap and being able to spot the concepts on either side of that gap. Do that and you're in the clear.

In summary, find the gap in the logic when reading a Justify stimulus. If you can (because the concepts are easily definable) and if you find it helpful, underline the two unlinked concepts that are on either side of the gap. Underlining can make it easier to work the choices because the concepts you need to link are marked on the paper in front of you. Whether you choose to underline or not, be as clear as possible on the two unlinked concepts.

Justify the Application Stimuli

Some Justify problems have a two-part stimulus that has a principle and its application. Here's an example:

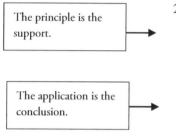

2. Principle: Employees of telemarketing agencies should never do anything that predisposes people to dislike the agencies' clients.

Application: (If an employee of a telemarketing agency has been told by a person the employee has called that he or she does not want to buy the product of a client of the agency, the employee should not try to talk that person into doing so)

Which one of the following, if true, justifies the given application of the principle above?

(A) Any employee of a telemarketing agency is likely to be able to determine whether trying to talk

When you face this type of Justify problem, understanding the stimulus is easy. The "principle" is the support, and the "application" is the conclusion. This should make sense because the principle is just a general rule while the application is the rule applied to a specific situation. The application draws a conclusion about a situation using the principle to support it.

Additional Thoughts on Justify Stimuli

Justify problems teach you to distill information as you identify the unlinked concepts because you must get at the core of each concept in order to spot the gap. This skill is extremely valuable because the whole Logical Reasoning section is about distilling information, mentally processing it, and reducing stimuli to their most important parts. As such, Justify problems are a solid foundation on which you will build your ability to critically process information.

Let's shift gears slightly for a note on what's yet to come. In the problem sets and drills at the end of this chapter, we use some conditional diagramming to make ideas from the stimulus as clear as possible. Conditional diagramming is generally not needed when *working* Justify problems because finding the gap is such a powerful focus for this type. However, diagramming conditional relationships can be rather helpful when reviewing Justify problems, and we recommend it as a way of furthering your understanding of conditionals and logic.

Choices

Justify problems have some challenging, dense stimuli, but working the choices is not difficult once you find the gap. As usual, it's a two-step process, beginning with elimination.

Step 1 – Eliminate

Assuming you found the right concepts when you worked the stimulus, eliminating three or all four incorrect choices doesn't take long. Just cross off each choice that fails to mention *both* concepts that are on either side of the gap. Don't worry about how the concepts are mentioned. For the eliminate step, all you care about is whether both concepts are present, not the way the choice relates them. If necessary, you'll analyze how the choice portrays the two concepts during the Confirm step.

For instance, consider the choices for the example about the running of the bulls, reprinted below. Eliminate choices without both of the unlinked concepts. The concepts are underlined to make the task simpler.

> Tomorrow is the running of the bulls in Pamplona and the runner turnout is expected to be large. Running with the bulls is quite <u>dangerous,</u> due to the possibility of getting trampled or gored. Yet, people come from all over the world regardless of this fact. So, people from all over the world will be <u>frightened</u> tomorrow as they run with the bulls.
>
> The conclusion of the argument follows logically if which one of the following is assumed?
>
> A)   Running with the bulls is the most risky tourist activity in Pamplona.
>
> B)   People who run with the bulls are frightened by dangerous activities.
>
> C)   People all over the world have a similar tolerance for fear.

Both (A) and (C) fail to mention "dangerous" as well as "frightened." (A) talks about risk, which could relate to the danger of running with the bulls, but it does not talk about fear. (C) talks about fear, but not about the *danger* of running with the bulls. (B) mentions both fear and danger, so keep it.

Step 2 - Confirm

On the majority of Justify problems, you can eliminate all four incorrect choices by checking each choice for the two unlinked concepts—those choices with only one of the concepts or with none get axed. When you're left with just one choice remaining, confirm that it links the two concepts and makes the argument valid. In the example about the running of the bulls, (B) says that dangerous activities frighten people who run with the bulls. This links the support that running with the bulls is dangerous to the conclusion that those who run with the bulls will be frightened. With the information in (B) added to the argument, the concepts connect, and the argument is valid logically.

The way (B) fits into the running with the bulls argument becomes especially clear when you look at how the argument and choice are represented in conditional diagrams.

running w/ bulls	→ dangerous activity	(support piece)
dangerous activity	→ frightened	(B)
running w/ bulls	→ frightened	(conclusion)

You will rarely have two choices remaining after the elimination step. When you do, examine each choice to see which correctly links the two concepts. The incorrect choice will be obvious; it will not properly link the concepts, and it will leave the argument invalid. For instance, take a look at the choice below from the example about the running of the bulls:

D)   Only dangerous sports can frighten people.

(D) has both unlinked concepts, so you would not eliminate it during step 1. However, (D) does not link them *in the way we need*. It says that nothing else besides a dangerous sport can frighten people ("*only* dangerous sports can frighten people"), which means that dangerous sports are *necessary* for people to be frightened. Here is what a conditional diagram looks like for (D):

frightened → dangerous activity

But to make the argument whole, we need to show that dangerous sports actually do frighten people; that they are *sufficient* for people being frightened. That is what (B) does. Again, here is the conditional diagram for (B):

dangerous activity → frightened

See how these choices differ? Your conditional skills can be super helpful to quickly spot the correct choices of two possible choices like (B) and (D), which discuss both unlinked concepts.

Envision Most of the Time

On a Justify problem, you can <u>envision</u> fairly precisely what the correct answer will look like if you find the two unlinked concepts in the argument. The answer must be a link between those unlinked concepts that connects them in the proper way. Very often, you can envision an answer on Justify problems this way.

Envisioning is empowering because you can predict the correct answer purely from analyzing the stimulus, and that makes it much easier to work the choices. You simply compare each choice to your envisioned answer. Whenever possible, you want to envision a good answer for a Justify problem after reading the stimulus. Here is a visual representation of the flow of information as you work the choices:

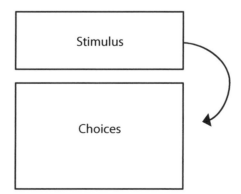

When you work the choices with an envisioned answer, you take your knowledge of the correct choice from the stimulus and apply it to the choices. You scrutinize each choice through the lens of your envisioned answer.

On the other hand, some Justify arguments have abstract gaps that are difficult to pinpoint. There will not be two clearly unlinked concepts. Instead, there will be a more general gap in the argument.

For these problems, focus less on identifying the two unlinked concepts because they are vague and hard to see on these problems. When you work the choices on one of these problems, <u>compare</u> each choice to the argument to see if the choice makes the conclusion valid. Ask yourself, "Does this choice connect part of the support to the conclusion, making the argument airtight?" This is how information flows as you compare the choices to the stimulus:

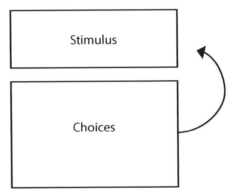

In a sense, you're trying out different links (choices) to see which one makes the stimulus "complete." This comparing method should look familiar because it is the approach on most Inference problems. When you spot an Obvious Inference, you can use the envision approach when working the choices.

Unlinked Concepts Drill

This drill will teach you to find the gap in a Justify stimulus and then use that gap to identify a choice that bridges it. These are the core Justify skills.

Directions

For each of the stimuli below, please do these steps:

- Bracket the conclusion.

- Locate the support. There is nothing to write for this step, but it will help you with step 3 because working through the support tends to uncover any Concept Jumps.

- Find the gap. Underline the two unlinked concepts.

- Determine which of the provided choices effectively plugs the gap.

Here is an example of a stimulus with the conclusion bracketed and the unlinked concepts underlined. The choice (C) fills the gap.

> When Teresa runs out of gas driving home, she is <u>late for dinner.</u>(So, because she ran out of gas driving home yesterday, she was <u>unhappy</u> yesterday)
>
> (C)   Being late for dinner makes Teresa unhappy.

1. Whoever is kind is loved by somebody or other, and whoever loves anyone is happy. It follows that whoever is kind is happy.

    The **conclusion follows logically** if which one of the following is assumed?

    (C)   Whoever is happy loves everyone.

    (D)   Whoever loves no one is loved by no one.

2. The solution to any environmental problem that is not the result of government mismanagement can only lie in major changes in consumer habits. But major changes in consumer habits will occur only if such changes are economically enticing. As a result, few serious ecological problems will be solved unless the solutions are made economically enticing.

    The **conclusion** drawn in the argument above **follows logically** if which one of the following is assumed?

    (A)   Few serious ecological problems are the result of government mismanagement.

    (B)   No environmental problems that stem from government mismanagement have solutions that are economically feasible.

3. Editorialist: Despite the importance it seems to have in our lives, money does not really exist. This is evident from the fact that all that would be needed to make money disappear would be a universal loss of belief in it. We witness this phenomenon on a small scale daily in the rises and falls of financial markets, whose fluctuations are often entirely independent of concrete causes and are the results of mere beliefs of investors.

    The **conclusion** of the editorialist's argument can be **properly drawn** if which one of the following is assumed?

    (A)   Anything that exists would continue to exist even if everyone were to stop believing in it.

    (B)   Only if one can have mistaken beliefs about a thing does that thing exist, strictly speaking.

    END OF SET

Drill Explanations

1. Whoever is kind is <u>loved by somebody or other</u>, and whoever <u>loves anyone</u> is happy (It follows that whoever is kind is <u>happy</u>.)

    (C)   Whoever is happy loves everyone.

    (D)   Whoever loves no one is loved by no one.

1) Conclusion. "It follows" is nice conclusion indicator. The conclusion says, "Whoever is kind is happy."

2) Support. We can sum up the first support piece as "kind people are loved by somebody." The next support piece is "people who love anyone are happy." Hmm… those two pieces don't connect. They sound like they do connect, but being *loved by* somebody and *loving* somebody are two different concepts.

3) Underline the unlinked concepts. During step two, we saw the subtle Concept Jump in one piece of support to the next. Note that the unlinked concepts here are between the support pieces, which is unusual. Almost always the unlinked concepts are between a support piece and *the conclusion*. Oh how those LSAT writers keep us on our toes!

4) Plug the gap. The argument proceeds thusly: If you're kind, then you're loved, and those who love are happy. Then, it connects the two ends of that chain to conclude that kind people are happy. Mind the gap: The argument jumps from "loved by" to "loves," so the correct choices will link these two concepts. It should state something to the effect of "if you are loved by somebody, then you love someone."

    (C)   Whoever is happy loves everyone.

This choice doesn't connect "loved by"—it's missing one of the two unlinked concepts, so you can eliminate it.

    (D)   Whoever loves no one is loved by no one.

This is a tricky choice because of its pervasive negativity, but it has both "loves" and "loved by." Let's analyze exactly what it's saying.

"If you love no one then you are loved by no one." Take the contrapositive of this statement and you get, "If you're loved by someone, then you love someone," which is exactly what you need. Sometimes you have to "translate" a choice to see that it is a match.

2. The solution to any environmental problem that is not the result of government mismanagement can only lie in major changes in consumer habits. But major changes in consumer habits will occur only if such changes are economically enticing. (As a result, few serious ecological problems will be solved unless the solutions are made economically enticing.)

   (A)   Few serious ecological problems are the result of government mismanagement.

   (B)   No environmental problems that stem from government mismanagement have solutions that are economically feasible.

1) Conclusion. "As a result" helps point us to the conclusion because it tells us that what follows is a summary of what came before. *If solutions are not made economically enticing, then few serious ecological problems will be solved.*

2) Support. Any environmental problem that is not the result of govt. mismanagement can only be solved by major changes in consumer habits, but those changes in consumer habits will only occur if the changes are economically enticing. If the government isn't responsible, then the only way to make a difference is consumers making a change, but they'll only do that if the change looks good economically.

3) Underline the unlinked concepts. This is one of those problems where you probably wouldn't be able to underline two simple unlinked concepts. Instead, you would need to contain the gap mentally or check the choices against the stimulus. The gap here is between concluding that "few serious ecological problems will be solved if the changes aren't economically enticing" and the support that "if an environmental problem isn't the result of governmental mismanagement, then the only way to solve it is through economically enticing consumers to change their habits." The conclusion contains the idea that a lot of the environmental problems aren't the result of governmental mismanagement, which you know because it says that "few serious ecological" issues will be solved without appealing to the consumers. But, the stimulus never states that the government is rarely responsible; it leaves that linking statement out, so the correct choice should state this link.

4) Plug the gap. You need a choice that states that few environmental problems are caused by governmental mismanagement. If you didn't spot this gap explicitly, then testing each of the choices against the info in the stimulus should still allow you to plug the gap effectively. Let's look at each of the choices.

   (A)   Few serious ecological problems are the result of government mismanagement.

This choice looks good; keep it.

   (B)   No environmental problems that stem from government mismanagement have solutions that are economically feasible.

This choice links environmental problems that are caused by governmental mismanagement to the solutions for those problems, but you need something that states how few of the problems are caused by governmental mismanagement, not something about the solutions for problems caused by government.

Let's come back to (A). With this choice in place, the conclusion is supported, and the gap is plugged. Solutions must be made economically enticing because that is the only way to fix environmental problems that need changes in consumer behavior. As (A) makes clear, most of the environmental problems are not caused by governmental mismanagement, so consumer changes are the only way to solve the issues (as the argument assumes).

Note that this problem doesn't have super-definable unlinked concepts. Instead, it has a more abstract gap that you must plug with a link that's not included in the stimulus.

3. Editorialist: Despite the importance it seems to have in our lives, (money does not really exist.) This is evident from the fact that all that would be needed to make money disappear would be a universal loss of belief in it. We witness this phenomenon on a small scale daily in the rises and falls of financial markets, whose fluctuations are often entirely independent of concrete causes and are the results of mere beliefs of investors.

   (A)   Anything that exists would continue to exist even if everyone were to stop believing in it.

   (B)   Only if one can have mistaken beliefs about a thing does that thing exist, strictly speaking.

1) Conclusion. We find the conclusion early in this stimulus. The whole stimulus supports the idea that money doesn't exist.

2) Find the support. The support—signaled by "this is evident from"—is that money would disappear if there were a universal loss of belief in it. The rest of the stimulus gives support for the idea that there could be a universal loss of belief in money.

3) Find the gap. In this case, the support doesn't connect to the conclusion. Just because money would disappear if there were a universal loss of belief in it doesn't logically mean it doesn't exist. The unlinked concepts are *belief* in something and that thing's *existence*.

4) Plug the gap. We just need to show that anything that can disappear from a universal loss of belief in it does not really exist.

Let's look at the choices.

   (A)   Anything that exists would continue to exist even if everyone were to stop believing in it.

This choice requires some translation in order to see what it actually means. It is not immediately attractive, but let's break down what it's saying. Something is thought to exist if everyone stops believing in that thing, and yet it continues to exist. If people stop believing in something and that thing disappeared (as the argument claims is the case with money), then you know that that thing doesn't truly exist because it would need to continue to exist, and not disappear, in order to truly exist. This is sort of a shitty LSAT problem, but it's a real one. It's important that you see both the straightforward problems and the backwards ones, so this exercise is at least helpful in that regard... (A) looks good once analyzed, keep it.

   (B)   Only if one can have mistaken beliefs about a thing does that thing exist, strictly speaking.

(B) talks about "mistaken beliefs," but the argument does not, so you can eliminate it right away.

(A) effectively plugs the gap. It's worded very poorly, and you have to remember that the stimulus says that "all that would make money disappear would be a universal loss of belief in it" in order to understand that that means it does not really exist. (A) states that, if money were real, it would not disappear just because people stopped believing in it. But according to the stimulus, money can disappear, so that means it doesn't exist. With (A), the conclusion is nicely supported. (A) is correct.

Justify Review

Introduction

- Make an argument valid by finding the choice that links a gap in the stimulus.
- Difficulty arises in identifying which concepts are unlinked.

Stem

- The stem will talk about the conclusion being properly inferred or use a variation on the word "justify" and have you fill the gap using a principle.
- Stem stamp: "J"

Stimulus

- The stimuli for Justify problems all have a Missing Link Flaw in the argument. This gap comes between two Unlinked Concepts.
- Justify the Application Stimuli have a principle (which is the support) and an application (which is the conclusion).
- Step 1 – Find the conclusion and bracket it. Look for helpful indicators.
- Step 2 – Find the support.
  - With a Logic Chain, where many pieces of support link up, find the key supporting link.
- Step 3 – Find the gap.
  - This often requires you to see the Unlinked Concepts on either side of the gap, which you can underline if that helps keep them clear.
  - Unlinked Concepts are almost always between the conclusion and the primary support.
  - During steps 1 and 2, a Concept Jump (when the argument jumps from one concept to another) can show you the gap.
  - On most Justify problems, you can envision a good answer by finding the unlinked concepts in the stimulus. That makes working the choices much easier.

Choices

- Step 1 – Eliminate choices that don't fill the gap.
- Step 2 – Confirm the only remaining choice or work the final two choices by analyzing whether each choice makes the conclusion properly inferred.
- On more difficult Justify problems, the gap will be abstract. When you work the choices, focus on finding the choice that makes the conclusion valid by comparing each choice to the argument.

Techniques Summary

- Core focus: Find Gap.
- Stimulus:
  - Bracket the conclusion and find the support.
  - Then, find the two unlinked concepts.
- Choices: Eliminate choices that do not fill the gap.

Justify Technique Set

Directions

- Technique Summary: For each problem, pause working the problem and read the Technique Summary after you read the stem and stamp it. As you complete the rest of the problem, actively apply the techniques.

- Time Limit: There is no time limit for completing the problems, so do your best to answer each correctly.

- Review: For each problem, read the explanation intently to check that you used the techniques properly. Also, use the explanation to improve your understanding of how the problem works.

- Milk every drop of learning out of a problem and its explanation before moving on so that your skills build steadily during this set.

1. The proposed change to the patent system is bound to have a chilling effect on scientific research. Under current rules, researchers have one full year after the initial publication of a new discovery to patent the discovery. This allows research results to be shared widely prior to the patent application. The proposed change would have the application precede initial publication, which would delay the communication of discoveries.

   The conclusion drawn above follows logically if which one of the following is assumed?

   (A) The proposed change will encourage more patent applications to be filed.

   (B) Dramatic advances in scientific research have occurred while the current patent system has been in place.

   (C) Delays in the communication of discoveries will have a chilling effect on scientific research.

   (D) Most researchers oppose the proposed change to the patent system.

   (E) The current rules for patent applications facilitate progress in scientific research by rewarding the communication of discoveries.

Techniques Summary

- Core focus: Find Gap.

- Stimulus:
  - Bracket the conclusion and find the support.
  - Then, find the two unlinked concepts.

- Choices: Eliminate choices that do not fill the gap.

1. (The proposed change to the patent system is bound to have a <u>chilling effect</u> on scientific research.)Under current rules, researchers have one full year after the initial publication of a new discovery to patent the discovery. This allows research results to be shared widely prior to the patent application. The proposed change would have the application precede initial publication, which would delay <u>the communication of discoveries.</u>

The **conclusion** drawn above **follows logically** if which one of the following is assumed?

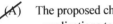 (A) The proposed change will encourage more patent applications to be filed.

(B) Dramatic advances in scientific research have occurred while the current patent system has been in place.

((C)) Delays in the communication of discoveries will have a chilling effect on scientific research.

(D) Most researchers oppose the proposed change to the patent system.

(E) The current rules for patent applications facilitate progress in scientific research by rewarding the communication of discoveries.

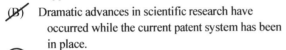

Type: Justify

<u>Stem</u> – You're asked which choice allows the conclusion to follow logically if it is assumed to be true. That's a Justify problem stem.

<u>Stimulus</u> – 1) Find the Conclusion. The stimulus has a lot of information, so remember to hold onto the conclusion as you go through the support and background info when looking for an assumption. The conclusion comes in the first sentence. The change to the patent system will have a chilling effect on scientific research.

2) Support. The next two sentences provide background information. The final sentence provides the main support that, should the application precede initial publication, it would cause a delay in the communication of discoveries.

3) Find the Gap. Connecting the conclusion and support, you've boiled down the argument to its essential parts. The chilling effect on research (from the conclusion) is supported by the delay in the communication of discoveries. Would a delay actually have a chilling effect, though? It seems that the argument has linked a "delay in communication" with a "chilling effect" on scientific research without justification. It's hard to say one way or the other if that would actually be the case, and the argument certainly doesn't make that connection explicit. These are the two unlinked concepts, and there lies the gap in the argument.

<u>Choices</u> – The correct choice will describe a link between delayed communication and a chilling effect on scientific research.

1) Eliminate. (A) doesn't talk about the "delay" nor about the "chilling effect," so it doesn't even touch the gap you're trying to fill. (B) does not treat the gap either, instead talking about the scientific advances that have taken place under the current patent system. (C) makes a direct link between a delay in communication of discoveries and a chilling effect on research, which is spot-on. Let's hold on to (C). (D) provides information about how researchers feel about the change, which is irrelevant to the immediate information in the stimulus. (E) deals with scientific research and communication of discoveries, but it provides information about the current rules as opposed to the proposed change. Because the proposed change is the subject of the argument, (E) is out.

2) Confirm. Winner, winner, (C)hicken dinner—(C) is confirmed because it links delays in the communication of discoveries to the chilling effect on scientific research.

2. Business ethicist: Managers of corporations have an obligation to serve shareholders as the shareholders would want to be served. Therefore, corporate managers have an obligation to act in the shareholders' best interest.

   The business ethicist's conclusion follows logically if which one of the following is assumed?

   (A) Corporate managers are always able to discern what is in the best interest of shareholders.

   (B) Shareholders would want to be served only in ways that are in their own best interest.

   (C) A corporate manager's obligations to shareholders take precedence over any other obligations the manager may have.

   (D) The shareholders have interests that can best be served by corporate managers.

   (E) All shareholders want to be served in identical ways.

Techniques Summary

- Core focus: Find Gap.
- Stimulus:
  - Bracket the conclusion and find the support.
  - Then, find the two unlinked concepts.
- Choices: Eliminate choices that do not fill the gap.

2. Business ethicist: Managers of corporations have an obligation to serve shareholders as the shareholders would <u>want to be served</u>. **Therefore,** (corporate managers have an obligation to act in the shareholders' <u>best interest.</u>)

J   The business ethicist's **conclusion follows logically** if which one of the following is assumed?

(A) Corporate managers are always able to discern what is in the best interest of shareholders.

(B) Shareholders would want to be served only in ways that are in their own best interest.

(C) A corporate manager's obligations to shareholders take precedence over any other obligations the manager may have.

(D) The shareholders have interests that can best be served by corporate managers.

(E) All shareholders want to be served in identical ways.

Type: Justify

<u>Stem</u> – The stem asks you what will make the conclusion follow logically, which is the mark of a Justify problem.

<u>Stimulus</u> – 1) Find the Conclusion. Your job is made easy by the conclusion indicator "therefore," which tells you that the second sentence is the conclusion. Put it in parentheses.

2) Find the Support. The first sentence is the only other idea provided in the stimulus, so it must be the support. Managers should serve shareholders as they would want to be served.

3) Find the Gap. We know the flaw is a Missing Link so we don't need to identify that. Instead, find the two concepts that do not link up. The conclusion talks about managers serving the shareholder's "best interest," but the support talks about a different concept: the shareholders being served as they would "want to be served." Underline those two concepts to make them stand out.

<u>Choices</u> – 1) Eliminate all choices that do not feature both concepts. Justify problems are ripe for quick elimination. (A) touches on "best interest" but not "serve want to be served," so we can eliminate it. (B) is a great match because it has both concepts and in the right relationship. Definitely hang onto this one as a possibility. (C) touches on neither concept, so cross it off! (D) sounds like it matches the "best interest" concept, but it is actually a little different. (D) talks about whether the shareholders have interests that can be served optimally by the managers. The concept in the stimulus is that the managers must act in the best interest of the shareholders, i.e. managers make the best decisions for them. Little distinctions like this are a big deal on the LSAT. (E) mentions neither of the concepts and talks about something that doesn't affect the conclusion at all. In finding the missing link, we are trying to make the argument airtight.

2) Confirm the remaining choice. Your overall goal in a Justify problem is to make the conclusion 100% valid, so make sure that (B) does that before you select it. The passage tells you that managers are obligated to serve shareholders in ways that the shareholders want to be served; this is the support. Here is a conditional diagram for (B):

Want Served $\rightarrow$ Best Interest

If you add in (B) (that shareholders only want to be served in ways that serve their own best interest), then the conclusion about acting in the shareholders' best interest is proven.

3. Social scientist: Since the body of thought known as Marxism claims to describe rigorously an inexorable historical movement toward the socialization of the means of production, it should be regarded as a scientific theory. Thus, certain interpreters, in taking Marxism as a political program aimed at radically transforming society, have misconstrued it.

The social scientist's conclusion follows logically if which one of the following is assumed?

(A) The description that Marxism gives of certain historical phenomena in the economic sphere is as rigorous as it is claimed to be.

(B) The aims of science are incompatible with the aims of those who would seek to transform society by political means.

(C) Only bodies of thought consisting purely of rigorous description are scientific theories.

(D) Scientific theories cannot be correctly interpreted to be, or to imply, political programs.

(E) The means of production will inevitably become socialized regardless of any political programs designed to make that occur.

Techniques Summary

- Core focus: Find Gap.
- Stimulus:
  - Bracket the conclusion and find the support.
  - Then, find the two unlinked concepts.
- Choices: Eliminate choices that do not fill the gap.

3. Social scientist: Since the body of thought known as Marxism claims to describe rigorously an inexorable historical movement toward the socialization of the means of production, it should be regarded as a <u>scientific theory</u>. (Thus, certain interpreters, in taking Marxism as a <u>political program aimed at radically transforming society</u>, have misconstrued it.)

J   The social scientist's conclusion follows logically if which one of the following is assumed?

   (A) The description that Marxism gives of certain historical phenomena in the economic sphere is as rigorous as it is claimed to be.

   (B) The aims of science are incompatible with the aims of those who would seek to transform society by political means.

   (C) Only bodies of thought consisting purely of rigorous description are scientific theories.

   (D) Scientific theories cannot be correctly interpreted to be, or to imply, political programs.

   (E) The means of production will inevitably become socialized regardless of any political programs designed to make that occur.

Type: Justify

Stem – The stem asks you what will make the conclusion follow logically, indicating that this is a Justify problem. Be sure to write a "J" next to the stem. Move to the stimulus. Be ready to identify the parts of an argument and find the unconnected concepts.

Stimulus – 1) Find the Conclusion. Sweet, "thus" is an obvious conclusion indicator, so bracket the second sentence. The conclusion is thickly phrased, so translate it. "Marxism is not a political program aimed at radically transforming society."

2) Find the Support. The first sentence is the only other one in the stimulus, so it must be the support. The support is that Marxism is a scientific theory and reasons are given for that.

3) Find the Gap. The conclusion says that Marxism is not a political program aimed at transforming society and the support says that Marxism is a scientific theory. Underline those concepts. The jump is between something being a scientific theory and it not being a political program.

Choices – 1) Eliminate choices that do not feature both concepts. (A) only reiterates the support without discussing the "political program" concept. (B) looks good at first because it seems to touch on both concepts, but under further analysis we see that it talks about the *aims* of science and the *aims* of those transforming society. Those are different concepts than scientific theories and political programs. (C) makes a distinction about what constitutes a scientific theory, and it doesn't mention how that disqualifies ideas from being political programs. (D) has both concepts and looks good; hold onto that puppy. (E) talks about political programs but not scientific theories.

2) Confirm the remaining choice. (D) says that scientific theories can never be political programs, and that is just what we envisioned for the link. Here's a conditional diagram:

scientific theory → ~political program

With that assumption in place, the support that Marxism is a scientific theory directly connects to the conclusion that Marxism is not a political program. (D) is correct.

4. Anyone who knows Ellsworth knows that he is bursting with self-righteousness, touting the idealism of his generation over the greed of the previous generation. So no one who knows him will be surprised that Ellsworth is offended by the suggestions in the media that he has engaged in unethical business practices.

The conclusion drawn above follows logically if which one of the following is assumed?

(A)   Everyone suspects self-righteous people of being, in actuality, unethical.

(B)   Ellsworth has been accused of unethical business practices before.

(C)   Hypocrites often hide behind righteous indignation.

(D)   Ellsworth is in fact innocent of all wrongdoing.

(E)   Everyone expects self-righteous people to be easily offended.

Techniques Summary

- <u>Core focus</u>: Find Gap.
- Stimulus:
  - Bracket the conclusion and find the support.
  - Then, find the two unlinked concepts.
- Choices: Eliminate choices that do not fill the gap.

4. Anyone who knows Ellsworth knows that he is bursting with <u>self-righteousness</u>, touting the idealism of his generation over the greed of the previous generation(So no one who knows him will be surprised that Ellsworth is <u>offended by the suggestions in the media</u> that he has engaged in unethical business practices.)

J   The conclusion drawn above follows logically if which one of the following is assumed?

   (A) Everyone suspects self-righteous people of being, in actuality, unethical.
   (B) Ellsworth has been accused of unethical business practices before.
   (C) Hypocrites often hide behind righteous indignation.
   (D) Ellsworth is in fact innocent of all wrongdoing.
   (E) Everyone expects self-righteous people to be easily offended.

Type: Justify

<u>Stem</u> – "Follows logically" is a Justify stem, so get ready to identify the parts of the argument.

<u>Stimulus</u> – 1) Find the Conclusion. "So" is a great indicator here. The conclusion is that people who know Ellsworth would find it normal that he is offended by the suggestion in the media.

2) Find the Support. We only have the one other idea besides the conclusion, so the support is that Ellsworth is very self-righteous.

3) Find the Gap. Being self-righteous does not connect with taking offense to the suggestions in the media (the conclusion). Underline those two concepts.

<u>Choices</u> – 1) Eliminate choices without both concepts. (A) connects being self-righteous to being unethical, but we need to connect that to being offended. (B) contains neither concept. Righteous indignation in (C) is similar to being offended, but being a hypocrite is not the same as being self-righteous. The concepts are warped in that choice. (D) contains neither concept. (E) is the last man standing, and fortunately it contains both concepts.

2) Confirm. If everyone expects self-righteous people to be easily offended and everyone who knows Ellsworth knows he is self-righteous, then it makes sense that no one would be surprised that he was offended by the media suggestions. We have a winner.

5. Censor: All anarchist novels have two objectionable characteristics: a subversive outlook and the depiction of wholesale violence. Therefore, it is permissible to ban any anarchist novel that would do more harm than good to society.

Which one of the following principles, if valid, most helps to justify the censor's reasoning?

(A) If a novel has a subversive outlook but does not depict wholesale violence, it is impermissible to ban it.

(B) If a novel depicts wholesale violence, then it is permissible to ban it if doing so would do more good than harm to society.

(C) It is permissible to ban a novel only if the novel has a subversive outlook and would do more harm than good to society.

(D) It is permissible to ban a novel that would cause society more harm than good if the novel has two or more objectionable characteristics.

(E) It is permissible to ban a novel that depicts wholesale violence only if that novel has at least one other objectionable characteristic.

Techniques Summary

- Core focus: Find Gap.
- Stimulus:
  - Bracket the conclusion and find the support.
  - Then, find the two unlinked concepts.
- Choices: Eliminate choices that do not fill the gap.

5. Censor: All anarchist novels have <u>two objectionable</u> <u>characteristics</u>: a subversive outlook and the depiction of wholesale violence.(Therefore, it is <u>permissible to ban any</u> <u>anarchist novel that would do more harm than good</u> to society.)

J Which one of the following principles, if valid, most helps to justify the censor's reasoning?

(A) If a novel has a subversive outlook but does not depict wholesale violence, it is impermissible to ban it.

(B) If a novel depicts wholesale violence, then it is permissible to ban it if doing so would do more good than harm to society.

(C) It is permissible to ban a novel only if the novel has a subversive outlook and would do more harm than good to society.

(D) It is permissible to ban a novel that would cause society more harm than good if the novel has two or more objectionable characteristics.

(E) It is permissible to ban a novel that depicts wholesale violence only if that novel has at least one other objectionable characteristic.

Type: Justify

Stem – "Justify" tells us that this is a Justify problem, so get ready to identify the parts of the argument.

Stimulus – 1) Find the Conclusion. "Therefore" indicates that the final sentence is the conclusion. It's okay to ban any anarchist novel that does more harm than good.

2) Find the Support. Why is it OK to ban any anarchist novel? Because they all have two objectionable characteristics. The characteristics themselves are support expansion, so it is not necessary to analyze those in depth.

3) Find the Gap. The argument does not have a link between the objectionable characteristics and banning a novel that does more harm than good.

Choices – 1) Eliminate choices without both concepts. The choices are principles, so they may be a little more general than other Justify choices. Yet, this doesn't affect how you work them. (A) talks about what makes a book impermissible to ban, and we need to hear about what makes a book permissible to ban. (B) and (C) only mention one of the objectionable characteristics, so eliminate them. (D) mentions two objectionable characteristics and banning a novel that would do more harm than good; keep it. (E) mentions two objectionable characteristics, but it doesn't touch on the more harm than good concept from the conclusion. You can eliminate this choice.

2) Confirm. (D) provides the link we need. If a novel has two (or more) objectionable characteristics and would do more harm than good, it can be banned. That is a direct link between the concepts in the support and in the conclusion.

6. Literary critic: A folktale is a traditional story told in an entertaining way, which may lead some to think that folktales lack deeper meaning. But this is not the case. A folktale is passed along by a culture for generations, and each storyteller adds something of his or her own to the story, and in this way folktales provide great insight into the wisdom of the culture.

The main conclusion of the literary critic's argument can be properly inferred if which one of the following is assumed?

(A) Any tale that is passed along by a culture for generations can provide great insight into the wisdom of that culture.

(B) Any tale that provides insight into the wisdom of a culture is deeply meaningful in some respect.

(C) Not every tale that lacks deep meaning or beauty is told solely for entertainment.

(D) Any tale with deep meaning provides great insight into the wisdom of the culture by which it has been passed on.

(E) A story that is told primarily for entertainment does not necessarily lack deeper meaning.

Techniques Summary

- Core focus: Find Gap.
- Stimulus:
  - Bracket the conclusion and find the support.
  - Then, find the two unlinked concepts.
- Choices: Eliminate choices that do not fill the gap.

6. Literary critic: A folktale is a traditional story told in an entertaining way, which may lead some to think that (folktales <u>lack deeper meaning</u>. But this is not the case.) A folktale is passed along by a culture for generations, and each storyteller adds something of his or her own to the story, and in this way folktales provide <u>great insight into the wisdom of the culture.</u>

The main conclusion of the literary critic's argument can be properly inferred if which one of the following is assumed?

J

 (A) Any tale that is passed along by a culture for generations can provide great insight into the wisdom of that culture.

(B) Any tale that provides insight into the wisdom of a culture is deeply meaningful in some respect.

 (C) Not every tale that lacks deep meaning or beauty is told solely for entertainment.

(D) Any tale with deep meaning provides great insight into the wisdom of the culture by which it has been passed on.

 (E) A story that is told primarily for entertainment does not necessarily lack deeper meaning.

Type: Justify

Stem – "Properly inferred" is the same as follows logically. This is a Justify problem, so mentally prepare to identify the parts of an argument and then find the unlinked concepts.

Stimulus – 1) Find the Conclusion. The conclusion is spread across two sentences here. It is that folktales do have deeper meaning.

2) Find the Support. The support is that folktales provide great insight into the wisdom of a culture.

3) Find the Gap. The unlinked concepts are pretty easy to see. The conclusion says that folktales have deep meaning, but the support only talks about providing great insight into the wisdom of the culture. Underline those two concepts in their respective parts of the argument.

Choices – 1) Eliminate choices without both concepts. (A) bolsters a part of the support and doesn't mention deeper meaning. (B) talks about both concepts, so keep it. (C) mentions something more than entertainment, but that is not great insight. (D) mentions both concepts so keep it. (E) doesn't mention great insight.

2) Confirm. You need to analyze (B) and (D) carefully. (B) connects the two concepts in the right direction, from the support to the conclusion. Here's a conditional diagram:

insight → deep meaning

(D) has the direction between the concepts backwards, so it doesn't make the argument valid. (D) tells us that tales with deep meaning have insight, but that does not indicate that tales with insight have deep meaning, which is what we need to connect the support to the conclusion. By contrast, (B) gives us what we need, and it is correct.

7.   Although Pluto has an atmosphere and is much larger than any asteroid, Pluto is not a true planet. Pluto formed in orbit around the planet Neptune and was then ejected from orbit around Neptune when Triton, Neptune's largest moon, was captured by Neptune's gravity.

The conclusion of the argument follows logically if which one of the following is assumed?

(A)   No celestial body can simultaneously be a moon and a planet.

(B)   Not all celestial bodies that have an atmosphere and orbit the sun are true planets.

(C)   If Pluto had not been ejected from its orbit around Neptune, Pluto would not have its current orbit around the sun and would still be a moon.

(D)   The size of a celestial body in orbit around the sun is not relevant to determining whether or not it is a true planet.

(E)   For a celestial body to be a true planet it must have formed in orbit around the sun exclusively.

Techniques Summary

- Core focus: Find Gap.

- Stimulus:

  o   Bracket the conclusion and find the support.

  o   Then, find the two unlinked concepts.

- Choices: Eliminate choices that do not fill the gap.

7. Although Pluto has an atmosphere and is much larger than any asteroid, (Pluto is <u>not a true planet.</u>) Pluto <u>formed in orbit around the planet Neptune and was then ejected from orbit around Neptune</u> when Triton, Neptune's largest <u>moon,</u> was captured by Neptune's gravity.

J   The conclusion of the argument follows logically if which one of the following is assumed?

(A) No celestial body can simultaneously be a moon and a planet.

(B) Not all celestial bodies that have an atmosphere and orbit the sun are true planets.

(C) If Pluto had not been ejected from its orbit around Neptune, Pluto would not have its current orbit around the sun and would still be a moon.

(D) The size of a celestial body in orbit around the sun is not relevant to determining whether or not it is a true planet.

(E) For a celestial body to be a true planet it must have formed in orbit around the sun exclusively.

Type: Justify
Tag: Contrapositive Choice

Stem – This is a classic Justify stem, so get ready to identify the parts of an argument and find the unlinked concepts.

Stimulus – 1) Find the Conclusion. The conclusion comes before the support. Pluto is not a true planet. Ouch, sorry Pluto, this argument is calling you out.

2) Find the Support. The support for this hurtful conclusion is that Pluto formed in orbit around Neptune and then was shot off. We don't need to go into the sub details about when Pluto was shot off.

3) Find the Gap. Why is Pluto not a true planet? Because it formed around Neptune. But, there's no connection between a true planet and how it was formed (specifically, that it wasn't formed around another planet). Those are our unlinked concepts.

Choices – 1) Eliminate. (A) doesn't mention Pluto's forming and ejection. A moon is mentioned in the expansion of the support, but that concept is irrelevant here. (B) talks about some opposing points that the argument brought up right away, which are neither here nor there. It doesn't mention Pluto's forming. (C) brings up a hypothetical situation, which is not relevant. (D) doesn't mention Pluto's forming. (E) is all that is left, so let's confirm it.

2) Confirm. (E) connects a celestial body's formation to what makes it a true planet. Pluto does not meet the requirement of forming around the sun, so it is not a true planet. Here is a diagram of this choice:

true planet $\rightarrow$ formed around the sun

(E) is correct.

8. University president: We will be forced to reduce spending next year if we do not increase our enrollment. So, if we are to maintain the quality of the education we provide, we must market our programs more aggressively. Without such marketing we will be unable to increase our enrollment.

The conclusion of the university president's argument can be properly drawn if which one of the following is assumed?

(A) The university will not maintain the quality of the education it provides if it increases its enrollment.

(B) The university will not need to reduce spending next year if it increases its enrollment.

(C) The university will increase its enrollment if it markets its programs more aggressively.

(D) The university will not maintain the quality of the education it provides if it reduces spending next year.

(E) The university will not need to reduce spending next year if it markets its programs more aggressively.

Techniques Summary

- <u>Core focus</u>: Find Gap.
- Stimulus:
  o Bracket the conclusion and find the support.
  o Then, find the two unlinked concepts.
- Choices: Eliminate choices that do not fill the gap.

8. University president: We will be forced to <u>reduce spending</u> next year if we do not increase our enrollment. (So, if we are to <u>maintain the quality</u> of the education we provide, we must market our programs more aggressively.) Without such marketing we will be unable to increase our enrollment.

    The conclusion of the university president's argument can be properly drawn if which one of the following is assumed?

    (A) The university will not maintain the quality of the education it provides if it increases its enrollment.

    (B) The university will not need to reduce spending next year if it increases its enrollment.

    (C) The university will increase its enrollment if it markets its programs more aggressively.

    (D) The university will not maintain the quality of the education it provides if it reduces spending next year.

    (E) The university will not need to reduce spending next year if it markets its programs more aggressively.

Type: Justify
Tags: Soft Conclusion

Stem – "Conclusion… properly drawn" tells us that this is a Justify problem. Move to the stimulus to identify the argument's parts and find the unlinked concepts.

Stimulus – This is the longest stimulus that you have faced in this type so far, and it is more complex.

1) Find the Conclusion. "So" is a conclusion indicator. The conclusion is that they need to market their programs more aggressively if they wish to maintain the quality of the education they provide.

2) Find the Support. There are two pieces of support on each side of the conclusion. One piece is that the school will be unable to increase enrollment without aggressive marketing. The other piece is that the school will be forced to reduce spending if enrollment doesn't pick up. We can link these and see that the school will reduce spending without aggressive marketing. That link makes the support easier to understand.

3) Find the Gap. The conclusion talks about maintaining the quality of education, but the support "ends" with reducing spending. Those concepts sound similar, but they are unlinked. Even if the school did have to reduce spending, they could be more efficient with what they do spend and still provide the same level of education.

Choices – 1) Eliminate. (A) doesn't mention reducing spending; further, it confuses parts of the argument. (B) doesn't mention any part of the conclusion. It also takes the conditional in the first sentence and negates both terms without swapping them. Here are the correct diagrams:

> no increase $\rightarrow$ reduce spending
>
> increase $\rightarrow$ ~ reduce spending

(C) does not mention reducing spending. (D) has both concepts, so hang onto this one. (E) does not mention quality of education.

2) Confirm. With (D) in place, the support piece about spending links directly to the conclusion, and the argument is justified. (D) is correct.

END OF SET

Justify Challenge Sets

Directions

- Technique Summary: Before you attempt a Set, read the Technique Summary to further engrain the techniques.

- Time Limit: There is no time limit for each Set, so work every problem carefully. Aim for 100% accuracy on each Set even on the most difficult problems.

- Mark problems that you are unsure on, so that you can review them even if you answer them correctly.

- Review: Attempt each Set and then review your work for those problems before moving on to the next Set. Review only the problems you missed and those you *marked for review.*

- First *self-review* each problem: analyze the correct choice and why it's correct. Refer to the stimulus to help with that. Next, analyze any incorrect choices that were tempting. Figure out why they are incorrect, again using the stimulus. After you self-review the problem, carefully read the problem explanation. As you read the explanation, analyze how well you used the techniques and look for aspects of the problem you overlooked during your self-review.

Challenge Set 1

Techniques Summary

- Core focus: Find Gap.

- Stimulus:
  - Bracket the conclusion and find the support.
  - Then, find the two unlinked concepts.

- Choices: Eliminate choices that do not fill the gap.

1. Mike: Tom did not tell me that I could use his computer, but it would not be wrong for me to use it anyway. Last week Tom used Mary's bicycle even though she had not told him he could use it.

   Which one of the following principles, if valid, would most help to justify Mike's reasoning?

   (A) Using the possessions of others without their permission is not always theft.

   (B) Generally one should tell the truth, but there are cases in which it is permissible not to.

   (C) If people have used your property without your permission, it is not wrong for you to use their property without their permission.

   (D) It is permissible to treat people in a way that is similar to the way in which they have treated others.

   (E) Using another person's property is wrong if the person is harmed by that use.

2. Editorial: It is usually desirable for people to have access to unregulated information, such as is found on the Internet. But a vast array of misinformation will always show up on the Internet, and it is difficult to determine which information is accurate. Accurate information is useless unless it can easily be distinguished from misinformation; thus, the information on the Internet should somehow be regulated.

   Which one of the following principles, if valid, most helps to justify the editorial's argument?

   (A) It is never possible to regulate misinformation without restricting people's access to accurate information.

   (B) Even if information is regulated, accurate information is often indistinguishable from misinformation.

   (C) Regulation of information makes it easy for people to distinguish between accurate information and misinformation.

   (D) It is acceptable for people to have access to a vast array of misinformation only if accurate information is never overlooked as a result.

   (E) It is usually more desirable for people to have access to useless, unregulated misinformation than it is for them to have access only to accurate but regulated information.

3. Principle: A law whose purpose is to protect wild animal populations should not be enforced against those whose actions do not threaten wild animal populations.

   Application: Even though there is a law against capturing wild snakes, which was enacted to protect wild snake populations, snake charmers who violate this law should not be prosecuted.

   Which one of the following, if true, most justifies the above application of the principle?

   (A) Since there are relatively few snake charmers and they each capture relatively few snakes per year, snake charmers have a minimal effect on wild populations.

   (B) Many attempts to prosecute snake charmers under this law have failed because prosecutors lacked adequate knowledge of the procedures used to capture snakes.

   (C) Very few, if any, snake charmers are aware that there is a law that prohibits the capture of wild snakes.

   (D) Snake populations are much less threatened than the populations of several other species for which capture is legal.

   (E) Snake charmers capture wild snakes only because they believe they would be unable to earn a living otherwise.

4. Very little is known about prehistoric hominid cave dwellers. However, a recent study of skeletons of these hominids has revealed an important clue about their daily activities: skeletal fractures present are most like the type and distribution of fractures sustained by rodeo riders. Therefore, it is likely that these cave dwellers engaged in activities similar to rodeo riders—chasing and tackling animals.

   Which one of the following principles, if valid, most helps to justify the argumentation above?

   (A) The primary source of clues about the lives of prehistoric hominids is their skeletal remains.

   (B) The most important aspect of prehistoric life to be studied is how food was obtained.

   (C) If direct evidence as to the cause of a phenomenon is available, then indirect evidence should not be sought.

   (D) If there is a similarity between two effects, then there is probably a similarity between their causes.

   (E) The frequency with which a hazardous activity is performed is proportional to the frequency of injuries resulting from that activity.

END OF SET

Set 1 Key & Explanations

1. D

2. C

3. A

4. D

1. Mike: Tom did not tell me that I could use his computer, but (it would not be wrong for me to use it anyway) Last week Tom used Mary's bicycle even though she had not told him he could use it.

J Which one of the following principles, if valid, would most help to justify Mike's reasoning?

(A) Using the possessions of others without their permission is not always theft.

(B) Generally one should tell the truth, but there are cases in which it is permissible not to.

(C) If people have used your property without your permission, it is not wrong for you to use their property without their permission.

(D) It is permissible to treat people in a way that is similar to the way in which they have treated others.

(E) Using another person's property is wrong if the person is harmed by that use.

Type: Justify
Flaw: Missing Link

Stem – The stem asks us to identify which of the choices *most helps to justify* the reasoning. That's a Justify problem stem.

Stimulus – 1) Find the Conclusion. Looking at the stimulus, you have a pretty straightforward argument to break down. The first clause is background information, and then the conclusion finishes out the first sentence. It would not be wrong for Mike to use Tom's computer.

2) Find the Support. The last sentence is a comparison with the way Mike wants to use Tom's computer: "Last week Tom used Mary's bicycle even though she had not told him he could use it." Mike is using this comparison as the basis for his conclusion, so this is the main support.

3) Find the Gap. The gap will reside in the reasoning, specifically how the support is used to make the conclusion valid. The conclusion about whether or not it would be wrong to use Tom's computer is based on Tom's use of Mary's bicycle without her approval. Mike assumes that the two circumstances are related. However, he never explicitly states that it is okay to treat Tom's possessions in a manner similar to how Tom has treated others' possessions. Consequently, there is a Missing Link in the argument

between these concepts. Let's consider the choices in light of this missing logical link in Mike's argument.

Choices – 1) Eliminate. (A) starts off on the right track but then brings up theft, which is irrelevant to the stimulus. This choice appeals to one's common sense, but it's out because it's unrelated. (B) is similar to (A) in that it deals with concepts not present in the stimulus. Using someone else's property may be an issue of personal morals, but nowhere in the stimulus is truth telling discussed. (B) is out. (C) is a principle that can be readily applied to the stimulus, so let's hold onto it. (D) also looks good, so hold onto it, too. (E) is like (A) and (B). It talks about borrowing as it harms an individual, which is nowhere in the stimulus.

2) Confirm. With the eliminate step complete, let's review the choices still in the running. (C) looks good, but on second thought it states that if people use *your* property without *your* permission, then you can use their property. Mike did not let Tom borrow *his own* property. Mike is actually completely removed from the borrower and the borrowee, Tom and Mary. For this reason, (C) appears to be a dud. Little details like this are important in so many Logical Reasoning problems. Constantly push yourself to understand the precise details. (D), on the other hand, is spot-on. It links the unlinked concepts, namely Mike's belief that if Tom borrowed Mary's stuff without getting permission, then it's okay to use Tom's stuff without getting permission. (D) is correct.

2. Editorial: It is usually desirable for people to have access to unregulated information, such as is found on the Internet. But a vast array of misinformation will always show up on the Internet, and it is difficult to <u>determine which information is accurate</u>. Accurate information is useless unless it can easily be distinguished from misinformation; **(thus**, the information on the Internet should somehow be regulated.**)**

    Which one of the following principles, if valid, most helps to justify the editorial's argument?

     (A)   It is never possible to regulate misinformation without restricting people's access to accurate information.

     (B)   Even if information is regulated, accurate information is often indistinguishable from misinformation.

    (C)   Regulation of information makes it easy for people to distinguish between accurate information and misinformation.

    (D)   It is acceptable for people to have access to a vast array of misinformation only if accurate information is never overlooked as a result.

     (E)   It is usually more desirable for people to have access to useless, unregulated misinformation than it is for them to have access only to accurate but regulated information.

Type: Justify
Flaw: Missing Link

<u>Stem</u> – This is a classic Justify stem. It asks you which choice justifies the editorial argument. Be ready to identify the parts of the stimulus.

<u>Stimulus</u> – 1) Find the Conclusion. "Thus" is a clear indicator of the conclusion. In this stimulus, the conclusion is that information on the Internet should somehow be regulated.

2) Find the Support. Our conclusion has two key pieces of support: misinformation will always show up on the Internet; and, it is difficult to determine which information is accurate. That second support piece is reiterated just before the conclusion, so we know that it is an important piece of support and possibly the primary support.

3) Find the gap: Even though this is a long Stimulus with a lot of information, the unlinked concepts are fairly straightforward: determining which information is accurate and regulating Information on the Internet. To link the gap, we'll need a choice that explains how regulating information on the Internet can make it easier to determine which information is accurate.

<u>Choices</u> – 1) Eliminate choices without both unlinked concepts. (A) doesn't even come close. It discusses regulating misinformation when our conclusion is all about regulating information. Also, restricting people's access to accurate information has nothing to do with the argument, which proposes a solution to help people find accurate information. (B) includes both unlinked concepts. Hold onto (B). (C) also includes both concepts, so let's keep that one as well. (D) doesn't mention regulating information at all. Eliminate it. (E) sort of mentions both concepts, but it seems to stray from the argument. Our conclusion is that information should be regulated, so why would it be more desirable for people to have access to useless, unregulated information than accurate, regulated information? This is almost the opposite of the conclusion. Eliminate it.

2) Confirm. When we compare (B) and (C), (C) is a much better choice to support our conclusion. (B) – If regulating information will not make it easier to determine which information is accurate, then there is no point to regulate that information in the first place. This choice doesn't support our conclusion. On the other hand, (C) is the best choice because it explains that regulation of information makes it easy for people to determine which information is accurate.

3. Principle: A law whose purpose is to protect wild animal populations should not be enforced against those whose <u>actions do not threaten wild animal populations.</u>

Application: Even though there is a law against capturing wild snakes, which was enacted to protect wild snake populations(<u>snake charmers who violate this law</u> should not be prosecuted.)

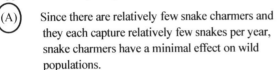

Which one of the following, if true, most justifies the above application of the principle?

(A) Since there are relatively few snake charmers and they each capture relatively few snakes per year, snake charmers have a minimal effect on wild populations.

(B) Many attempts to prosecute snake charmers under this law have failed because prosecutors lacked adequate knowledge of the procedures used to capture snakes.

(C) Very few, if any, snake charmers are aware that there is a law that prohibits the capture of wild snakes.

(D) Snake populations are much less threatened than the populations of several other species for which capture is legal.

(E) Snake charmers capture wild snakes only because they believe they would be unable to earn a living otherwise.

Type: Justify
Flaw: Missing Link
Tags: Principle & Application

<u>Stem</u> – "Most justifies the above application of the principle" tells you this is a Justify problem.

<u>Stimulus</u> – 1) Find the Conclusion. This is a Principle and Application Stimulus, so we know that the Application contains our conclusion. The conclusion is simple: snake charmers who violate a law against capturing wild snakes should not be prosecuted.

2) Find the Support. In a Principle and Application Stimulus, the Principle contains the primary support. Like the conclusion, the support is relatively simple: a law that protects wild animal populations should not be enforced against those who do not threaten the wild animal populations.

3) Find the Gap. The support tells us that laws should not be enforced against those who don't threaten animal populations, and the conclusion tells us snake charmers should not be prosecuted. There is clearly a missing link between those who don't threaten animal populations and snake charmers who violate a law against capturing wild snakes. In order to fill the gap, we will need to find a choice that explains that snake charmers do not threaten animal populations. If we can find something like that, then this argument will be 100% airtight.

<u>Choices</u> – 1) Eliminate choices without both unlinked concepts. (A) looks pretty nice. It discusses snake charmers, and "a minimal effect on wild populations" sounds pretty similar to actions that do not threaten wild animal populations. Let's keep (A) and go through the remaining choices. (B) mentions snake charmers, but it doesn't discuss actions that do not threaten wild animal populations. (C) also touches on snake charmers but misses the second unlinked concept. (D) talks about snakes, but it doesn't mention snake charmers explicitly. Also, it talks about wild populations that are threatened, but it has nothing to do with the actions that affect those wild populations. (E) mentions snake charmers, but, again, this choice misses the unlinked concept of actions that do not threaten wild animal populations.

2) Confirm. We're left with (A), which actually provides a nice link. If snake charmers have a minimal effect on wild populations, then their actions do not threaten wild animal populations, so snake charmers who violate a law against capturing wild snakes should not be prosecuted.

4. Very little is known about prehistoric hominid cave dwellers. However, a recent study of skeletons of these hominids has revealed an important clue about their daily activities: <u>skeletal fractures present are most like the type and distribution of fractures sustained by rodeo riders.</u> (**Therefore**, it is likely that these cave dwellers <u>engaged in activities similar to rodeo riders</u>)–chasing and tackling animals.

Which one of the following principles, if valid, most helps to justify the argumentation above?

(A) The primary source of clues about the lives of prehistoric hominids is their skeletal remains.

(B) The most important aspect of prehistoric life to be studied is how food was obtained.

(C) If direct evidence as to the cause of a phenomenon is available, then indirect evidence should not be sought.

(D) If there is a similarity between two effects, then there is probably a similarity between their causes.

(E) The frequency with which a hazardous activity is performed is proportional to the frequency of injuries resulting from that activity.

Type: Justify
Flaw: Missing Link

<u>Stem</u> – "Most helps to justify the argumentation" tells you this is a Justify problem.

<u>Stimulus</u> – 1) Find the Conclusion. The indicator "therefore" sets you up nicely to find the conclusion. The argument concludes that cave dwellers engaged in activities similar to modern rodeo riders.

2) Find the Support. The primary support to our conclusion is that skeletal fractures in cave dweller remains are similar to those sustained by modern-day rodeo riders.

3) Find the Gap. The gap may not seem obvious initially, but as we examine how the support and the conclusion interplay it isn't too hard to see. The conclusion proposes that cave dwellers engaged in similar activities to rodeo riding because they had similar skeletal fractures. The unlinked concepts are fairly specific: skeletal fractures that are most like those sustained by rodeo riders and activities similar to rodeo riders. As we consider these, we realize that one is a cause and one is an effect, but on an LSAT argument we can't necessarily assume the cause and effect relationship is valid. We don't have enough information to assume that similar effects – skeletal fractures – were influenced by similar causes – activities such as chasing and tackling animals. As we dig into the choices, we want to fill this gap and find something that addresses the disconnect between these two.

<u>Choices</u> – 1) Eliminate choices without both unlinked concepts. (A) talks about skeletal remains, but not skeletal fractures, our effect. Also, it doesn't come close to mentioning the cause. (B) misses the mark as well. The activities that are similar to rodeo riding may have been related to how cave dwellers obtained food, but this has nothing to do with our gap because it fails to mention the effect, skeletal fractures. (C) talks about evidence, which could refer to our effect since skeletal fractures are the evidence for the support. Also, "cause" could refer to activities similar to rodeo riding. It looks shaky, but hang onto (C). (D) may not mention our unlinked concepts specifically, but it discusses similarity in effects and similarity in causes. Let's hang onto (D) as well. (E) mentions a hazardous activity, which could refer to activities similar to rodeo riding. "Injuries resulting from that activity" could refer to skeletal fractures. Let's hang onto (E).

2) Confirm. After elimination, we're left with (C), (D), and (E). Let's take a closer look at them and see which one makes the argument 100% airtight. (C) is more about evidence than the relationship between cause and effect. We don't know anything about direct and indirect evidence from the argument, so on closer examination (C) doesn't fill our gap. Although (D) doesn't dig into to the specifics of the argument, it does a very good job of supporting the argument. The gap is between skeletal fractures – an effect – and activities similar to rodeo riding – a cause. In order to fill the gap, we need a choice that shows that skeletal fractures similar to those sustained by rodeo riders were probably caused by activities similar to rodeo riding. Essentially, we need something that proves that similar effects have similar causes. That's exactly what (D) introduces. By contrast, (E) discusses the frequency of the hazardous activity and the frequency of the resulting injuries. The argument doesn't give us much about frequency at all, so this one doesn't come close to filling the gap. On the other hand, (D) does an excellent job of filling the gap, and it is correct.

Challenge Set 2

Techniques Summary

- <u>Core focus</u>: Find Gap.
- Stimulus:
  - Bracket the conclusion and find the support.
  - Then, find the two unlinked concepts.
- Choices: Eliminate choices that do not fill the gap.

1. Everything that is commonplace and ordinary fails to catch our attention, so there are things that fail to catch our attention but that are miracles of nature.

   The conclusion of the argument follows logically if which one of the following is assumed?

   (A) Only miracles of nature fail to be ordinary and commonplace.

   (B) Some things that are ordinary and commonplace are miracles of nature.

   (C) Some things that are commonplace and ordinary fail to catch our attention.

   (D) Everything that fails to catch our attention is commonplace and ordinary.

   (E) Only extraordinary or unusual things catch our attention.

2. Curator: Critics have rightly claimed that removing the centuries-old grime from the frescoes of Michelangelo will expose them to acids formed by the combination of water vapor in human breath with pollutants in the air. Notwithstanding this fact, the restoration should continue, for the frescoes in their present condition cannot be seen as they appeared when painted by Michelangelo.

   Which one of the following principles, if valid, most helps to justify the curator's reasoning?

   (A) The decision as to whether an artwork merits restoration or not should depend on its greatness as judged by aesthetic standards alone.

   (B) An artwork possesses aesthetic value only if there are people who observe and appreciate it.

   (C) It is acceptable to risk future damage to an artwork if the purpose is to enable it to be appreciated in its original form.

   (D) It is right to spend large amounts of money on the restoration of an old artwork if this restoration makes the artwork accessible to large numbers of people.

   (E) A picture that has become encrusted with grime over a long period can no longer be regarded as the same work of art as that painted by the artist.

3. Most apartments on the upper floors of The Vista Arms apartment building have scenic views. So there is in the building at least one studio apartment with scenic views.

The conclusion of the argument follows logically if which one of the following is assumed?

(A)   All of the apartments on the lower floors of the building have scenic views.

(B)   All of the apartments in the building have scenic views.

(C)   Most of the apartments in the building are studio apartments.

(D)   Most of the apartments with scenic views are on the upper floors of the building.

(E)   Most of the apartments on the upper floors of the building are studio apartments.

4. Curator: A magazine recently ran a very misleading story on the reaction of local residents to our controversial art exhibit. They quoted the responses of three residents, all of whom expressed a sense of moral outrage. These quotations were intended to suggest that most local residents oppose the exhibit; the story failed to mention, however, the fact that the three residents are all close friends.

Which one of the following principles most helps to justify the curator's argumentation?

(A)   It is misleading to present the opinions of people with no special expertise on a subject as though they were experts.

(B)   It is misleading to present the opinions of people on only one side of an issue when the population is likely to be evenly divided on that issue.

(C)   It is misleading to present the opinions of a few people as evidence of what the majority thinks unless the opinions they express are widely held.

(D)   It is misleading to present testimony from close friends and thereby imply that they must agree with each other.

(E)   It is misleading to present the opinions of a potentially nonrepresentative sample of people as if they represent public opinion.

END OF SET

Set 2 Key & Explanations

1. B
2. C
3. E
4. E

1. Everything that is commonplace and ordinary fails to catch our attention (**so** there are things that fail to catch our attention but that are miracles of nature)

    J The conclusion of the argument follows logically if which one of the following is assumed?

    (A) Only miracles of nature fail to be ordinary and commonplace.

    (B) Some things that are ordinary and commonplace are miracles of nature.

    (C) Some things that are commonplace and ordinary fail to catch our attention.

    (D) Everything that fails to catch our attention is commonplace and ordinary.

    (E) Only extraordinary or unusual things catch our attention.

Type: Justify
Flaw: Missing Link
Tags: Quantifiers

Stem – "Conclusion … follows logically" tells you this will be Justify problem. Let's identify the parts of the argument.

Stimulus – 1) Find the Conclusion. This is a simple one-sentence stimulus. The indicator "so" helps point us toward the conclusion: that some things that fail to catch our attention are miracles of nature.

2) Find the Support. If the second clause in our one-sentence stimulus is the conclusion, then the first clause must be the support. In this case, our support is that everything commonplace and ordinary fails to catch our attention.

3) Find the Gap. In this stimulus, we're only given two concepts, so it isn't very difficult to see that they are related but unlinked. The two concepts are things that are commonplace and ordinary and miracles of nature. Everything that is commonplace and ordinary fails to catch our attention, and some things that fail to catch our attention are miracles of nature. We need a choice that ties these two together. It will probably explain that miracles of nature can be commonplace and ordinary. Let's see what we find in the choices.

Choices – 1) Eliminate choices without both unlinked concepts. (A) mentions both miracles of nature and ordinary and commonplace, so hang to this one. (B) also mentions both concepts, so we'll need to hang onto that one, too. (C) mentions commonplace and ordinary, but it doesn't mention miracles of nature. (D) also mentions commonplace and ordinary but overlooks miracles of nature. (E) discusses "extraordinary or unusual things," which is actually a New Concept. It doesn't even come close to including both of our unlinked concepts.

2) Confirm. After elimination, we're left with (A) and (B). (A) doesn't give us what we need to make this argument 100% valid. If miracles of nature are the only things that fail to be ordinary and commonplace, then how can we conclude that some things that fail to catch our attention are miracles of nature? By contrast, (B) gives us a nice link for our gap. All things that are commonplace and ordinary fail to catch our attention. If *some* things that are ordinary and commonplace are also miracles of nature, then *some* things that fail to catch are attention are miracles of nature. (B) gives us what we need to prove the conclusion, and it is correct.

2. Curator: Critics have rightly claimed that removing the centuries-old grime from the frescoes of Michelangelo will expose them to acids formed by the combination of water vapor in human breath with pollutants in the air. (Notwithstanding this fact, <u>the restoration should continue,</u>) <u>for the frescoes in their present condition cannot be seen as they appeared when painted by Michelangelo.</u>

Which one of the following principles, if valid, most helps to justify the curator's reasoning?

(A) The decision as to whether an artwork merits restoration or not should depend on its greatness as judged by aesthetic standards alone.

(B) An artwork possesses aesthetic value only if there are people who observe and appreciate it.

(C) It is acceptable to risk future damage to an artwork if the purpose is to enable it to be appreciated in its original form.

(D) It is right to spend large amounts of money on the restoration of an old artwork if this restoration makes the artwork accessible to large numbers of people.

(E) A picture that has become encrusted with grime over a long period can no longer be regarded as the same work of art as that painted by the artist.

Type: Justify
Flaw: Missing Link

Stem – "Most helps to justify" is a classic Justify stem, so we need to be ready to identify the parts of the argument.

Stimulus – 1) Find the Conclusion. This stimulus has a lot of information about the restoration of frescoes painted by Michelangelo, but that shouldn't prevent you from locating the conclusion quickly. The phrase "notwithstanding this fact" acts as a type of indicator, but it also adds to our conclusion. The conclusion is that the restoration should continue despite concerns that it may harm the frescoes. It's not enough to say that restoration should continue alone. We need to understand that restoration could be detrimental to the frescoes, but nevertheless restoration should continue.

2) Find the Support. The primary support comes directly after our conclusion. The restoration should continue because the frescoes cannot be seen as they originally appeared when Michelangelo painted them.

3) Find the Gap. The gap may not seem quite as obvious in this argument, but we start to see two unlinked concepts when we consider the conclusion and its primary support. Actually, the long first sentence becomes pretty helpful. We know that the restoration could cause damage to the frescoes. Nevertheless, the restoration should continue so that people can see the frescoes as Michelangelo originally painted them. There's a missing link in this logic between continuing restoration despite the risks and ensuring people can see the frescoes as they originally appeared. When we look through the choices, we want to look for two

concepts: continuing risky restoration and ensuring people can see the frescoes' original appearance.

Choices – 1) Eliminate choices without both unlinked concepts. (A) misses the mark. It sort of talks about restoration, but the bit about greatness as judged by aesthetic standards has nothing to do with the argument. (B) discusses aesthetic value, which isn't related to our unlinked concepts whatsoever. (C) is a little tricky. Although it doesn't mention restoration explicitly, it actually touches on both of our unlinked concepts. We know that restoration could risk future damage to an artwork, so that is a very similar restatement of our concept that risky restoration should continue. "Appreciated in its original form" also sounds a lot like our second concept that people should see the frescoes as they were originally painted. Let's hang onto (C). (D) discusses the cost of restoration and making artwork accessible, neither of which are our unlinked concepts. (E) sort of touches on our concept that people should see the frescoes in their original condition, but it doesn't discuss restoration.

2) Confirm. The only choice left is (C), which provides a nice link. If it is acceptable to risk future damage through restoration for the purpose of ensuring people can see the frescoes in their original form, then the restoration should continue. (C) makes our argument 100% airtight, and it is correct.

3. Most <u>apartments on the upper floors</u> of The Vista Arms apartment building have scenic views **(So** there is in the building at least one <u>studio apartment</u> with scenic views. **)**

The conclusion of the argument follows logically if which one of the following is assumed?

(A) All of the apartments on the lower floors of the building have scenic views.

(B) All of the apartments in the building have scenic views.

(C) Most of the apartments in the building are studio apartments.

(D) Most of the apartments with scenic views are on the upper floors of the building.

(E) Most of the apartments on the upper floors of the building are studio apartments.

Type: Justify
Flaw: Missing Link
Tags: Quantifiers

<u>Stem</u> – The question stem asks you to identify an assumption that the argument relies upon but does not state. This is a Justify stem.

<u>Stimulus</u> – 1) Find the Conclusion. "So" is a nice indicator that marks the conclusion. "There is in the building at least one studio apartment with scenic view."

2) Find the Support. The only possible support is the first sentence, which states that most apartments on the upper floor of the apartment building have scenic views.

3) Find the Gap. Hmm… There's a missing word there. The conclusion talks about "studio apartments," while the support only talks about the apartments on the "upper floors." Maybe it was a mistake on the part of the argument and apartment and studio apartment are the same thing? Never, ever side with the argument. If it slips up in any way, as the argument does in all Justify stimuli, focus on the Missing Link and turn it into your success. The argument never links *apartments on the upper floor* with *studio apartments*. The stem wants us to identify the central assumption in the argument, so let's look for a choice that fills the gap between apartments on the upper floors and studio apartments.

<u>Choices</u> – 1) Eliminate:.(A) talks about the lower floors, which, while not discussed and potentially a missing link, does not connect the two concepts that need a link: apartments on the upper floors and studio apartments. (A) is out. (B) never touches on the idea of studio apartments, so it doesn't treat the unlinked concepts. Even if all apartments have scenic views, there may be no studio apartments—(B) doesn't tell you enough to be sure. (B) is out, too. (C) talks about one of the unlinked concepts but not both. You can't do much with the idea that most of the apartments are studio apartments because that could mean that 80% of them are studio apartments, all of which are on the lower floors. (C) doesn't link the concepts, so it's out. (D) claims most of the apartments on the upper floors have scenic views, which is nice for them, but it does not say anything at all about studio apartments. On to (E), which mentions both apartments on the upper floors as well as studio apartments. You've eliminated everything else, and (E) looks good. Let's move on to the confirmation step.

2) Confirm. (E) claims that most of the apartments on the upper floors are studio apartments, which validates the conclusion that, if most of the apartments on the upper floors have scenic views, then at least one studio apartment has scenic views. On the LSAT, "most" means an amount more than 50%. If most of the apartments on the upper floors have scenic views and most of the upper-floor apartments are studio apartments, then you have an overlap of two amounts, both "most" or >50%. When we combine the quantifiers, most and most indicate "at least one," while the actual number could in fact be much greater. (E) is correct.

4. Curator: (A magazine recently ran a <u>very misleading story</u> on the reaction of local residents to our controversial art exhibit.) They quoted the responses of three residents, all of whom expressed a sense of moral outrage. These quotations were intended to suggest that most local residents oppose the exhibit; <u>the story failed to mention, however, the fact that the three residents are all close friends.</u>

Which one of the following principles most helps to justify the curator's argumentation?

(A) It is misleading to present the opinions of people with no special expertise on a subject as though they were experts.

(B) It is misleading to present the opinions of people on only one side of an issue when the population is likely to be evenly divided on that issue.

(C) It is misleading to present the opinions of a few people as evidence of what the majority thinks unless the opinions they express are widely held.

(D) It is misleading to present testimony from close friends and thereby imply that they must agree with each other.

(E) It is misleading to present the opinions of a potentially nonrepresentative sample of people as if they represent public opinion.

Type: Justify
Flaw: Missing Link

<u>Stem</u> – "Most helps to justify" tells you this is a Justify problem. Be ready to dissect the parts of the argument.

<u>Stimulus</u> – 1) Find the Conclusion. In this argument, the conclusion comes first. A magazine ran a very misleading story. It's not a particularly obvious conclusion. But "misleading" is a subjective word, so the Curator will need explain why the magazine story is misleading.

2) Find the Support. The magazine story intended to suggest that most local residents oppose the exhibit, but the only residents quoted are three close friends. So, the magazine article was misleading because the three residents who expressed moral outrage are three close friends who probably do not represent the opinions of most local residents.

3) Find the Gap. There's an obvious gap between the support and the conclusion: how does quoting just three residents who are close friends make a magazine article misleading? Remember that the story was intended to suggest that most residents oppose the art exhibit, so the argument implies that the opinions of three close friends do not represent public opinion as a whole because three friends probably all share the same opinion, not a diverse set of opinions. To fill this gap, we will need a choice that shows how or why quoting three close friends can make a magazine article misleading.

<u>Choices</u> – 1) Eliminate choices without both unlinked concepts. (A) mentions misleading, but we're not looking for the opinions of people with no special expertise. We need a choice that discusses quoting three close friends who may not represent the diversity of opinions of most local residents. (B) seems to touch on both unlinked concepts to a degree, but it actually expands beyond the concept of the three close friends. The argument implies that the three close friends were not a good representation of public opinion. We don't know whether or not the population is evenly divided; we just know that the three close friends didn't express the opinions of most local residents, so (B) doesn't discuss that unlinked concept. (C) is very similar. Our unlinked concept is the opinions of three close friends that probably do not represent the majority. We don't know for sure what the majority thinks; we just know that the opinions of three close friends probably do not represent most local residents' opinion on the exhibit. Much like (B), (C) pushes us further than our unlinked concept. (D) is the first choice that mentions the three close friends, but like (B) and (C), it doesn't properly address the concept. The concept is that three close friends do not represent public opinion accurately. We're not concerned with whether or not they agree because they're close friends. We just need a choice that understands that the three close friends are probably not an accurate representation of the public opinion as a whole. By contrast, (E) gives us exactly what we need. It discusses misleading and the opinions of a few people who probably do not represent public opinion as a whole.

2) Confirm. We're left with (E), which is an excellent choice to fill our gap. The magazine article was misleading because it presented only the opinions of three close friends. Those three close friends are probably not a good representation of the opinions of most local residents, and presenting opinions that are potentially nonrepresentative of public opinion is misleading. That's a pretty solid argument.

Challenge Set 3

This is a difficult Group, so take your time on each problem and be careful with the choice you select.

Techniques Summary

- Core focus: Find Gap.

- Stimulus:

  o   Bracket the conclusion and find the support.

  o   Then, find the two unlinked concepts.

- Choices: Eliminate choices that do not fill the gap.

1.   Principle: If the burden of a proposed policy change would fall disproportionately on people with low incomes, that policy change should not be made.

   Application: The city of Centerburgh plans to reintroduce rock salt as a road de-icing agent, after having stopped its use several years ago on the grounds that it accelerated the corrosion of automobiles. Although the city claims that cars are now better protected from salt's corrosive properties than they were even as recently as five years ago, the city's plan should be halted.

   Which one of the following, if true of Centerburgh, most justifies the above application of the principle?

   (A)   Individuals with low incomes are more likely to use public transportation and are less likely to drive cars than are individuals with higher incomes.

   (B)   Road maintenance is primarily funded by local sales taxes, which disproportionately burden people with low incomes.

   (C)   Cars now cost twice what they did when rock salt was last used as a road de-icing agent.

   (D)   People with low incomes are more likely to purchase older vehicles than are people with higher incomes.

   (E)   Among drivers, those with low incomes are less likely than those with higher incomes to use roads that have been treated with deicing agents.

2.   Educator: Traditional classroom education is ineffective because education in such an environment is not truly a social process and only social processes can develop students' insights. In the traditional classroom, the teacher acts from outside the group and interaction between teachers and students is rigid and artificial.

   The educator's conclusion follows logically if which one of the following is assumed?

   (A)   Development of insight takes place only if genuine education also occurs.

   (B)   Classroom education is effective if the interaction between teachers and students is neither rigid nor artificial.

   (C)   All social processes involve interaction that is neither rigid nor artificial.

   (D)   Education is not effective unless it leads to the development of insight.

   (E)   The teacher does not act from outside the group in a nontraditional classroom.

3. Essayist: It is much less difficult to live an enjoyable life if one is able to make lifestyle choices that accord with one's personal beliefs and then see those choices accepted by others. It is possible for people to find this kind of acceptance by choosing friends and associates who share many of their personal beliefs. Thus, no one should be denied the freedom to choose the people with whom he or she will associate.

Which one of the following principles, if valid, most helps to justify the essayist's argument?

(A) No one should be denied the freedom to make lifestyle choices that accord with his or her personal beliefs.

(B) One should associate with at least some people who share many of one's personal beliefs.

(C) If having a given freedom could make it less difficult for someone to live an enjoyable life, then no one should be denied that freedom.

(D) No one whose enjoyment of life depends, at least in part, on friends and associates who share many of the same personal beliefs should be deliberately prevented from having such friends and associates.

(E) One may choose for oneself the people with whom one will associate, if doing so could make it easier to live an enjoyable life.

4. Economics professor: Marty's Pizza and Checkers Pizza are the two major pizza parlors in our town. Marty's sold coupon books including coupons good for one large plain pizza at any local pizza parlor, at Marty's expense. But Checkers refused to accept these coupons, even though they were redeemed by all other local pizza parlors. Accepting them would have cost Checkers nothing and would have satisfied those of its potential customers who had purchased the coupon books. This shows that Checkers's motive in refusing to accept the coupons was simply to hurt Marty's Pizza.

Which one of the following, if assumed, enables the economics professor's conclusion to be properly drawn?

(A) Any company that refuses to accept coupons issued by a competitor when doing so would satisfy some of the company's potential customers is motivated solely by the desire to hurt that competitor.

(B) Any company that wishes to hurt a competitor by refusing to accept coupons issued by that competitor will refuse to accept them even when accepting them would cost nothing and would satisfy its potential customers.

(C) At least one company has refused to accept coupons issued by its major local competitor simply in order to hurt that competitor, even though those coupons were accepted by all other local competitors.

(D) Any company that accepts its major competitor's coupons helps its competitor by doing so, even if it also satisfies its own actual or potential customers.

(E) If accepting coupons issued by a competitor would not enable a company to satisfy its actual or potential customers, then that company's refusal to accept the coupons is motivated by the desire to satisfy customers.

END OF SET

Set 3 Key & Explanations

These are difficult problems so do a careful review of each one to rapidly improve your Justify skills. Milk every drop of learning from these problems.

1. D

2. D

3. C

4. A

1. Principle: If the burden of a proposed policy change would <u>fall disproportionately on people with low incomes, that policy change should not be made.</u>

    Application: The city of Centerburgh plans to reintroduce rock salt as a road deicing agent, after having stopped its use several years ago on the grounds that it accelerated the corrosion of automobiles. Although the city claims that cars are now better protected from salt's corrosive properties than they were even as recently as five years ago <u>(the city's plan should be halted.)</u>

    J Which one of the following, if true of Centerburgh, most justifies the above application of the principle?

    (A) Individuals with low incomes are more likely to use public transportation and are less likely to drive cars than are individuals with higher incomes.

    (B) Road maintenance is primarily funded by local sales taxes, which disproportionately burden people with low incomes.

    (C) Cars now cost twice what they did when rock salt was last used as a road de-icing agent.

    (D) People with low incomes are more likely to purchase older vehicles than are people with higher incomes.

    (E) Among drivers, those with low incomes are less likely than those with higher incomes to use roads that have been treated with deicing agents.

Type: Justify
Flaw: Missing Link
Tag: Principle & Application Stimuli

<u>Stem</u> – "Justifies" tells us the problem type. We are looking for information about the city that will justify how the Principle (general rule) is applied.

<u>Stimulus</u> – 1) Find the Conclusion. The conclusion is in the extra-long Application here. The conclusion is that the plan to reintroduce rock salt as a road de-icing agent should be halted.

2) Find the Support. The support is found in the Principle. If a policy change has a burden that falls on the poor more than others, it should be halted.

3) Find the Gap. Why does using rock salt burden the poor more than everyone else? This is not given, but that is what we need. The fact that the plan should be halted for the city means it must be a greater burden for the poor. We need something here that sets the poor apart from everyone else.

Notice the fact that newer cars are more protected from salt corrosion than older ones. That may come in handy.

<u>Choices</u> – 1) Eliminate. (A) talks about how the poor drive less than others, so they should be hurt *less* by the salt. This does the opposite of what we need. (B) talks about road maintenance placing a higher burden on the poor, but nothing in the rock salt plan talks about more road maintenance. This difference does not provide the link we need. (C) talks about overall car cost going up, but that doesn't necessarily mean the poor are hurt more than others by road salt. (D) gives us something that separates the poor from everyone else – they drive older vehicles. How does that relate to rock salt? Not sure, but let's keep it. (E) gives us a difference between the poor and everyone else, but like (A) it is in the wrong direction. If those with low incomes drive on road with deicing agents less, then they should be hurt by the rock salt less, too.

2) Confirm. (D) talks about the poor driving older vehicles, and the application of the principle said that older vehicles get hurt more by rock salt. Bingo – this links the poor being disproportionally burdened by the policy to canceling the plan for rock salt as a deicing agent.

This is a challenging Justify problem that doesn't fit perfectly with our unlinked concepts approach. However, as long as you see that you need to link low-income people being hurt more by the change with the specifics of the change, the problem is very doable. Another key is using the setup given in the application about the specific nature of the policy change (the info on older cars being less protected against rock salt).

2.   Educator: (Traditional classroom education is ineffective) because education in such an environment is not truly a social process and only social processes can develop students' insights. In the traditional classroom, the teacher acts from outside the group and interaction between teachers and students is rigid and artificial.

The educator's **conclusion follows logically** if which one of the following is assumed?

J

 (A)   Development of insight takes place only if genuine education also occurs.

 (B)   Classroom education is effective if the interaction between teachers and students is neither rigid nor artificial.

 (C)   All social processes involve interaction that is neither rigid nor artificial.

(D)   Education is not effective unless it leads to the development of insight.

 (E)   The teacher does not act from outside the group in a nontraditional classroom.

Type: Justify
Flaw: Missing Link
Tag: First-Line Conclusion

Stem – "Conclusion follows logically" = a Justify problem.

Stimulus – 1) Find the Conclusion. It comes right away. Traditional classroom education is ineffective.

2) Find the Support. The rest of the stimulus supports the first-line conclusion. The key support pieces are that education in a classroom environment is not a social process, and only social processes can develop student insights.

3) Find the Gap. The support ends with the idea that the current educational environment does not develop *student insights*. That concept is never linked to the conclusion that traditional classroom education is *ineffective*. The correct choice will link those two concepts.

Choices – 1) Eliminate choices that do not feature both Unlinked Concepts. (A) doesn't have the concept of education being ineffective. (B) and (C) don't mention the development of insight. (D) mentions both concepts, so keep it. (E) doesn't mention either concept.

2) Confirm. (D) provides the link we need by stating that the development of insight is a requirement for effective education. Because we know that traditional classroom education does not develop student insight, it is therefore ineffective and the conclusion follows logically. Here is the conditional diagram for (D):

Effective education → develops insight

(D) is correct and is also a valid point in the real world. Developing insight—the capacity to gain an accurate and deep intuitive understanding of a person or thing—is certainly a requirement of effective education. We are helping you develop insight on the LSAT right now!

3. Essayist: It is much <u>less difficult to live an enjoyable life</u> if one is able to make lifestyle choices that accord with one's personal beliefs and then see those choices accepted by others. It is possible for people to find this kind of acceptance by choosing friends and associates who share many of their personal beliefs (**Thus**, no one should be <u>denied the freedom</u> to choose the people with whom he or she will associate.)

Which one of the following **principles**, if valid, most helps to **justify** the essayist's argument?

(A) No one should be denied the freedom to make lifestyle choices that accord with his or her personal beliefs.

(B) One should associate with at least some people who share many of one's personal beliefs.

(C) If having a given freedom could make it less difficult for someone to live an enjoyable life, then no one should be denied that freedom.

(D) No one whose enjoyment of life depends, at least in part, on friends and associates who share many of the same personal beliefs should be deliberately prevented from having such friends and associates.

(E) One may choose for oneself the people with whom one will associate, if doing so could make it easier to live an enjoyable life.

Type: Justify
Flaw: Missing Link

Stem – You're asked to find the principle that allows the argument's reasoning to be justified—that's a Justify problem stem.

Stimulus – 1) Find the Conclusion. No one should be denied the freedom to choose the people with whom he or she will associate.

2) Find the Support. It's less difficult to live an enjoyable life if you're able to choose those with whom you associate.

3) Find the Gap. The argument never connects the idea that doing something that makes it much less difficult to live a enjoyable life is a freedom that shouldn't be denied. There's a Missing Link that should connect these two Unlinked Concepts.

Choices – The correct choice will provide a link between doing something that makes it much less difficult to live a meaningful life and being denied that freedom.

1) Eliminate. (A) links "denied the freedom" with an action that accords with one's belief. Thus, it has one half of the unlinked concepts, but it fails to connect "denied the freedom" to something that makes it "less difficult to live an enjoyable life." (B) says that one should associate with at least some people who share many of one's personal beliefs, which does nothing to connect the two unlinked concepts of denied freedom and living an enjoyable life. (C) says that, if a freedom can make it less difficult for someone to live an enjoyable life, then no one should be denied that freedom, which perfectly connects the unlinked concepts—keep it. (D) says that no one whose enjoyment of life depends on friends and associates who share similar beliefs should be deliberately prevented from having such friends and associates. That idea goes beyond the information in the argument to make a statement about those whose lives depend on associating with certain friends and associates. (E) says that one can choose whom they'll associate with if it makes their life more enjoyable. That doesn't talk about being denied a freedom, so it's out.

2) Confirm. (C) links the two parts of the Missing Link: a certain thing that makes it less difficult to lead an enjoyable life and being denied the freedom to do that thing. (C) is correct.

4. Economics professor: Marty's Pizza and Checkers Pizza are the two major pizza parlors in our town. Marty's sold coupon books including coupons good for one large plain pizza at any local pizza parlor, at Marty's expense. But Checkers refused to accept these coupons, even though they were redeemed by all other local pizza parlors. Accepting <u>them would have cost Checkers nothing and would have satisfied those of its potential customers who had purchased the coupon books</u>(This shows that Checkers's motive in refusing to <u>accept the coupons was simply to hurt Marty's Pizza.</u>)

Which one of the following, if assumed, enables the economics professor's conclusion to be properly drawn?

(A) Any company that refuses to accept coupons issued by a competitor when doing so would satisfy some of the company's potential customers is motivated solely by the desire to hurt that competitor.

(B) Any company that wishes to hurt a competitor by refusing to accept coupons issued by that competitor will refuse to accept them even when accepting them would cost nothing and would satisfy its potential customers.

(C) At least one company has refused to accept coupons issued by its major local competitor simply in order to hurt that competitor, even though those coupons were accepted by all other local competitors.

(D) Any company that accepts its major competitor's coupons helps its competitor by doing so, even if it also satisfies its own actual or potential customers.

(E) If accepting coupons issued by a competitor would not enable a company to satisfy its actual or potential customers, then that company's refusal to accept the coupons is motivated by the desire to satisfy customers.

Type: Justify
Flaw: Missing Link

<u>Stem</u> – "Enables the … conclusion to be properly drawn" tells us this is a Justify problem.

<u>Stimulus</u> – 1) Find the Conclusion. "This shows" helps direct you to the conclusion. In refusing to accept Marty's coupons even though it could benefit them, Checker's motive was to hurt Marty's.

2) Find the Support. In the argument, we learn that Checker's refused to accept Marty's coupons even though accepting them would have cost Checker's nothing and could have satisfied some of their customers. So, the primary support for the conclusion is that Checkers could have benefited from accepting the coupons or, more specifically, it would not have hurt them to accept the coupons. In this way, we can see that their motivation to refuse the coupons must have been for another reason.

3) Find the Gap. There's a clear gap between the support and the conclusion. The conclusion tells us that Checker's motive in refusing the coupons was to harm Marty's. The support tells us that accepting the coupons would not have been detrimental to Checker's and could have been beneficial in some way. We need to find a link between these two concepts – something that explains why refusing to accept the coupons indicates a motive to harm Marty's. As we look through the choices, our two unlinked concepts are motivation to do harm and refusing coupons even though accepting them would cost nothing and could satisfy some customers.

<u>Choices</u> – 1) Eliminate choices without both unlinked concepts. (A) talks about refusing to accept coupons even though doing so would satisfy some customers. Also, (A) discusses a company's motivation to hurt a competitor. Hang onto (A). (B) seems to discuss both concepts as well, so let's keep it, too. (C) sort of mentions a motivation to harm a competitor, but it mentions other local competitors accepting the coupons. We're looking for a choice that talks about how accepting the coupons would cost nothing and could satisfy customers, so eliminate (C). (D) talks about helping a competitor, which is a different concept. We don't know anything about helping a competitor; we're concerned with a company's motivation to harm its competitor. (E) mentions a motivation to satisfy customers. We're looking for a motivation to harm competitors. Also, we know that accepting the coupons could satisfy customers, so clearly Checker's was not motivated by that aim.

2) Confirm. We're left with (A) and (B). (A) does an excellent job of filling the gap. It introduces a neat conditional that helps support the argument: if a company refuses to accept coupons when doing so would satisfy some customers, then that company is motivated solely by the desire to hurt its competitor. This conditional links refusing to accept the coupons to a motivation to harm a competitor, which is exactly what we need to make this argument 100% airtight. On the other hand, (B) introduces a similar conditional, but it doesn't give us the same support. (B) proposes that, if a company wishes to hurt a competitor by refusing to accept coupons, then it will refuse them even if doing so would cost nothing and would satisfy customers. That doesn't fill our gap. We need a choice that shows that a company's sole motive is to hurt its competitor if it refuses coupons that might be beneficial in some ways. (B) doesn't give us what we need. By contrast, (A) fills our gap nicely, and it is correct.

Challenge Set 4

This is a very difficult Set, so take your time on each problem and be careful with the choice you select.

Techniques Summary

- <u>Core focus</u>: Find Gap.
- Stimulus:
  - Bracket the conclusion and find the support.
  - Then, find the two unlinked concepts.
- Choices: Eliminate choices that do not fill the gap.

1. Because dried peat moss, which is derived from sphagnum moss, contains no chemical additives and is a renewable resource, many gardeners use large amounts of it as a soil conditioner in the belief that the practice is environmentally sound. They are mistaken. The millions of acres of sphagnum moss in the world contribute more oxygen to the atmosphere than do all of the world's rain forests combined, and the garden soil industry is depleting these areas much faster than they can renew themselves.

Which one of the following principles, if valid, most helps to justify the argument's reasoning?

(A) Using a product may be environmentally unsound even if the product is a renewable resource and contains no chemical additive.

(B) A practice is not environmentally sound if it significantly reduces the amount of oxygen entering the atmosphere.

(C) A practice is environmentally sound if it helps to protect rain forests that contribute large amounts of oxygen to the atmosphere.

(D) If the environmental benefits of a practice outweigh the environmental costs, that practice can be legitimately considered environmentally sound.

(E) If the practices of an industry threaten a vital resource, those practices should be banned.

2. Editorial: It is clear that what is called "health education" is usually propaganda rather than education. Propaganda and education are never the same thing. The former is nothing but an attempt to influence behavior through the repetition of simplistic slogans, whereas the latter never involves such a method. Though education does attempt to influence behavior, it does so by offering information in all its complexity, leaving it up to the individual to decide how to act on that information. Sadly, however, propaganda is much more successful than education.

The conclusion drawn by the editorial follows logically if it is assumed that what is called "health education" usually

(A) does not leave it up to the individual to decide how to act on information

(B) does not offer information in all its complexity

(C) does not involve the repetition of simplistic slogans

(D) attempts to influence behavior solely by repeating simplistic slogans

(E) is very successful in influencing people's behavior

3. Although the geological record contains some hints of major meteor impacts preceding mass extinctions, there were many extinctions that did not follow any known major meteor impacts. Likewise, there are many records of major meteor impacts that do not seem to have been followed by mass extinctions. Thus the geological record suggests that there is no consistent causal link between major meteor impacts and mass extinctions.

Which one of the following assumptions enables the argument's conclusion to be properly inferred?

(A)   If there were a consistent causal link between major meteor impacts and mass extinctions, then all major meteor impacts would be followed by mass extinctions.

(B)   Major meteor impacts and mass extinctions cannot be consistently causally linked unless many mass extinctions have followed major meteor impacts.

(C)   Of the mass extinctions that did not follow any known major meteor impacts, few if any followed major meteor impacts of which the geological record contains no hints.

(D)   If there is no consistent causal link between major meteor impacts and mass extinctions, then not all mass extinctions could have followed major meteor impacts.

(E)   There could be a consistent causal link between major meteor impacts and mass extinctions even if not every major meteor impact has been followed by a mass extinction.

4. If Skiff's book is published this year, Professor Nguyen vows she will urge the dean to promote Skiff. Thus, if Skiff's book is as important and as well written as Skiff claims, he will be promoted, for Nguyen will certainly keep her promise, and the dean will surely promote Skiff if Nguyen recommends it.

The argument's conclusion can be properly inferred if which one of the following is assumed?

(A)   Skiff's book will be published this year if it is as important as he claims it is.

(B)   Skiff needs to publish a book before he can be promoted.

(C)   Professor Nguyen believes that Skiff's book is well written.

(D)   Skiff's book will not be published unless it is as important and as well written as he claims it is.

(E)   Skiff will not be promoted unless Professor Nguyen urges the dean to do so.

END OF SET

Set 4 Key & Explanations

These are difficult problems so do a careful review of each one to rapidly improve your Justify skills. Milk every drop of learning from these problems.

      1. B

      2. D

      3. A

      4. A

1.   Because dried peat moss, which is derived from sphagnum moss, contains no chemical additives and is a renewable resource(many gardeners use large amounts of it as a soil conditioner in the belief that the practice is <u>environmentally sound</u>. They are mistaken.)The millions of acres of sphagnum moss in the world contribute <u>more oxygen to the atmosphere</u> than do all of the world's rain forests combined, and the garden soil industry is depleting these areas much faster than they can renew themselves.

  Which one of the following principles, if valid, most helps to justify the argument's reasoning?

   (A)   Using a product may be environmentally unsound even if the product is a renewable resource and contains no chemical additive.

   (B)   A practice is not environmentally sound if it significantly reduces the amount of oxygen entering the atmosphere.

   (C)   A practice is environmentally sound if it helps to protect rain forests that contribute large amounts of oxygen to the atmosphere.

   (D)   If the environmental benefits of a practice outweigh the environmental costs, that practice can be legitimately considered environmentally sound.

   (E)   If the practices of an industry threaten a vital resource, those practices should be banned.

Type: Justify
Flaw: Missing Link
Tag: Opposing View Conclusion

<u>Stem</u> – "Justify" tell us this is a Justify problem. Enter the argument looking for its parts and the unlinked concepts.

<u>Stimulus</u> – 1) Find the Conclusion. The conclusion is that using peat moss as a soil conditioner is not environmentally sound. The conclusion is stated bluntly: "they are mistaken." The conclusion argues that the belief that using lots of peat moss is environmentally sound is incorrect.

2) Find the Support. The support is that the moss contributes oxygen to the atmosphere, and the stocks of moss are being depleted.

3) Find the Gap. Something being environmentally unsound is not linked to the concept of oxygen production. Even though these concepts sound compatible, logically they are not the same.

<u>Choices</u> – 1) Eliminate. (A) doesn't mention oxygen production. (B) looks great. (C) also mentions both concepts. (D) does not mention oxygen production, and it is too vague to be correct. (E) talks about banning an industry, but it doesn't mention the concept of environmental soundness.

2) Confirm. Analyze (B) and (C) carefully. (B) directly connects reducing oxygen in the atmosphere to being environmentally unsound. Here's a diagram:

      Reduces oxygen → environmentally unsound

That is the exact connection we need to justify the reasoning. (C) is different. It talks about environmentally sound practices, which is not the concept we need. We need environmentally *unsound* practices. (C) also focuses on rain forests, not oxygen production. For these reasons, (C) is incorrect. Here is what its conditional diagram would look like:

      Protects rainforests → environmentally sound

2. Editorial (**It is clear** that what is called "health education" is usually propaganda rather than education) Propaganda and education are never the same thing. The former is nothing but an attempt to influence behavior through the repetition of simplistic slogans, whereas the latter never involves such a method. Though education does attempt to influence behavior, it does so by offering information in all its complexity, leaving it up to the individual to decide how to act on that information. Sadly, however, propaganda is much more successful than education.

The conclusion drawn by the editorial follows logically if it is assumed that what is called "health education" usually

(A) does not leave it up to the individual to decide how to act on information

(B) does not offer information in all its complexity

(C) does not involve the repetition of simplistic slogans

(D) attempts to influence behavior solely by repeating simplistic slogans

(E) is very successful in influencing people's behavior

Type: Justify
Flaw: Missing Link

Stem – "Conclusion … follows logically" tells you that this is a Justify problem, but this stem is different from everything we've seen before. This stem asks you to complete a sentence that describes "health education," which could be one of our unlinked concepts.

Stimulus – 1) Find the Conclusion. The phrase "it is clear" acts as an indicator for the conclusion. "Health education" is usually propaganda rather than education.

2) Find the Support. Instead of giving you clear support for the conclusion, this argument dives into the differences between propaganda and education. According to our conclusion, "health education" is usually propaganda, so we should focus on the argument's description of propaganda because the stem asked us about "health education."

3) Find the Gap. Because the support doesn't explain what makes "health education" usually propaganda, there is a clear gap between these two unlinked concepts. What does the argument tell us about propaganda? It is never the same thing as education; it is nothing but an attempt to influence behavior through repeating slogans. It is much more successful than education. We need to find a choice that ties "health education" to this description of propaganda.

Choices – 1) Eliminate choices without both unlinked concepts. The stem gave us the unlinked concept of "health education," so we only need to look for choices that describe propaganda. (A) and (B) both describe the opposite of education. We know that education offers information in all its complexity and leaves it up to the individual to decide how to act on information. Although propaganda and education are never the same thing, propaganda is not necessarily the opposite of education. Even if "health education" usually does not leave it up to the individual and usually does not offer information in all its complexity, that doesn't necessarily mean that it is propaganda. There could be many other means of influencing behavior that do neither of those things and are not propaganda. (C) does not describe propaganda at all. In fact, (C) would prove that "health education" is not propaganda. On the other hand, (D) offers a description of propaganda, using a concrete fact about propaganda from the argument. Let's hang onto this one. (E) doesn't necessarily describe propaganda. We know that propaganda is much more successful than education in influencing people's behavior. That doesn't mean that propaganda is the only means to influence behavior that is successful. Education could be a very successful way to influence behavior, too, as long as propaganda is much more successful, relatively speaking.

2) Confirm. (D) is the best choice. Propaganda is nothing but an attempt to influence behavior through the repetition of simplistic slogans. If "health education" attempts to influence behavior solely by repeating simplistic slogans, then "health education" must be propaganda.

3. Although the geological record contains some hints of major meteor impacts preceding mass extinctions, there were many extinctions that did not follow any known major meteor impacts. Likewise, there are many records of major meteor impacts that do not seem to have been followed by mass extinctions. (**Thus** the geological record suggests that there is no consistent causal link between major meteor impacts and mass extinctions.)

J   Which one of the following assumptions enables the argument's conclusion to be properly inferred?

(A) If there were a consistent causal link between major meteor impacts and mass extinctions, then all major meteor impacts would be followed by mass extinctions.

(B) Major meteor impacts and mass extinctions cannot be consistently causally linked unless many mass extinctions have followed major meteor impacts.

(C) Of the mass extinctions that did not follow any known major meteor impacts, few if any followed major meteor impacts of which the geological record contains no hints.

(D) If there is no consistent causal link between major meteor impacts and mass extinctions, then not all mass extinctions could have followed major meteor impacts.

(E) There could be a consistent causal link between major meteor impacts and mass extinctions even if not every major meteor impact has been followed by a mass extinction.

Type: Justify
Flaw: Missing Link

Stem – "Enables the argument's conclusion to be properly inferred" tells you this is a Justify problem.

Stimulus – 1) Find the Conclusion. "Thus" is a nice indicator for the conclusion that the geological record suggests that there is no consistent causal link between major meteor impacts and mass extinctions.

2) Find the Support. There are two key pieces of support: there were many extinctions that did not follow major meteor impacts; and, there are many major meteor impacts that were not followed by mass extinctions. The most important piece of support is the second, though, because our conclusion concerns the causal link between major meteor impacts and mass extinctions. It doesn't matter if extinctions occurred without a meteor impact. We're only concerned with what happened following a meteor impact.

3) Find the Gap. The gap on this problem is pretty obvious. Our unlinked concepts are major meteor impacts that were not followed by mass extinctions and no consistent causal link between major meteor impacts and mass extinctions. To support the conclusion, these two unlinked concepts form a nice conditional. If many some meteor impacts were not followed by mass extinctions, then there is no consistent causal link between

major meteor impacts and mass extinctions. Let's see if that shows up in the choices.

Choices – 1) Eliminate choices without both unlinked concepts. (A) might look like it doesn't include our unlinked concepts, but it's actually the contrapositive of the conditional we just put together. Hang onto (A), and let's look through the remaining choices. (B) looks to include both concepts, so let's remember how to work with unless. (B) says this: if many mass extinctions did not follow meteor impacts, then there is no consistent causal link. That doesn't include both unlinked concepts. We're not concerned with mass extinctions that did not follow meteor impacts. (C) doesn't talk about either concept. It discusses mass extinctions that followed major meteor impacts, but it's not specific enough to our unlinked concepts. (D) mentions no consistent causal link between major meteor impacts and mass extinctions, but it fails to mention major meteor impacts that were not followed by mass extinctions. We're not concerned with mass extinctions that did not follow meteor impacts because that has nothing to do with our cause and effect relationship. (E) seems to include both unlinked concepts, so we'll want to keep it as well.

2) Confirm. We're left with (A) and (E). Let's look at (E) first. (E) sort of undermines our argument. We need to prove that there is no consistent causal link between major meteor impacts and mass extinctions. If (E) were true, then our conclusion isn't valid. We wouldn't have any information explaining that there is no consistent causal link if some major meteor impacts were not followed by mass extinctions. On the other hand, (A) provides the contrapositive of the conditional that we thought could fill out gap. If some major meteor impacts were not followed by mass extinctions, then there is no consistent causal link between the two. If there were a consistent causal link, then all major meteor impacts would be followed by mass extinctions. That's pretty nice, and (A) is correct.

4. If Skiff's book is published this year, Professor Nguyen vows she will urge the dean to promote Skiff. (Thus, if Skiff's book is as important and as well written as Skiff claims, he will be promoted,) for Nguyen will certainly keep her promise, and the dean will surely promote Skiff if Nguyen recommends it.

J   The argument's conclusion can be properly inferred if which one of the following is assumed?

(A) Skiff's book will be published this year if it is as important as he claims it is.

(B) Skiff needs to publish a book before he can be promoted.

(C) Professor Nguyen believes that Skiff's book is well written.

(D) Skiff's book will not be published unless it is as important and as well written as he claims it is.

(E) Skiff will not be promoted unless Professor Nguyen urges the dean to do so.

Type: Justify
Flaw: Missing Link
Tag: Soft Conclusion

Stem – "Properly inferred" and "is assumed" tell us this is a Justify problem.

Stimulus – 1) Find the Conclusion. "Thus" at the beginning of the second sentence tells you that the conclusion is "if skiffs book is as important and well written as he claims, he will be promoted." The "for" later in that sentence tells you that support is coming and the conclusion is done. This is a conditional conclusion.

2) Find the Support. There are three pieces of support spread across the first sentence and the end of the second sentence. Basically, the entire passage that is not the conclusion is support. You don't need to dissect the support too much.

3) Find the Gap. When you read the first sentence and the conclusion, the concepts that do not link should become clear. The argument jumps from the book being published (part of the support in the first sentence) to the book being important and well written. Those are not the same thing, but the test writers hope you will not notice that concept switch.

Choices – 1) Eliminate. (A) has both "book is published" and "book is as important as he says," your two concepts. Keep it. (B) does not have the book is important concept. It sounds like (C) contains the well-written concept, but it actually does not; that piece is that the book is as well written as Skiff says it is. Also, (C) doesn't contain the published concept. (D) has both concepts, so keep it. (E) has neither concept.

2) Confirm. Let's take a closer look at our two remaining choices. (A) doesn't need to have the "as well written" part of the concept because it tells you that the fact that the book is as important as he says is *sufficient* for it to get published. Here's the diagram for (A):

important as he says → published

Knowing that, if the book is important, it gets published is all you need to link the concepts correctly and make the argument valid. Here is how that works: if you know the book is published, you know that Nguyen will urge the dean to promote and the dean will promote him if urged.

(D) doesn't connect both concepts in the right way. It says that in order for the book to be published, it must be as important and well written as he says. Diagram:

published → important & well written

The choice only gives us a requirement for publication; it doesn't tell us that the book being as important and well written as he says is sufficient for publication. (A) does just that.

Set 5

This is a very difficult Set, so take your time on each problem and be careful with the choice you select.

Techniques Summary

- Core focus: Find Gap.
- Stimulus:
    - Bracket the conclusion and find the support.
    - Then, find the two unlinked concepts.
- Choices: Eliminate choices that do not fill the gap.

1. Dried parsley should never be used in cooking, for it is far less tasty and healthful than fresh parsley is.

    Which one of the following principles, if valid, most clearly helps to justify the argument above?

    (A)   Fresh ingredients should be used in cooking whenever possible.

    (B)   Only the tastiest ingredients should ever be used in cooking.

    (C)   Ingredients that should never be used in cooking are generally neither tasty nor healthful.

    (D)   Parsley that is not both tasty and healthful should never be used in cooking.

    (E)   In cooking, dried ingredients are inferior to fresh ingredients.

2. Scientist: Physicists claim that their system of careful peer review prevents scientific fraud in physics effectively. But biologists claimed the same thing for their field 20 years ago, and they turned out to be wrong. Since then, biologists have greatly enhanced their discipline's safeguards against scientific fraud, thus preventing further major incidents. It would be conducive to progress in physics if physicists were to do the same thing.

    The conclusion of the scientist's argument is most strongly supported if which one of the following is assumed?

    (A)   Major incidents of scientific fraud in a scientific discipline are deleterious to progress in that discipline.

    (B)   Very few incidents of even minor scientific fraud have occurred in biology over the last 20 years.

    (C)   No system of careful peer review is completely effective in preventing scientific fraud in any scientific discipline.

    (D)   Twenty years ago the system of peer review in biology was less effective in preventing scientific fraud than the system of peer review in physics is today.

    (E)   Over the years, there have been relatively few, if any, major incidents of scientific fraud in physics.

3. Acquiring complete detailed information about all the pros and cons of a product one might purchase would clearly be difficult and expensive. It is rational not to acquire such information unless one expects that the benefits of doing so will outweigh the cost and difficulty of doing so. Therefore, consumers who do not bother to acquire such information are thereby behaving rationally.

The conclusion of the argument is properly drawn if which one of the following is assumed?

(A) Rational consumers who do not expect that the benefits outweigh the cost and difficulty of acquiring detailed information about a product they might purchase usually do not bother to acquire such information.

(B) Whenever it is rational not to acquire detailed information about a product, it would be irrational to bother to acquire such information.

(C) The benefits of acquiring detailed information about a product one might purchase usually do not outweigh the cost and difficulty of doing so.

(D) Rational consumers usually expect that the benefits of acquiring detailed information about a product they might purchase would not outweigh the cost and difficulty of doing so.

(E) Consumers who do not bother to acquire complete detailed information about a product they might purchase do not expect that the benefits of acquiring such information will outweigh the cost and difficulty of doing so.

4. Ethicist: Marital vows often contain the promise to love "until death do us part." If "love" here refers to a feeling, then this promise makes no sense, for feelings are not within one's control, and a promise to do something not within one's control makes no sense. Thus, no one—including those making marital vows—should take "love" in this context to be referring to feelings.

The ethicist's conclusion follows logically if which one of the following is assumed?

(A) None of our feelings are within our control.

(B) People should not make promises to do something that is not within their control.

(C) "Love" can legitimately be taken to refer to something other than feelings.

(D) Promises should not be interpreted in such a way that they make no sense.

(E) Promises that cannot be kept do not make any sense.

END OF SET

Set 5 Key & Explanations

Review these problems *very* thoroughly. Out of the entire Set, you'll get the most learning out of reviewing and mastering these super-difficult problems.

    1. B

    2. A

    3. E

    4. D

1. (Dried parsley should <u>never be used in cooking</u>,)for it is far <u>less tasty and healthful than fresh</u> parsley is.

J   Which one of the following principles, if valid, most clearly helps to justify the argument above?

    (A)   Fresh ingredients should be used in cooking whenever possible.

    (B)   Only the tastiest ingredients should ever be used in cooking.

    (C)   Ingredients that should never be used in cooking are generally neither tasty nor healthful.

    (D)   Parsley that is not both tasty and healthful should never be used in cooking.

    (E)   In cooking, dried ingredients are inferior to fresh ingredients.

Type: Justify
Flaw: Missing Link

Stem – "Justify" tell us this is a Justify problem. Enter the argument looking for its parts and the unlinked concepts.

Stimulus – 1) Find the Conclusion. "For" in the middle of the sentence indicates the *support* follows. That means that what came before "for" is the conclusion: dried parsley should never be used in cooking.

2) Find the Support. Dried parsley is less tasty and healthful than fresh.

3) Find the Gap. We are told two ways that dried parsley is inferior to fresh, but neither of those is directly connected to *never using it* in cooking. The first concept is a comparison: "less tasty" does not mean the same thing as "not tasty." This may be important in the choices.

Choices – 1) Eliminate. (A) – "Used whenever possible" is not strong enough, as we need something that tells when it is not okay to use ingredients. (B) looks good because it limits the ingredients in cooking to the tastiest. Keep it. (C) talks about ingredients that are not tasty or healthful. It contains an absolute value for the ingredients, not a relative one like the support of the argument, so eliminate it. (D) does the same thing as (C). (E) contains a relative comparison, but it neglects to mention not using the ingredients in cooking, which is a concept we need.

Being clear that one of the concepts was a relative comparison was important in knowing which choices to eliminate.

2) Confirm. (B) says that you shouldn't use ingredients that are not the tastiest in cooking. That provides the link you need. If dried parsley is not the tastiest version of parsley, then it should never be used in cooking. This successfully connects the support to the conclusion.

The correct choice didn't mention being less healthful at all. That is fine because the fact that dried parsley should never be used in cooking is fully established through the link talking about tastiness. The principle connects that quality alone to never being used in cooking.

Below are the conditional diagrams for the support, link and conclusion.

Support:

    dried parsley → less tasty & healthful

Link:

    less tasty → never used in cooking

Conclusion:

    dried parsley → never used in cooking

2. Scientist: Physicists claim that their system of careful peer review prevents scientific fraud in physics effectively. But biologists claimed the same thing for their field 20 years ago, and they turned out to be wrong. Since then, biologists have greatly enhanced their discipline's safeguards against scientific fraud, thus <u>preventing further major incidents</u> (It would be <u>conducive to progress in physics</u> if physicists were to do the same thing.)

The conclusion of the scientist's argument is most strongly supported if which one of the following is assumed?

(A) Major incidents of scientific fraud in a scientific discipline are deleterious to progress in that discipline.

(B) Very few incidents of even minor scientific fraud have occurred in biology over the last 20 years.

(C) No system of careful peer review is completely effective in preventing scientific fraud in any scientific discipline.

(D) Twenty years ago the system of peer review in biology was less effective in preventing scientific fraud than the system of peer review in physics is today.

(E) Over the years, there have been relatively few, if any, major incidents of scientific fraud in physics.

Type: Justify
Flaw: Missing Link

Stem – The stem asks you which choice most strongly supports the argument, so this is a classic Justify stem.

Stimulus – 1) Find the Conclusion. This argument's conclusion comes at the very end. It would be conducive to progress in physics if physicists followed the lead of biologists by greatly enhancing safeguards against scientific fraud.

2) Find the Support. The key support is that 20 years ago biologists – like physicists – utilized a system of peer review, but it did not prevent scientific fraud effectively. Since then, biologists have worked hard to protect against scientific fraud, and they have been able to prevent major incidents of scientific fraud.

3) Find the Gap. There is pretty obvious gap in the logic here. If physicists do the same thing that biologists have done over the past 20 years, then they would enhance their safeguards against scientific fraud, which would likely prevent major incidents. But what does that have to do with progress in physics? The gap is between major incidents of scientific fraud and progress in that field. More than likely, we'll need to find a choice that explains that preventing those major incidents helps bolster progress. Or by contrast, we may find a choice that shows that major incidents of scientific fraud stifle progress.

Choices – 1) Eliminate choices without both unlinked concepts. (A) mentions both major incidents of scientific fraud and progress, so let's hang onto this choice. (B) talks about minor incidents of scientific fraud, which is a very different concept from major incidents of scientific fraud. There is also no mention of progress. (C) misses the mark completely. We know that peer review is not effective for preventing scientific fraud because it did not work for biologists, but that doesn't support our conclusion because it doesn't mention our unlinked concepts. (D) is similar in that it doesn't mention the unlinked concepts, so it doesn't attempt to fill the gap and will probably not give us the support we need for this argument. (E) mentions major incidents of scientific fraud, but it has nothing about progress. If anything, (E) might undermine our argument. If there aren't major incidents, then why should physicists follow the lead of biologists and enhance their safeguards against scientific fraud?

2) Confirm. After elimination, the only choice remaining is (A), which does an excellent job of filling our gap. If major incidents of scientific fraud are deleterious to progress, then physicists should enhance their safeguards against scientific fraud to promote progress. In this way, we now have a link between progress in physics and major incidents of scientific fraud, which is exactly what we need to make this argument 100% airtight.

3. Acquiring complete detailed information about all the pros and cons of a product one might purchase would clearly be difficult and expensive. It is <u>rational not to acquire such</u> information unless one expects that the <u>benefits</u> of doing so will outweigh the cost and difficulty of doing so. **Therefore** (consumers who do not bother to acquire such information are thereby behaving rationally)

    The **conclusion of the argument is properly** drawn if which one of the following is assumed?

    (A) Rational consumers who do not expect that the benefits outweigh the cost and difficulty of acquiring detailed information about a product they might purchase usually do not bother to acquire such information.

    (B) Whenever it is rational not to acquire detailed information about a product, it would be irrational to bother to acquire such information.

    (C) The benefits of acquiring detailed information about a product one might purchase usually do not outweigh the cost and difficulty of doing so.

    (D) Rational consumers usually expect that the benefits of acquiring detailed information about a product they might purchase would not outweigh the cost and difficulty of doing so.

    (E) Consumers who do not bother to acquire complete detailed information about a product they might purchase do not expect that the benefits of acquiring such information will outweigh the cost and difficulty of doing so.

Type: Justify
Flaw: Missing Link
Tags: Dropped Concept

<u>Stem</u> – The stem asks you to determine which answer allows the conclusion to be properly drawn, which is a Justify stem.

<u>Stimulus</u> – 1) Find the Conclusion. Consumers who do not bother to acquire information about a product are acting rationally in not doing so. Note the indicator "therefore."

2) Find the Support. The support states that acquiring this info is difficult and expensive. And it also says that it's rational not to collect this information, except in a case where the benefits of collecting the data would outweigh the costs and difficulties of collecting it.

3) Find the Gap. This argument has a Dropped Concept: the idea that it's not rational to not collect data on a product if the benefits outweigh the costs of doing so. The argument says that it's rational not to collect information about the pros and cons of a product unless you expect that there will be benefits to collecting that information. Then, it concludes that those who don't collect the info are rational. But what happened to the expected benefits? The argument has a Missing Link between the rationality of not acquiring info and the idea that one should acquire the information if you can expect to benefit from that knowledge.

<u>Choices</u> – The correct answer will link the idea that consumers who don't collect the information are rational and the idea that it's rational to collect information on a product if you expect to benefit from having done so. Basically, you need an answer that qualifies the rational consumer. It's only rational not to collect the information if you don't see any benefit from it.

1) Eliminate. (A) is a wordy little dingus. It says that rational customers who don't think the benefits outweigh the cost of getting info usually don't get that info. This choice focuses on the wrong group of people; it talks about people who *don't expect* any benefits from collecting data on a product, but you need an answer that talks about people who *don't collect* data because that's what the conclusion is about. It's a small difference in wording, but it's a big difference in meaning. (B) says that it would be irrational to bother to acquire information in a situation where you know that it's rational *not* to acquire that information. That doesn't talk about the idea of *expecting benefit* from acquiring information, so it's out. (C) says that the benefits usually don't outweigh the costs, but that's irrelevant because the argument is about whether or not people *expect* the benefits to outweigh the costs, not if they actual do outweigh the costs. (D) says that rational consumers *usually* expect the benefits of acquiring information to outweigh the costs, but the argument never talks about what customers do often or infrequently. (E) says that customer who don't acquire info don't expect there to be benefits for doing so. This connects the Unlinked Concepts; move on to confirm it.

2) Confirm. (E) says that those who don't bother getting the information don't expect any benefit from getting that information. This connects the Dropped Concept to the conclusion—not gathering info is only rational if you don't expect a benefit. That's your Missing Link. (E) is correct.

4. Ethicist: Marital vows often contain the promise to love "until death do us part." If "love" here refers to a feeling, then this promise makes no sense, for feelings are not within one's control, and a promise to do something not within one's control makes no sense. (**Thus**, no one—including those making marital vows—should take "love" in this context to be referring to feelings.)

The ethicist's conclusion follows logically if which one of the following is assumed?

  (A)   None of our feelings are within our control.

  (B)   People should not make promises to do something that is not within their control.

  (C)   "Love" can legitimately be taken to refer to something other than feelings.

(D)   Promises should not be interpreted in such a way that they make no sense.

  (E)   Promises that cannot be kept do not make any sense.

Type: Justify
Flaw: Missing Link

Stem – "Conclusion follows logically" tells you this is a Justify problem. Be ready to identify the parts of the argument.

Stimulus – 1) Find the Conclusion. "Thus" is a nice indicator for the conclusion, but this conclusion is a little complicated. In the context of a promise, no one should take "love" as referring to feelings. It's important to understand that the conclusion means that no one should *interpret* "love" as referring to feelings in that specific context of a promise.

2) Find the Support. The second sentence of the argument provides the crux of the primary support. A promise to do something not within one's control makes no sense. "Love" often refers to a feeling, and feelings are not within one's control. If "love" refers to a feeling in the context of a marital vow, then the promise makes no sense because any promise to do something not within one's control makes no sense. It's a pretty complicated piece of support, but the key is understanding that a promise to do something one can't control makes no sense and that feelings (i.e. "love") are not within one's control.

3) Find the Gap. In this argument, the gap may not seem altogether obvious. From a simple perspective, the conclusion might seem to follow logically from the support, but this is an LSAT problem, so we need to examine it further. If someone interpreted "love" in a promise as referring to a feeling, then that promise would not make sense. So why shouldn't they do that? There's our gap; the argument doesn't tell us that no one should think that "love" refers to a feeling in this context. It might seem simple that no one should do that, but we need a piece of information that says just that to make this conclusion valid. The choices will probably not be as explicit, so we need to just look for something that tells us people should not make promises that don't make sense.

Choices – 1) On this problem, we probably won't be able to simply eliminate choices without both unlinked concepts because our unlinked concepts are not clearly defined. Instead, we need to look for a choice that tells us that promises should not be understood in a way that they make no sense. (A) misses the mark. The argument already tells us that feelings are not within our control, so we don't need (A) to prove our conclusion. (B) is close, but let's see if something comes up that is more specific to the conclusion. (C) stretches beyond what we know. The argument only refers to "love" as it refers to a feeling. That doesn't necessarily mean that "love" can't be more than just a feeling, but our conclusion refers to "love" in this specific context of a feeling. So, (C) doesn't support our conclusion whatsoever. (D) is very nice on the other hand. Promises should not be interpreted in such a way that they make no sense. If "love" is used in the context of a feeling, then the promise is interpreted in a way that makes no sense. This is exactly what we need. By contrast, (E) pushes us toward a New Concept: keeping promises. The argument doesn't have any concern with whether or not a promise can be kept; we're only worried about whether or not a promise makes sense.

2) Confirm. (D) is the best choice to support our conclusion. We liked the look of (B) initially, but the conclusion is about the understanding of a promise. Because the conclusion is not talking about making promises, (B) doesn't give us the support we need. On the other hand, (D) helps fill the gap, and it is correct.

Justify Test Set

Practice your Justify techniques with time pressure.

Directions

- Time Limit: There is a 15-minute time limit for this 11-problem set. Pace with your watch and set a timer. Guess on any problems you do not reach, just as you will on the official LSAT.

- Mark problems you are unsure of as you attempt the set.

- Bubble Sheet: Like all timed sets, fill in your answers in the bubble sheet for this Test Set.

- Review: Review only problems that you answered incorrectly and those that you marked as unsure. First self-review each problem, then carefully read the explanation.

1. Guideline: It is improper for public officials to influence the award of contracts or to perform other acts related to their office in a way that benefits themselves. Even the appearance of such impropriety should be avoided.

    Application: Greenville's mayor acted improperly in urging the award of the city's street maintenance contract to a company owned and operated by one of the mayor's relatives, whose business would have been in serious financial trouble had it not been awarded the contract.

    Which one of the following principles most helps in justifying the application of the guideline?

    (A)   Public officials, when fulfilling their duties, should be held to higher standards than private individuals.

    (B)   Publicly funded contracts should be awarded based primarily on cost and the reliability of the contractor.

    (C)   Creating the appearance of impropriety is as blameworthy as acting improperly.

    (D)   Awarding a contract to a financially troubled business should be regarded as taking excessive risk.

    (E)   Benefiting one's family or friends should be regarded as benefiting oneself.

2. Geneticist: Billions of dollars are spent each year on high-profile experiments that attempt to link particular human genes with particular personality traits. Though such experiments seem to promise a new understanding of human nature, they have few practical consequences. Meanwhile, more mundane and practical genetic projects—for example, those that look for natural ways to make edible plants hardier or more nutritious—are grossly underfunded. Thus, funding for human gene research should be reduced while funding for other genetic research should be increased.

    Which one of the following principles, if valid, most helps to justify the geneticist's reasoning?

    (A)   Experiments that have the potential to help the whole human race are more worthwhile than those that help only a small number of people.

    (B)   Experiments that focus on the genetics of plants are more practical than those that focus on the genetics of human nature.

    (C)   Experiments that help prevent malnutrition are more worthwhile than those that help prevent merely undesirable personality traits.

    (D)   Experiments that have modest but practical goals are more worthwhile than those that have impressive goals but few practical consequences.

    (E)   Experiments that get little media attention and are not widely supported by the public are more valuable than are those that get much media coverage and have wide public support.

3. For each action we perform, we can know only some of its consequences. Thus the view that in no situation can we know what action is morally right would be true if an action's being morally right were the same as the action's having the best consequences.

The conclusion follows logically if which one of the following is assumed?

(A) On some occasions we can come to learn that it is morally wrong to perform a certain action.

(B) On some occasions we can know what action is morally right.

(C) Knowing that an action has the best consequences requires knowing all the consequences of that action.

(D) Only the immediate consequences of our actions are relevant in determining whether they are morally right.

(E) An action may be morally right for one particular person without being morally right for all people.

4. Principle: Employees of telemarketing agencies should never do anything that predisposes people to dislike the agencies' clients.

Application: If an employee of a telemarketing agency has been told by a person the employee has called that he or she does not want to buy the product of a client of the agency, the employee should not try to talk that person into doing so.

Which one of the following, if true, justifies the given application of the principle above?

(A) Any employee of a telemarketing agency is likely to be able to determine whether trying to talk someone into buying the product of a client of the agency after the person has said that he or she does not want to will likely engender animosity toward the client.

(B) Some employees of telemarketing agencies are unlikely to be certain about whether trying to talk someone into buying the product of a client of the agency after the person has said that he or she does not want to will likely engender animosity toward the client.

(C) Any employee of a telemarketing agency who tries to get someone to buy the product of a client of the agency after the person has said that he or she does not want to will engender animosity toward the client.

(D) Some people that an employee of a telemarketing agency calls to ask them to buy the product of a client of the agency will refuse to do so even though they are not predisposed to dislike the client.

(E) People who are already predisposed to dislike the client of a telemarketing agency are more likely to refuse to buy the product of that client than are people who are predisposed to like the client.

5. Doctor: It is wrong for medical researchers to keep their research confidential, even if the companies for which they work would rather that they do so. If research results are not shared, the development of effective medical treatments may be delayed, and thus humans may suffer unnecessarily.

Which one of the following principles, if valid, most helps to justify the doctor's argument?

(A) Medical researchers should never engage in any behavior that they know will cause humans to suffer.

(B) If the most important moral principle is to prevent human suffering, then it is wrong for medical researchers to keep their research confidential.

(C) Medical researchers should not keep information confidential if it is possible that sharing that information would prevent some unnecessary human suffering.

(D) Medical researchers should always attempt to develop effective medical treatments as rapidly as they can while fulfilling their other moral obligations.

(E) It is wrong for any company to ask its medical researchers to keep their research confidential, if failure to share the research might delay development of effective medical treatments.

6. The only preexisting recordings that are transferred onto compact disc are those that record companies believe will sell well enough on compact disc to be profitable. So, most classic jazz recordings will not be transferred onto compact disc, because few classic jazz recordings are played on the radio.

The conclusion above follows logically if which one of the following is assumed?

(A) Few of the preexisting recordings that record companies believe can be profitably transferred to compact disc are classic jazz recordings.

(B) Few compact discs featuring classic jazz recordings are played on the radio.

(C) The only recordings that are played on the radio are ones that record companies believe can be profitably sold as compact discs.

(D) Most record companies are less interested in preserving classic jazz recordings than in making a profit.

(E) No recording that is not played on the radio is one that record companies believe would be profitable if transferred to compact disc.

7. Resident: Residents of this locale should not consider their loss of farming as a way of life to be a tragedy. When this area was a rural area it was economically depressed, but it is now a growing bastion of high-tech industry with high-wage jobs, and supports over 20 times the number of jobs it did then.

Which one of the following, if true, does the most to justify the conclusion of the resident's argument?

(A) Farming is becoming increasingly efficient, with the result that fewer farms are required to produce the same amount of food.

(B) The development of high-tech industry is more valuable to national security than is farming.

(C) Residents of this locale do not value a rural way of life more than they value economic prosperity.

(D) Many residents of this locale have annual incomes that are twice what they were when the locale was primarily agricultural.

(E) The loss of a family farm is often perceived as tragic even when no financial hardship results.

8. Because no other theory has been able to predict it so simply and accurately, the advance of the perihelion of Mercury is sometimes cited as evidence in support of Einstein's theory of general relativity. However, this phenomenon was already well known when Einstein developed his theory, and he quite probably adjusted his equations to generate the correct numbers for the perihelion advance. Therefore, accounting for this advance should not be counted as evidence in support of Einstein's theory.

Which one of the following principles, if valid, most helps to justify the argument above?

(A) Unless a phenomenon predicted by a scientific theory is unknown at the time the theory is developed, the theory should not be credited with the discovery of that phenomenon.

(B) A phenomenon that is predicted by a scientific theory should not count as evidence in favor of that theory unless the theory was developed with that phenomenon in mind.

(C) Unless a theory can accurately account for all relevant phenomena that are already well known at the time of its development, it cannot be regarded as well supported.

(D) If a theory is adjusted specifically to account for some particular phenomenon, a match between that theory and that phenomenon should not count as evidence in favor of the theory.

(E) If a theory is adjusted to generate the correct predictions for some phenomenon that is already known to the scientist developing the theory, the theory should not be counted as predicting that phenomenon.

9. Principle: Only if a professor believes a student knowingly presented someone else's ideas without attribution should the professor make an official determination that the student has committed plagiarism.

Application: It is not the case that Professor Serfin should make an official determination that Walters committed plagiarism in the term paper about Willa Cather that Walters wrote for Serfin's class.

Which one of the following, if true, justifies the above application of the principle?

(A) Professor Serfin does not have completely compelling evidence to conclude that Walters presented someone else's ideas as if they were his own in the term paper about Willa Cather.

(B) If Walters had realized that the main thesis of his term paper is identical to the main thesis of a book he had read, Walters would have attributed the idea to the book.

(C) Although the main thesis of Walters's term paper is identical to that of a book that he did not cite, Professor Serfin is convinced that Walters did not knowingly try to pass anyone else's ideas off as his own.

(D) Walters does not believe that Professor Serfin should make an official determination that he plagiarized.

(E) Professor Serfin has no intention of making an official determination that Walters plagiarized in the class.

10. Judge: The defendant admits noncompliance with national building codes but asks that penalties not be imposed because he was confused as to whether national or local building codes applied to the area in which he was building. This excuse might be acceptable had he been charged with noncompliance with local codes, but since he is charged with noncompliance with national codes, his excuse is unacceptable.

Which one of the following principles, if valid, most helps to justify the judge's reasoning?

(A) Local codes and national codes must not overlap with each other.

(B) Local codes may be less strict, but not more strict, than national codes.

(C) Any behavior required by national codes is also required by local codes.

(D) Ignorance of the difference between two codes is not an adequate excuse for noncompliance.

(E) A behavior that is in compliance with one law is not necessarily in compliance with another.

11. Physician: The rise in blood pressure that commonly accompanies aging often results from a calcium deficiency. This deficiency is frequently caused by a deficiency in the active form of vitamin D needed in order for the body to absorb calcium. Since the calcium in one glass of milk per day can easily make up for any underlying calcium deficiency, some older people can lower their blood pressure by drinking milk.

The physician's conclusion is properly drawn if which one of the following is assumed?

(A) There is in milk, in a form that older people can generally utilize, enough of the active form of vitamin D and any other substances needed in order for the body to absorb the calcium in that milk.

(B) Milk does not contain any substance that is likely to cause increased blood pressure in older people.

(C) Older people's drinking one glass of milk per day does not contribute to a deficiency in the active form of vitamin D needed in order for the body to absorb the calcium in that milk.

(D) People who consume high quantities of calcium together with the active form of vitamin D and any other substances needed in order for the body to absorb calcium have normal blood pressure.

(E) Anyone who has a deficiency in the active form of vitamin D also has a calcium deficiency.

END OF SET

Test Set Key

Nice job completing the Justify Test Set. Check your work with the Key below.

1. E
2. D
3. C
4. C
5. C
6. E
7. C
8. D
9. C
10. C
11. A

Test Set Explanations

1. Guideline: It is improper for public officials to influence the award of contracts or to perform other acts related to their office in a way that <u>benefits themselves</u>. Even the appearance of such impropriety should be avoided.

    Application (Greenville's mayor acted improperly in urging the award of the city's street maintenance contract to a company owned and operated by one of the mayor's relatives) whose business would have <u>been in serious financial trouble had it not been awarded the contract.</u>

    Which one of the following principles most helps in justifying the application of the guideline?

    (A) Public officials, when fulfilling their duties, should be held to higher standards than private individuals.

    (B) Publicly funded contracts should be awarded based primarily on cost and the reliability of the contractor.

    (C) Creating the appearance of impropriety is as blameworthy as acting improperly.

    (D) Awarding a contract to a financially troubled business should be regarded as taking excessive risk.

    (E) Benefiting one's family or friends should be regarded as benefiting oneself.

Type: Justify
Flaw: Missing Link
Tag: Principle & Application

Stem – This is a classic Justify stem, and more specifically this problem uses a Principle and Application stimulus. That should help us as we identify the parts of the argument.

Stimulus – 1) Find the Conclusion. When we see the Principle and Application setup, we know that the conclusion comes in the application. The conclusion is simple: Greenville's mayor acted improperly in urging the award of a contract to a company owned by one of the mayor's relatives.

2) Find the Support. In many Principle and Application setups, the primary support comes in the "principle" section (or in the case of this problem, the "guideline"). In this argument, the key support for the mayor acting improperly is that the contract benefited one of the mayor's relatives, whose business would have been in rough shape without the contract.

3) Find the Gap. The argument's conclusion tells us that the mayor acted improperly in awarding a contract that benefited a relative. The "guideline" section of the argument helps us see the gap. We know that it is improper for public officials to act in a way that benefits themselves. That is the only definition we know of what constitutes improper behavior. In this example, though, the mayor acted in a way that benefited a relative, so why is that

improper? There's our gap. Our two unlinked concepts are benefiting oneself and benefiting a relative. If we can find something in the choices that connects the two, we'll be able to make this argument valid.

Choices – 1) Eliminate choices without both unlinked concepts. (A) doesn't really come close. (B) talks about awarding contracts based on cost and reliability of the contractor, which has nothing to do with whether or not the public official or a relative benefit from the contract. (C) discusses the appearance of impropriety, but we're talking about a specific instance in which a public official acted improperly. (D) talks about awarding a contract to a financially troubled business, which the mayor clearly did, but we're concerned about the mayor's personal benefitting from the contract. On the other hand, (E) is the only choice that mentions both of our unlinked concepts.

2) Confirm. After elimination, we're left with (E), which provides the support we need for this conclusion. If benefiting one's family should be regarded as benefiting oneself, then the mayor clearly acted improperly in awarding a contract to help a relative's business.

2. Geneticist: Billions of dollars are spent each year on high-profile experiments that attempt to link particular human genes with particular personality traits. Though such experiments seem to promise a new understanding of human nature, <u>they have few practical consequences</u>. Meanwhile, more mundane and practical genetic projects—for example, those that look for natural ways to make edible plants hardier or more nutritious—are grossly underfunded. (**Thus**, <u>funding for human gene research should be reduced while funding for other genetic research should be increased.</u>)

Which one of the following principles, if valid, most helps to justify the geneticist's reasoning?

(A) Experiments that have the potential to help the whole human race are more worthwhile than those that help only a small number of people.

(B) Experiments that focus on the genetics of plants are more practical than those that focus on the genetics of human nature.

(C) Experiments that help prevent malnutrition are more worthwhile than those that help prevent merely undesirable personality traits.

(D) Experiments that have modest but practical goals are more worthwhile than those that have impressive goals but few practical consequences.

(E) Experiments that get little media attention and are not widely supported by the public are more valuable than are those that get much media coverage and have wide public support.

Type: Justify
Flaw: Missing Link

<u>Stem</u> – "Most helps to justify" tells you this is a Justify problem.

<u>Stimulus</u> – 1) Find the Conclusion. The indicator "thus" helps direct you to the argument's conclusion. Funding for human gene research should be reduced while funding for other genetic research should be increased.

2) Find the Support. Although human gene research seems to promise a new understanding of human nature, these experiments have few practical consequences. By contrast, more mundane genetic projects are more practical and are grossly underfunded.

3) Find the Gap. On this problem, there is a clear gap between appropriating funding and the practicality of genetic experiments. The conclusion argues that funding for human genetic research – which has few practical consequences – should be reduced. By contrast, funding for other genetic research – which is more mundane but also more practical – should be increased. So, our two unlinked concepts are experiments being worthy of funding and the practicality of those experiments. To fill our gap, we need something that explains that more practical experiments are worthy of more funding than less practical experiments even when those less practical experiments might have loftier goals.

<u>Choices</u> – 1) Eliminate choices without both unlinked concepts. (A) discusses the scope of experiments and their potential to help people. That doesn't tie into either of our concepts. (B) discusses the practicality of some genetics experiments, but it has nothing to do with funding. (C) discusses experiments that are more worthwhile. An experiment that is more worthwhile would be more worthy of funding, but that doesn't really concern the practicality of the experiments as explicitly as we need. (D) talks about experiments with practical goals being more worthwhile than those with few practical consequences. Although (D) doesn't mention funding specifically, "worthwhile" gives us what we need to cover that concept. Hang onto (D). (E) mentions the value of experiments, which ties into our concept of funding. Nevertheless, media attention and public support have nothing to do with our unlinked concept of the practicality of experiments, so this choice misses the mark.

2) Confirm. After elimination, we're left with (D), which gives us the support we need for this conclusion. If more practical experiments are more worthwhile than those with few practical consequences, then the more practical experiments deserve more funding while those with impressive but impractical goals deserve less. That's exactly what we need to fill the gap.

3. For each action we perform, we can <u>know only some of its</u> <u>consequences</u>(**Thus** the view that in no situation can we know what action is morally right would be true if an action's being morally right were the same as the action's <u>having the best consequences.</u>)

J   The **conclusion follows logically** if which one of the following is assumed?

 (A)   On some occasions we can come to learn that it is morally wrong to perform a certain action.

 (B)   On some occasions we can know what action is morally right.

(C)   Knowing that an action has the best consequences requires knowing all the consequences of that action.

 (D)   Only the immediate consequences of our actions are relevant in determining whether they are morally right.

 (E)   An action may be morally right for one particular person without being morally right for all people.

Type: Justify
Flaw: Missing Link
Tag: Soft Conclusion, Conditionals

<u>Stem</u> – "Conclusion follows logically" tells us that this is a Justify problem.

<u>Stimulus</u> – 1) Find the Conclusion. "Thus" indicates that the final sentence is the conclusion. It is a Soft Conclusion: we can never know that an action is morally right in a situation *if* being morally right is the same as having the best consequences. That latter half about best consequences is basically support tied up in the conclusion.

2) Find the Support. This comes in the first sentence; it is that we can only know some of the consequences of actions we perform.

3) Find the Gap. The support concept that we can only know some of the consequences of an action is unconnected to the concept in the conclusion about having the best consequences. The correct answer will link these two concepts.

<u>Choices</u> – 1) Eliminate. (A) doesn't mention best consequences. (B) provides a different, opposite conclusion to the stimulus, so it cannot be correct. (C) links the two concepts we need to link, so keep it. (D) doesn't talk about either of our unlinked concepts. (E) is vague and doesn't affect the conclusion.

2) Confirm. (C) links the concepts of best consequences to knowing all the consequences from the support. Here is its diagram:

Action best conseq. → knowing all conseq.

This links makes the conclusion valid by showing that an action being morally right means knowing all the consequences of an action, which we are told is not possible. (C) is correct.

4. Principle: Employees of telemarketing agencies should never do anything that predisposes people to dislike the agencies' clients.

Application: (If an employee of a telemarketing agency has been told by a person the employee has called that he or she does not want to buy the product of a client of the agency, the employee should not try to talk that person into doing so.)

J Which one of the following, if true, justifies the given application of the principle above?

(A) Any employee of a telemarketing agency is likely to be able to determine whether trying to talk someone into buying the product of a client of the agency after the person has said that he or she does not want to will likely engender animosity toward the client.

(B) Some employees of telemarketing agencies are unlikely to be certain about whether trying to talk someone into buying the product of a client of the agency after the person has said that he or she does not want to will likely engender animosity toward the client.

(C) Any employee of a telemarketing agency who tries to get someone to buy the product of a client of the agency after the person has said that he or she does not want to will engender animosity toward the client.

(D) Some people that an employee of a telemarketing agency calls to ask them to buy the product of a client of the agency will refuse to do so even though they are not predisposed to dislike the client.

(E) People who are already predisposed to dislike the client of a telemarketing agency are more likely to refuse to buy the product of that client than are people who are predisposed to like the client.

Type: Justify
Flaw: Missing Link
Tag: Principle & Application Stimulus

Stem – The word "justifies" in the stem tells you that this is a Justify problem, and this one features a Principle and Application Stimulus.

Stimulus – 1) Find the Conclusion. The conclusion is the Application of the Principle. Here, the conclusion is that an employee should not try to talk a person into buying a product when that person said she was not interested.

2) Find the Support. The support is the Principle. This makes sense because the principle is applied to the situation in the conclusion. Here, the support is that the employees should never take actions that would make the person on the phone dislike the client.

3) Find the Gap. You know that one concept will be in the principle and one will be in the application because the unlinked concepts always span the conclusion and support. This allows their link to make the conclusion valid.

Predisposing people to dislike the clients does not connect with the employee talking a person into buying something the person said she does not want. Sure, in real life, we might think that someone trying to sell us something we don't want would make us dislike the company they are trying to sell for, but here that relationship is not established.

Choices – 1) Eliminate choices without both concepts. (A) contains both concepts, even though what it says about them sounds wrong. Keep it for now. (B) is quite similar to (A); keep it, too. (C) is a stronger version of (A) and (B), definitely a keeper. (D) doesn't mention the concept of talking the person into buying. (E) also doesn't mention that concept.

2) Confirm the choice that links the concepts correctly. Analyze (A), (B), and (C) with an eye toward whether they tell us that trying to talk someone into buying when they have already said no will make them dislike the clients. (A) says that the employees can tell when they are trying to talk someone into buying whether it will make that person dislike the client. Whether they can tell is not the same as the talking into causing the dislike. We need a direct connection here. (B) says the same thing as (A) but that some employees cannot tell. Again, not what we need.

(C) links the two concepts correctly. It says that an employee trying to talk the person into buying WILL cause that animosity towards the client. With (C) in place, the application of the principle is fully justified.

5. Doctor (It is wrong for medical researchers to <u>keep their research confidential</u>,) even if the companies for which they work would rather that they do so. If research results are not shared, the development of effective medical treatments may be delayed, and <u>thus humans may suffer unnecessarily</u>.

    J Which one of the following principles, if valid, most helps to justify the doctor's argument?

    (A) Medical researchers should never engage in any behavior that they know will cause humans to suffer.

    (B) If the most important moral principle is to prevent human suffering, then it is wrong for medical researchers to keep their research confidential.

    (C) Medical researchers should not keep information confidential if it is possible that sharing that information would prevent some unnecessary human suffering.

    (D) Medical researchers should always attempt to develop effective medical treatments as rapidly as they can while fulfilling their other moral obligations.

    (E) It is wrong for any company to ask its medical researchers to keep their research confidential, if failure to share the research might delay development of effective medical treatments.

Type: Justify
Flaw: Missing Link
Tag: Logic Chain

<u>Stem</u> – "Most helps to justify" is a classic Justify problem stem.

<u>Stimulus</u> – 1) Find the Conclusion. In this argument, the conclusion comes first. It is wrong for medical researchers to keep their research confidential.

2) Find the Support. The support comes in the form of a Logic Chain. Research results not shared → development of effective medical treatments may be delayed → unnecessary human suffering.

3) Find the Gap. In this problem, we need to find a way to support the conclusion that keeping medical research confidential is wrong. The supporting Logic Chain tells us that not sharing medical research can lead to unnecessary human suffering. Obviously, anything that can lead to unnecessary human suffering would be considered wrong, so our two unlinked concepts are keeping medical research confidential and unnecessary human suffering. If we can find a choice that shows that sharing medical research (not keeping it confidential) can prevent unnecessary human suffering, then we'll be able to fill this gap and make the argument 100% airtight.

<u>Choices</u> – 1) Eliminate choices without both unlinked concepts. (A) discusses human suffering, but it doesn't give us anything about keeping information confidential. (B) mentions human suffering and, more specifically, preventing it, and (B) also mentions keeping medical research confidential. Hang onto this one. (C) also mentions keeping information confidential and preventing unnecessary human suffering, so let's keep this choice as well. (D) talks about developing effective medical treatments quickly and fulfilling moral obligations. Neither of those ideas match our unlinked concepts. (E) mentions keeping research confidential and failing to share the development of effective medical treatments. Even though our logic chain tells us that delaying the development of treatments could lead to unnecessary human suffering, this choice doesn't really cover our unlinked concepts properly because it introduces the new concept that it is wrong for a company to ask its researchers to keep their research confidential. (E) comes close to covering our unlinked concepts, but we're not concerned with the right or wrong actions of a company. We want to know about unnecessary human suffering and how it shows that keeping medical research confidential is wrong.

2) Confirm. After elimination, we're left with (B) and (C). (B) looks decent, but it talks about the most important moral principle. Preventing unnecessary human suffering doesn't necessarily have to be the most important human principle to show that keeping medical research confidential is wrong. That also doesn't give us enough support to make this argument valid. On the other hand, (C) fills our gap nicely. If it is possible that sharing medical research could prevent human suffering, then it would be wrong to keep medical research confidential. That's a neat link between keeping medical research confidential and unnecessary human suffering, which is exactly what we need to support this argument.

228 | Chapter 6

6. The only preexisting recordings that are transferred onto compact disc are those that record companies believe will sell well enough on compact disc to be profitable. (So, most classic jazz recordings will not be transferred onto compact disc) because few classic jazz recordings are played on the radio.

The **conclusion** above **follows logically** if which one of the following is assumed?

(A) Few of the preexisting recordings that record companies believe can be profitably transferred to compact disc are classic jazz recordings.

(B) Few compact discs featuring classic jazz recordings are played on the radio.

(C) The only recordings that are played on the radio are ones that record companies believe can be profitably sold as compact discs.

(D) Most record companies are less interested in preserving classic jazz recordings than in making a profit.

(E) No recording that is not played on the radio is one that record companies believe would be profitable if transferred to compact disc.

Type: Justify
Flaw: Missing Link
Tag: Conditionals, Confusing Choice

Stem – "Conclusion follows logically" = Justify problem.

Stimulus – 1) Find the Conclusion. "So" indicates that the conclusion is coming. Most classic jazz recordings will not be transferred to CD.

2) Find the Support. There are two pieces of support. The first sentence of the stimulus tells us that recordings are only transferred onto compact disc when the record companies think that the CDs will be profitable after paying for the transferring. The second piece of support is signaled by "because:" few classic jazz recordings are played on the radio.

3) Find the Gap. Profitability of the recording after transferring it to CD is never linked to the concept of being played on the radio. This gap is the source of this Missing Link flaw.

Choices – 1) Eliminate. (A) talks about the entire group of preexisting recordings and how jazz recordings fit in there. This is extraneous information, and it does not mention how radio play fits in. (B) doesn't mention profitability. (C) mentions both concepts, so keep it. (D) mentions making a profit, but not in relation to being played on the radio. (E) also has both concepts, so keep it as well.

2) Confirm. Analyze (C) carefully. (C) says that only recordings that record companies believe will be profitable as CDs are played on the radio. The problem is that this choice leaves out the idea of being profitable *after the cost of being transferred* to CD. This is a crucial idea for the link.

(E) gives you the link you need, but it uses a double negative so it is difficult to understand. The "no" and "not" cancel out, so (E) says that if a recording is played on the radio then record companies believe it would be profitable if transferred to compact disc. Here's the conditional diagram:

Radio → Profitable if Transferred

(E) is correct.

7. Resident (Residents of this locale should not consider their loss of farming as a way of life to be a tragedy) When this area was a rural area it was economically depressed, but it is now a growing bastion of high-tech industry with high-wage jobs, and supports over 20 times the number of jobs it did then.

J Which one of the following, if true, does the most to justify the conclusion of the resident's argument?

(A) Farming is becoming increasingly efficient, with the result that fewer farms are required to produce the same amount of food.

(B) The development of high-tech industry is more valuable to national security than is farming.

(C) Residents of this locale do not value a rural way of life more than they value economic prosperity.

(D) Many residents of this locale have annual incomes that are twice what they were when the locale was primarily agricultural.

(E) The loss of a family farm is often perceived as tragic even when no financial hardship results.

Type: Justify
Flaw: Missing Link

Stem – "Does the most to justify the conclusion" tells us this is a Justify problem.

Stimulus – 1) Find the Conclusion. In this argument, the conclusion comes first. Residents of this community should not view the loss of a rural way of life as a tragedy.

2) Find the Support. The support for the conclusion is that the area has seen huge economic growth in the high-tech industry since it changed from its rural roots. By contrast, the community was economically depressed when it was a rural area.

3) Find the Gap. In this argument, the gap is between the new economic growth and success of the high-tech industry and the old rural way of life in the community. In order to fill the gap, we need a choice that ties these two together in a way that supports the conclusion. If the residents should not view the shift away from a rural way of a life as a tragedy, then we need a link that shows that residents of the community should see that shift toward economic prosperity as a positive development and not a tragedy.

Choices – 1) Eliminate choices without both unlinked concepts. (A) discusses the rural way of life, but it doesn't tell us anything about the new economic growth and success. Instead, it talks about the efficiency of modern farming, which has nothing to do with our unlinked concepts. (B) talks about the development of the high-tech industry and farming. Let's hang onto this one. (C) mentions the rural way of life and economic prosperity, both of which tie into our unlinked concepts. It also talks about residents of the locale and what they value. Let's keep (C) also and look at the other choices. (D) discusses the increase in many resident's incomes since the community shifted away from its agricultural focus. That ties into our concept of economic growth and the old rural way of life. Let's keep (D). (E) discusses the shift away from agriculture, but it doesn't talk about the new economic growth.

2) Confirm. After elimination, we're left with (B), (C), and (D). (B) mentions both of our unlinked concepts, but what does this argument have to do with national security? If the development of the high-tech industry and consequent economic growth is more valuable to national security than farming, that's great, but that doesn't support our conclusion that the residents should not see the shift as a tragedy. (D) tells us that many residents have much stronger incomes than when the community's economy was based on agriculture, which could provide some support. Nevertheless, we need a choice that ties the older rural way of life to the new economic growth and success in a way that supports the conclusion that residents should not view the change as a tragedy. (C) does just that. If these residents value economic prosperity more than they value their traditional rural way of life, then they should not see the loss of farming as a tragedy. Clearly, the local economy has benefited significantly from the change to the high-tech industry, and the residents should not see the loss of farming as tragic if they value economic prosperity. (C) gives us a nice link and just what we need to make this argument valid.

8. Because no other theory has been able to predict it so simply and accurately, the advance of the perihelion of Mercury is sometimes cited as evidence in support of Einstein's theory of general relativity. However, this phenomenon was already well known when Einstein developed his theory, and he quite probably adjusted his equations to generate the correct numbers for the perihelion advance (**Therefore**, accounting for this advance should not be counted as evidence in support of Einstein's theory)

    Which one of the following principles, if valid, most helps to justify the argument above?

    (A) Unless a phenomenon predicted by a scientific theory is unknown at the time the theory is developed, the theory should not be credited with the discovery of that phenomenon.

    (B) A phenomenon that is predicted by a scientific theory should not count as evidence in favor of that theory unless the theory was developed with that phenomenon in mind.

    (C) Unless a theory can accurately account for all relevant phenomena that are already well known at the time of its development, it cannot be regarded as well supported.

    (D) If a theory is adjusted specifically to account for some particular phenomenon, a match between that theory and that phenomenon should not count as evidence in favor of the theory.

    (E) If a theory is adjusted to generate the correct predictions for some phenomenon that is already known to the scientist developing the theory, the theory should not be counted as predicting that phenomenon.

Type: Justify
Flaw: Missing Link

Stem – "Justify" tells us that this is a Justify problem. Go into the stimulus ready to analyze an argument and locate the unlinked concepts.

Stimulus – 1) Find the Conclusion. "Therefore" tells us that the final sentence is the conclusion. The fact that Einstein's theory accounts for the advance of the perihelion of Mercury should not count as evidence for the theory; it shouldn't give one more reason to believe in Einstein's theory.

2) Find the Support. The stimulus begins with some opposing information: no other theory has been able to predict the advance as well as Einstein's. But, that goes against the conclusion. The support for the conclusion is that Einstein knew about and accounted for the advance of perihelion when he created his theory. So, of course the theory predicts it well.

3) Find the Gap. The stimulus says that Einstein thought about the advance when he created his theory and perhaps tweaked his equations in the theory to match the advance well. The stimulus

jumps from that to the conclusion about the advance not counting in support of Einstein's theory. We need a direct link between those two.

Choices – 1) Eliminate choices without both concepts. (A) talks about the theory *discovering* a phenomenon, which is not the right concept. (B) and (C) do not mention Einstein adjusting his theory to match the phenomenon, so cut 'em. (D) has both concepts we need. (E) sounds good at first, but it confuses the concept in the conclusion. The conclusion in the stimulus talks about accounting for the phenomenon counting as evidence, not about predicting the phenomenon, as Einstein's theory did well.

2) Confirm. (D) gives us the link between Einstein adjusting his theory to match the phenomenon and the fact that the theory predicts the advance so well not counting as evidence in favor of the theory. That connection justifies the conclusion of the argument.

9. Principle: Only if a professor believes a student knowingly presented someone else's ideas without attribution should the professor make an official determination that the student has committed plagiarism.

   Application: (It is not the case that Professor Serfin should make an official determination that Walters committed plagiarism in the term paper about Willa Cather that Walters wrote for Serfin's class.)

   J Which one of the following, if true, justifies the above application of the principle?

   (A) Professor Serfin does not have completely compelling evidence to conclude that Walters presented someone else's ideas as if they were his own in the term paper about Willa Cather.

   (B) If Walters had realized that the main thesis of his term paper is identical to the main thesis of a book he had read, Walters would have attributed the idea to the book.

   (C) Although the main thesis of Walters's term paper is identical to that of a book that he did not cite, Professor Serfin is convinced that Walters did not knowingly try to pass anyone else's ideas off as his own.

   (D) Walters does not believe that Professor Serfin should make an official determination that he plagiarized.

   (E) Professor Serfin has no intention of making an official determination that Walters plagiarized in the class.

Type: Justify
Flaw: Missing Link
Tag: Principle & Application Stimulus

Stem – "Justifies" tells us that this is a Justify problem, and it features a Principle and Application stimulus.

Stimulus – 1) Find the Conclusion. The Application is the conclusion: Professor Serfin should *not* make a determination that Walters committed plagiarism.

2) Find the Support. The Principle is the support: to say that a student committed plagiarism, a professor must believe a student knowingly presented someone else's ideas without attribution. This is a very specific requirement, so use that when you work the choices.

3) Find the Gap. The application of the principle says that Professor Serfin should not say that Walters committed plagiarism, but that is not directly linked with the rule of when to say that a student did commit plagiarism. We need to take the general rule given and apply it to Professor Serfin and Walters situation. The underlining in the support helps you stay focused on exactly the concept that the application needs to match.

Choices – 1) Eliminate choices without both concepts. (A) talks about evidence to conclude, but we need to know what Prof Serfin believes. Eliminate (A). (B) only talks about Walters, again not mentioning anything about Prof Serfin's belief. (C) mentions Professor Serfin not believing that Walters knowingly presented other ideas, so keep it. (D), like (B), talks about Walters perspective, which is not what we need. (E) mentions Professor Serfin, but not his beliefs. It also doesn't mention Walters presenting someone else's ideas as his own.

Paying close attention to the specific nature of the principle here was really helpful in eliminating choices that did not talk about Professor Serfin's view.

2) Confirm. (C) works in justifying the application of the principle because it explicitly mentions Professor Serfin being convinced that Walters did not try to pass off someone else's ideas. That is the crucial aspect of the support (which is general in nature) that we needed to link to its application in this specific situation.

10. Judge: The defendant admits noncompliance with national building codes but asks that penalties not be imposed because he was confused as to whether national or local building codes applied to the area in which he was building. This excuse might be acceptable had he been charged with <u>noncompliance with local codes,</u> but **since** he is charged with <u>noncompliance with national codes</u>(his excuse is unacceptable.)

Which one of the following principles, if valid, most helps to justify the judge's reasoning?

(A) Local codes and national codes must not overlap with each other.

(B) Local codes may be less strict, but not more strict, than national codes.

(C) Any behavior required by national codes is also required by local codes.

(D) Ignorance of the difference between two codes is not an adequate excuse for noncompliance.

(E) A behavior that is in compliance with one law is not necessarily in compliance with another.

Type: Justify
Flaw: Missing Link

Stem – "Most helps to justify" is a classic Justify problem stem. Be ready to identify the parts of the argument.

Stimulus – 1) Find the Conclusion. The clause beginning with the word "since" is a nice indicator for the conclusion, which comes at the end of the argument. The defendant's excuse that he was confused as to whether national or local building codes applied is unacceptable.

2) Find the Support. The primary support is that the defendant is charged with noncompliance with national codes. His excuse is that he wasn't sure which codes applied. If he were charged with noncompliance of local codes, then that excuse might be acceptable.

3) Find the Gap. According to the conclusion, the defendant's excuse is unacceptable. Even though it might be acceptable if he were charged with noncompliance with local codes, he is charged with noncompliance of national codes, and his excuse is not valid. The gap in this argument is simple: what is the relationship between local and national codes? If we can find a link between the two that shows that the defendant's excuse could be considered unacceptable, then we'll have what we need to support the conclusion. Our unlinked concepts are national codes and local codes.

Choices – 1) Eliminate choices without both unlinked concepts. (A) mentions both national codes and local codes, so let's hang onto that one. (B) also mentions both types of codes, so we can keep (B) as well. (C) also talks about both of our unlinked concepts, so we'll need to keep this choice, too. (D) sort of touches on the two codes, but it talks about them in the context of ignorance of the differences, which isn't one of our unlinked concepts. It also talks about what makes an excuse inadequate, which might sound tempting, but we need information about the relationship between local codes and national codes to support this argument. (E) talks about behavior and compliance with different laws. That doesn't really cover our unlinked concepts.

2) Confirm. After elimination, we're left with (A), (B), and (C). (A) doesn't help us understand the relationship between national codes and local codes and why that relationship would make the defendant's excuse unacceptable. If the local codes and national codes must not overlap, then it's possible that the defendant's excuse could be considered acceptable, so (A) sort of undermines the argument. (B) talks about which type of codes can be more or less strict. That doesn't really give us what we need. On the other hand, (C) provides a nice understanding of the relationship between national and local codes in a way that would make the defendant's excuse unacceptable. If the behaviors required by national codes are also required by local codes, then it doesn't matter which codes applied, so the defendant's excuse is unacceptable. Essentially, if the codes require the same behaviors, then noncompliance will be noncompliance in every instance. That's a relationship between national codes and local codes that gives us what we need to support the conclusion.

11. Physician: The rise in blood pressure that commonly accompanies aging often results from a calcium deficiency. This deficiency is frequently caused by a deficiency in the active form of vitamin D needed in order for the body to absorb calcium. **Since** the calcium in one glass of milk per day can easily make up for any underlying calcium deficiency, some older people (can lower their blood pressure by drinking milk.)

The physician's **conclusion is properly drawn** if which one of the following is assumed?

(A) There is in milk, in a form that older people can generally utilize, enough of the active form of vitamin D and any other substances needed in order for the body to absorb the calcium in that milk.

(B) Milk does not contain any substance that is likely to cause increased blood pressure in older people.

(C) Older people's drinking one glass of milk per day does not contribute to a deficiency in the active form of vitamin D needed in order for the body to absorb the calcium in that milk.

(D) People who consume high quantities of calcium together with the active form of vitamin D and any other substances needed in order for the body to absorb calcium have normal blood pressure.

(E) Anyone who has a deficiency in the active form of vitamin D also has a calcium deficiency.

Type: Justify
Flaw: Missing Link

Stem – "Conclusion is properly drawn if which is assumed" is a Justify problem stem.

Stimulus – 1) Find the Conclusion. The argument concludes that some older people can lower their blood pressure by drinking milk.

2) Find the Support. As you age, blood pressure rises, and this rise can result from calcium deficiency. The deficiency is caused by a lack of active vitamin D. Milk has enough calcium, so drinking milk should help old people to lower their blood pressure.

3) Find the Gap. The argument never states how drinking milk—even though it has calcium—will account for the vitamin D deficiency needed to absorb the calcium. Thus, the argument assumes a link between milk and vitamin D, but only states one between milk and calcium. Milk and vitamin D are our unlinked concepts.

Choices – The correct choice will state a link between drinking milk and getting active vitamin D.

1) Eliminate. (A) says that there's enough active vitamin D in milk for the body to absorb calcium. That's exactly what you're looking for—hold onto it. (B) says that milk doesn't have anything that would increase blood pressure, which is comforting, but ultimately it's unrelated to any important information in the argument. (C) says that drinking milk doesn't make you lose any more vitamin D, but this choice says nothing about the current issue of vitamin D deficiency in old people; it just says it won't get worse. (D) says that people who consume high amounts of calcium along with vitamin D have normal blood pressure. But where are they getting the vitamin D? That's still left out, but it's a vital part of the argument. (E) says that anyone with a deficiency in vitamin D also has a calcium deficiency. That does nothing to link the milk intake to vitamin D increase.

2) Confirm. (A) is good. It links drinking milk to getting vitamin D, and thus it justifies the argument's conclusion that drinking milk can indeed lower blood pressure in some older people. (A) is correct.

7 Linking Practice

Practice all the Linking skills you have built in this Module. First, the Linking Stems Drill helps you map Inference and Justify stems to the techniques for each type. Then, the Linking Practice Sets give you experience switching between Inference and Justify techniques on full problems.

Chapter Contents
Linking Stems Drill
Linking Practice Sets (Three sets of 7 problems)

Linking Stems Drill

Question stems are important. In order to successfully answer an LR problem, you first need to understand what the problem asks you to do. Thanks to all your targeted practice, the stem also triggers your set of techniques for the type. When you see a Justify stem and stamp it with a "J," the mantra "find the gap" should immediately come to mind.

The quicker you identify a stem and call to mind the key techniques, the more time you have to focus your attention on answering the problem. This Linking Stems Drill helps you practice your ability to do just that. In it, you'll find a mix of different Inference and Justify stems. You will classify and stamp each stem and then state the core focus for the question type. Here are the core focuses for each:

- I = "Start with (E), Prove and Move."
- J = "Find the Gap"

The core focus task is mental; you don't need to write it. That said, mentally rehearsing the focus for the problem type is the most important part of this drill. A stem stamp only has meaning if it activates the techniques for the type.

The core focus is an anchor for all of the techniques for a type, and it helps you pull them to mind. When you think, "Start with (E), Prove and Move" for an Inference problem, you are also thinking, "Understand the facts and look for an Obvious Inference" in the stimulus and "Eliminate unproven choices" as you work the choices. Every time you read the Techniques Summary for a type during the Technique and Challenge Sets, you were ingraining the techniques.

Directions

For each stem:

- Identify it as an Inference or Justify problem and stamp it.
- Mentally rehearse the key technique for the type. Do this for each stem.

Stems Drill Set One

Which one of the following principles, if valid, most helps to justify the essayist's argument?

If the statements above are true, which one of the following must also be true?

Which one of the following, if assumed, enables the economics professor's conclusion to be properly drawn?

Which one of the following can be properly inferred from the information above?

The statements above, if true, most strongly support which one of the following?

The conclusion of the scientist's argument is most strongly supported if which one of the following is assumed?

The conclusion of the argument is most strongly supported if which one of the following completes the passage

Which one of the following can be properly inferred from the information above?

END OF SET

Set One Answers

Verify that you stamped the stems properly with the list below.

J   Which one of the following principles, if valid, most helps to justify the essayist's argument?

I   If the statements above are true, which one of the following must also be true?

J   Which one of the following, if assumed, enables the economics professor's conclusion to be properly drawn?

I   Which one of the following can be properly inferred from the information above?

I   The statements above, if true, most strongly support which one of the following?

J   The conclusion of the scientist's argument is most strongly supported if which one of the following is assumed?

J   The conclusion of the argument is most strongly supported if which one of the following completes the passage?

I   Which one of the following can be properly inferred from the information above?

Stems Drill Set Two

For each stem, Stem stamp it, and then mentally state the type's core focus:

If all of the statements above are true, which one of the following must be true?

The physician's conclusion is properly drawn if which one of the following is assumed?

The science writer's statements, if true, most strongly support which one of the following?

If all of the interior decorator's statements are true, then which one of the following must be true?

If the statements above are true, which one of the following must also be true?

Which one of the following principles, if valid, most helps to justify the counselor's reasoning?

Which one of the following can be properly inferred from the computer scientist's statements?

Which one of the following, if assumed, enables the psychologist's conclusion to be properly drawn?

Which one of the following is most strongly supported by the aerobics instructor's statements?

END OF SET

Set Two Answers

I   If all of the statements above are true, which one of the following must be true?

J   The physician's conclusion is properly drawn if which one of the following is assumed?

I   The science writer's statements, if true, most strongly support which one of the following?

I   If all of the interior decorator's statements are true, then which one of the following must be true?

I   If the statements above are true, which one of the following must also be true?

J   Which one of the following principles, if valid, most helps to justify the counselor's reasoning?

I   Which one of the following can be properly inferred from the computer scientist's statements?

J   Which one of the following, if assumed, enables the psychologist's conclusion to be properly drawn?

I   Which one of the following is most strongly supported by the aerobics instructor's statements?

Linking Practice Sets

These timed Practice Sets combine all the Linking Skills you have built. Each Set mixes Inference and Justify problems, so you must switch back and forth between these two types and their techniques. Completing different tasks in rapid succession is one thing that makes the Logical Reasoning section difficult. And facing Inference and Justify problems, you will get to use your conditionals and reasoning (identifying argument parts) skills.

Directions

- <u>Time Limit:</u> There is a 9 minute time limit for this Practice set. Use a digital timer and pace with your watch. Guess on any problems you do not reach, just as you will on the official LSAT.

- Mark problems you are unsure of as you attempt the set.

- <u>Bubble Sheet:</u> Like all timed sets, fill in your answers in the bubble sheet for this Test Set.

   <u>Review:</u> Review only problems that you answered incorrectly and those that you marked as unsure. First self-review each problem, then carefully read the explanation. Explanations are only provided for the more difficult problems.

Practice Set 1

1. Parent: Pushing very young children into rigorous study in an effort to make our nation more competitive does more harm than good. Curricula for these young students must address their special developmental needs, and while rigorous work in secondary school makes sense, the same approach in the early years of primary school produces only short-term gains and may cause young children to burn out on schoolwork. Using very young students as pawns in the race to make the nation economically competitive is unfair and may ultimately work against us.

   Which one of the following can be inferred from the parent's statements?

   (A)   For our nation to be competitive, our secondary school curriculum must include more rigorous study than it now does.

   (B)   The developmental needs of secondary school students are not now being addressed in our high schools.

   (C)   Our country can be competitive only if the developmental needs of all our students can be met.

   (D)   A curriculum of rigorous study does not adequately address the developmental needs of primary school students.

   (E)   Unless our nation encourages more rigorous study in the early years of primary school, we cannot be economically competitive.

2. "Hot spot" is a term that ecologists use to describe those habitats with the greatest concentrations of species found only in one place—so-called "endemic" species. Many of these hot spots are vulnerable to habitat loss due to commercial development. Furthermore, loss of endemic species accounts for most modern-day extinctions. Thus, given that only a limited number of environmental battles can be waged, it would be reasonable for organizations dedicated to preserving species to _____.

   Which one of the following most logically completes the argument?

   (A)   try to help only those species who are threatened with extinction because of habitat loss

   (B)   concentrate their resources on protecting hot spot habitats

   (C)   treat all endemic species as equally valuable and equally in need of preservation

   (D)   accept that most endemic species will become extinct

   (E)   expand the definition of "hot spot" to include vulnerable habitats that are not currently home to many endangered species

3. Counselor: Hagerle sincerely apologized to the physician for lying to her. So Hagerle owes me a sincere apology as well, because Hagerle told the same lie to both of us.

   Which one of the following principles, if valid, most helps to justify the counselor's reasoning?

   (A) It is good to apologize for having done something wrong to a person if one is capable of doing so sincerely.

   (B) If someone tells the same lie to two different people, then neither of those lied to is owed an apology unless both are.

   (C) Someone is owed a sincere apology for having been lied to by a person if someone else has already received a sincere apology for the same lie from that same person.

   (D) If one is capable of sincerely apologizing to someone for lying to them, then one owes that person such an apology.

   (E) A person should not apologize to someone for telling a lie unless he or she can sincerely apologize to all others to whom the lie was told.

4. Some scientists have expressed reservations about quantum theory because of its counterintuitive consequences. But despite rigorous attempts to show that quantum theory's predictions were inaccurate, they were shown to be accurate within the generally accepted statistical margin of error. These results, which have not been equaled by quantum theory's competitors, warrant acceptance of quantum theory.

   Which one of the following principles most helps to justify the reasoning above?

   (A) A scientific theory should be accepted if it has fewer counterintuitive consequences than do its competitors.

   (B) A scientific theory should be accepted if it has been subjected to serious attempts to disprove it and has withstood all of them.

   (C) The consequences of a scientific theory should not be considered counterintuitive if the theory's predictions have been found to be accurate.

   (D) A theory should not be rejected until it has been subjected to serious attempts to disprove it.

   (E) A theory should be accepted only if its predictions have not been disproved by experiment.

5. There are 70 to 100 Florida panthers alive today. This represents a very large increase over their numbers in the 1970s, but their population must reach at least 250 if it is to be self-sustaining. Their current habitat is not large enough to support any more of these animals, however.

   If the statements above are true, which one of the following must also be true?

   (A) Some part of the panthers' current habitat is only of marginal quality.

   (B) If the population of Florida panthers ever exceeds 250, it will be self-sustaining.

   (C) Unless Florida panthers acquire a larger habitat, their population will not be self-sustaining.

   (D) The population of Florida panthers will never increase much beyond its current level.

   (E) Today, Florida panthers occupy a larger habitat than they did in the 1970s.

6. Essayist: Common sense, which is always progressing, is nothing but a collection of theories that have been tested over time and found useful. When alternative theories that prove even more useful are developed, they gradually take the place of theories already embodied in common sense. This causes common sense to progress, but, because it absorbs new theories slowly, it always contains some obsolete theories.

If all of the essayist's statements are true, then which one of the following must be true?

(A) At least some new theories that have not yet been found to be more useful than any theory currently part of common sense will never be absorbed into the body of common sense.

(B) Of the useful theories within the body of common sense, the older ones are generally less useful than the newer ones.

(C) The frequency with which new theories are generated prevents their rapid absorption into the body of common sense.

(D) Each theory within the body of common sense is eventually replaced with a new theory that is more useful.

(E) At least some theories that have been tested over time and found useful are less useful than some other theories that have not been fully absorbed into the body of common sense.

7. The government is being urged to prevent organizations devoted to certain views on human nutrition from advocating a diet that includes large portions of uncooked meat, because eating uncooked meat can be very dangerous. However, this purported fact does not justify the government's silencing the groups, for surely the government would not be justified in silencing a purely political group merely on the grounds that the policies the group advocates could be harmful to some members of society. The same should be true for silencing groups with certain views on human nutrition.

Which one of the following principles most helps to justify the reasoning in the argument?

(A) The government should not silence any group for advocating a position that a significant proportion of society believes to be beneficial.

(B) The government ought to do whatever is in the best interest of society.

(C) One ought to advocate a position only if one believes that it is true or would be beneficial.

(D) The government ought not to silence an opinion merely on the grounds that it could be harmful to disseminate the opinion.

(E) One ought to urge the government to do only those things the government is justified in doing.

END OF SET

Set 1 Key & Explanations

1. D

2. B (64/3, #1)

3. C

4. B (42/4, #15)

5. C (64/1, #2)

6. E (42/4, #26)

7. D (64/1, #12)

1. Parent: Pushing very young children into rigorous study in an effort to make our nation more competitive does more harm than good. Curricula for these young students must address their special developmental needs, and while rigorous work in secondary school makes sense, the same approach in the early years of primary school produces only short-term gains and may cause young children to burn out on schoolwork. Using very young students as pawns in the race to make the nation economically competitive is unfair and may ultimately work against us.

Which one of the following can be **inferred** from the parent's statements?

(A)   For our nation to be competitive, our secondary school curriculum must include more rigorous study than it now does.

(B)   The developmental needs of secondary school students are not now being addressed in our high schools.

(C)   Our country can be competitive only if the developmental needs of all our students can be met.

(D)   A curriculum of rigorous study does not adequately address the developmental needs of primary school students.

(E)   Unless our nation encourages more rigorous study in the early years of primary school, we cannot be economically competitive.

Type: Inference
Tags: Obvious Inference, Prove & Move

Stem – "inferred" is an Inference problem stem. Understand the facts then look for an Obvious Inference.

Stimulus – 1) Understand the facts. Pushing young students into a school system designed around rigorous study harms young students because it eventually leads to burnout in primary school students.

2) Look for an Obvious Inference. The "rigorous study" suggested to make our nation more competitive is not a good match for the needs of the *primary* schoolchildren; it may be successful for other levels of young students, but in primary school kids it leads to burnout. So, the rigorous study programs must not be appropriate for that young of a student.

Choices – The correct choice will infer that the rigorous study approach doesn't properly address what the primary schoolchildren need at that stage in their educational development. Eliminate starting with (E) and use the Prove and Move technique if you can prove a choice.

1) Eliminate. (E) infers that, if our nation doesn't encourage more rigorous study in the early years of primary school, we can't be economically competitive, but that inference assumes that improving out educational competitiveness is the *only* possible way to make our nation more *economically* competitive. That's not supported by the information in the stimulus, though, because there's nothing to lead you to believe that the education of schoolchildren is the only way to achieve economic competitiveness. (D) infers that a curriculum of rigorous study doesn't adequately address the developmental needs of primary school students; that's a good match for the Obvious Inference. Comparing (D) to the information in the stimulus, you know that rigorous study helps schoolchildren, but it causes primary school students to burn out on schoolwork. Thus, it must not adequately address the developmental needs of the schoolchildren as (D) describes. (D) is proven, so go ahead and Prove and Move.

3. Counselor: Hagerle sincerely <u>apologized to the physician</u> for lying to her(**So** Hagerle <u>owes me a sincere apology</u> as well)because Hagerle told the same lie to both of us.

Which one of the following **principles**, if valid, most helps to **justify** the counselor's reasoning?

(A) It is good to apologize for having done something wrong to a person if one is capable of doing so sincerely.

(B) If someone tells the same lie to two different people, then neither of those lied to is owed an apology unless both are.

(C) Someone is owed a sincere apology for having been lied to by a person if someone else has already received a sincere apology for the same lie from that same person.

(D) If one is capable of sincerely apologizing to someone for lying to them, then one owes that person such an apology.

(E) A person should not apologize to someone for telling a lie unless he or she can sincerely apologize to all others to whom the lie was told.

Type: Justify
Flaw: Missing Link

<u>Stem</u> – You're asked to identify which principle allows the reasoning to be justified—that's a Justify problem stem.

<u>Stimulus</u> – 1) Find the Conclusion. The argument concludes that Hagerle owes the speaker a sincere apology.

2) Find the Support. The argument states that Hagerle apologized to the physician for lying to her. Because Hagerle told the speaker the same lie, the speaker feels like she should get an apology, too.

3) Fing the Gap. It's pretty clear that there's a gap between apologizing to another person for a lie and apologizing to the counselor for the same lie. Just because Hagerle apologized to the physician doesn't mean you're entitled to one, too!

<u>Choices</u> – The correct answer will state that someone who apologizes to one person must apologize to another person if that other person was affected by the same lie as the first person. Or something to that effect—it probably won't be so wordy in the answer.

1) Eliminate. (A) states that it's good to apologize to someone if you're able to do so sincerely. That idea isn't related to the idea that you should apologize to one person if you've apologized to another person for the same lie. (B) says that, if a lie is told to two people, either both of them get an apology or none do. That's not quite what the argument is saying. While in the end both people lied-to would get an apology if the argument got its way, it is not arguing based on the all-or-none idea that everyone gets an apology or nobody does. (C) provides a nice link to our unlinked concepts. Someone is owed an apology if another person got an apology for the same lie. That looks more like the argument than (B) does. Hold onto (C). (D) says that if you're capable of sincerely apologizing for lying to somebody, then you owe that person an apology. But, the argument bases its conclusion on the fact that Hagerle apologized to the physician, not on the fact that Hagerle is capable of a sincere apology. (E) talks about whether or not a person should apologize for a lie. They should only do so, according to this choice, if they can sincerely apologize to all those to whom the lie was told. Again, that's not quite the reasoning used in the argument. The argument doesn't say, "You apologized to the physician, which shows you're capable of a sincere apology, so you should apologize to me." Rather, it says, "You apologized to the physician for a lie. You said that same lie to me, so apologize to me, too."

2) Confirm. (C) makes an explicit link between the idea that an apology to one person for a lie means that another person, told the same lie, should also get an apology. (C) is correct.

Practice Set 2

Directions

- Time Limit: There is a 10 minute time limit for this Practice Set. Use a digital timer and pace with your watch. Guess on any problems you do not reach, just as you will on the official LSAT.

- Mark problems you are unsure of as you attempt the set.

- Bubble Sheet: Like all timed sets, fill in your answers in the bubble sheet for this Test Set.

- Review: Review only problems that you answered incorrectly and those that you marked as unsure. First self-review each problem, then carefully read the explanation.

1. Editorial: One of our local television stations has been criticized for its recent coverage of the personal problems of a local politician's nephew, but the coverage was in fact good journalism. The information was accurate. Furthermore, the newscast had significantly more viewers than it normally does, because many people are curious about the politician's nephew's problems.

   Which one of the following principles, if valid, would most help to justify the reasoning in the editorial?

   (A) Journalism deserves to be criticized if it does not provide information that people want.

   (B) Any journalism that intentionally misrepresents the facts of a case deserves to be criticized.

   (C) Any journalism that provides accurate information on a subject about which there is considerable interest is good journalism.

   (D) Good journalism will always provide people with information that they desire or need.

   (E) Journalism that neither satisfies the public's curiosity nor provides accurate information can never be considered good journalism.

2. Small experimental vacuum tubes can operate in heat that makes semiconductor components fail. Any component whose resistance to heat is greater than that of semiconductors would be preferable for use in digital circuits, but only if that component were also comparable to semiconductors in all other significant respects, such as maximum current capacity. However, vacuum tubes' maximum current capacity is presently not comparable to that of semiconductors.

   If the statements above are true, which one of the following must also be true?

   (A) Vacuum tubes are not now preferable to semiconductors for use in digital circuits.

   (B) Once vacuum tubes and semiconductors have comparable maximum current capacity, vacuum tubes will be used in some digital circuits.

   (C) The only reason that vacuum tubes are not now used in digital circuits is that vacuum tubes' maximum current capacity is too low.

   (D) Semiconductors will always be preferable to vacuum tubes for use in many applications other than digital circuits.

   (E) Resistance to heat is the only advantage that vacuum tubes have over semiconductors.

3. Physics professor: Some scientists claim that superheated plasma in which electrical resistance fails is a factor in causing so-called "ball lightning." If this were so, then such lightning would emit intense light and, since plasma has gaslike properties, would rise in the air. However, the instances of ball lightning that I observed were of low intensity and floated horizontally before vanishing. Thus, superheated plasma with failed electrical resistance is never a factor in causing ball lightning.

   The physics professor's conclusion follows logically if which one of the following is assumed?

   (A) Superheated plasma in which electrical resistance fails does not cause types of lightning other than ball lightning.

   (B) The phenomena observed by the physics professor were each observed by at least one other person.

   (C) Ball lightning can occur as the result of several different factors.

   (D) Superheating of gaslike substances causes bright light to be emitted.

   (E) All types of ball lightning have the same cause.

4. Two different dates have been offered as the approximate end point of the last ice age in North America. The first date was established by testing insect fragments found in samples of sediments to determine when warmth-adapted open-ground beetles replaced cold-adapted arctic beetles. The second date was established by testing pollen grains in those same samples to determine when ice masses yielded to spruce forests. The first date is more than 500 years earlier than the second.

The statements above, if true, most strongly support which one of the following conclusions about the last ice age and its aftermath in North America?

(A) Toward the end of the ice age, warmth-adapted open-ground beetles ceased to inhabit areas where the predominant tree cover consisted of spruce forests.

(B) Among those sediments deposited toward the end of the ice age, those found to contain cold-adapted arctic beetle fragments can also be expected to contain spruce-pollen grains.

(C) Ice masses continued to advance through North America for several hundred years after the end of the ice age.

(D) The species of cold-adapted arctic beetle that inhabited areas covered by ice masses died out toward the end of the last ice age.

(E) Toward the end of the ice age, warmth-adapted open-ground beetles colonized the new terrain opened to them faster than soil changes and seed dispersion established new spruce forests.

5. One child pushed another child from behind, injuring the second child. The first child clearly understands the difference between right and wrong, so what was done was wrong if it was intended to injure the second child.

Which one of the following principles, if valid, most helps to justify the reasoning in the argument?

(A) An action that is intended to harm another person is wrong only if the person who performed the action understands the difference between right and wrong.

(B) It is wrong for a person who understands the difference between right and wrong to intentionally harm another person.

(C) Any act that is wrong is done with the intention of causing harm.

(D) An act that harms another person is wrong if the person who did it understands the difference between right and wrong and did not think about whether the act would injure the other person.

(E) A person who does not understand the difference between right and wrong does not bear any responsibility for harming another person.

6. Inez: The book we are reading, The Nature of Matter, is mistitled. A title should summarize the content of the whole book, but nearly half of this book is devoted to discussing a different, albeit closely related subject: energy.

Antonio: I do not think that the author erred; according to modern physics, matter and energy are two facets of the same phenomenon.

Which one of the following is most strongly supported by the conversation above?

(A) Inez believes that the book should be called *The Nature of Energy*.

(B) Antonio believes that there are no differences between matter and energy.

(C) Inez and Antonio disagree on whether matter and energy are related.

(D) Inez and Antonio disagree about the overall value of the book.

(E) Inez believes that the book's title should not mention matter without mentioning energy.

7. Curator: Our museum displays only twentieth-century works, which are either on loan from private collectors or in the museum's permanent collection. Prints of all of the latter works are available in the museum store. The museum store also sells prints of some works that are not part of the museum's permanent collection, such as Hopper's Nighthawks.

If the curator's statements are true, which one of the following must be true?

(A) Every print in the museum store is of a work that is either on loan to the museum from a private collector or part of the museum's permanent collection.

(B) Every print that is sold in the museum store is a copy of a twentieth-century work.

(C) There are prints in the museum store of every work that is displayed in the museum and not on loan from a private collector.

(D) Hopper's *Nighthawks* is both a twentieth-century work and a work on loan to the museum from a private collector.

(E) Hopper's *Nighthawks* is not displayed in the museum.

END OF SET

Set 2 Key & Explanations

1. C

2. A

3. E

4. E

5. B

6. E

7. C

1. Editorial: One of our local television stations has been criticized for its recent coverage of the personal problems of a local politician's nephew(**but** the coverage was in fact good journalism.)The information was accurate. Furthermore, the newscast had significantly more viewers than it normally does, because many people are curious about the politician's nephew's problems.

    J Which one of the following **principles**, if valid, would **most help to justify the reasoning** in the editorial?

    (A) Journalism deserves to be criticized if it does not provide information that people want.

    (B) Any journalism that intentionally misrepresents the facts of a case deserves to be criticized.

    (C) Any journalism that provides accurate information on a subject about which there is considerable interest is good journalism.

    (D) Good journalism will always provide people with information that they desire or need.

    (E) Journalism that neither satisfies the public's curiosity nor provides accurate information can never be considered good journalism.

Type: Justify
Flaw: Missing Link
Tags: Equated Concepts Jump, Opposing View Conclusion

Stem – You're asked to find the principle that, if valid, justifies the reasoning—that's a Justify problem.

Stimulus – 1) Find the Conclusion. This is an Opposing View Conclusion, noted by the initial statement and the mid-stimulus conclusion preceded by the indicator "but." The coverage of the local television stations was good journalism, despite the recent criticisms.

2) Find the Support. As support for the conclusion that the TV reporting was good journalism, the argument states that the information was accurate and the newscast had a good number of viewers due to general curiosity in the issue.

3) Find the Gap. The argument equates "good journalism" with "accurate information" on a subject that has a lot of interest. That gap might make sense in the real world, but in an LSAT problem these are unlinked concepts.

Choices – 1) Eliminate choices without both unlinked concepts. (A) says that journalism should be criticized if it doesn't provide info people want. There's no discussion of accuracy in that answer, so it's out. (B) is irrelevant because it talks about journalism that intentionally misrepresents the facts of a case, but the television reports in the argument provided accurate information. (C) says that any journalism that provides accurate info on a high-interest topic is good journalism. That's a direct match; it justifies the conclusion with a good link. (D) says that good journalism provides people with info they want or need, but again, there's no discussion of accuracy, just preference. (E) talks about what isn't good journalism, which isn't helpful. Knowing what doesn't make for good journalism tells you nothing about what does make for good journalism.

2) Confirm. (C) is your winner. It connects "good journalism" to "accurate information" and a large, interested audience. That's just the link you need in order to justify the argument's reasoning. (C) is correct.

2. Small experimental vacuum tubes can operate in heat that makes semiconductor components fail. Any component whose resistance to heat is greater than that of semiconductors would be preferable for use in digital circuits, but only if that component were also comparable to semiconductors in all other significant respects, such as maximum current capacity. However, vacuum tubes' maximum current capacity is presently not comparable to that of semiconductors.

If the statements above are true, which one of the following **must also be true**?

 (A) Vacuum tubes are not now preferable to semiconductors for use in digital circuits.

 (B) Once vacuum tubes and semiconductors have comparable maximum current capacity, vacuum tubes will be used in some digital circuits.

 (C) The only reason that vacuum tubes are not now used in digital circuits is that vacuum tubes' maximum current capacity is too low.

 (D) Semiconductors will always be preferable to vacuum tubes for use in many applications other than digital circuits.

(E) Resistance to heat is the only advantage that vacuum tubes have over semiconductors.

Type: Inference
Tags: Obvious Inference

Stem – "Must also be true" is an Inference problem stem. Understand the facts, and then look for an Obvious Inference.

Stimulus – 1) Understand the Facts. You're told about two different types of component: vacuum tubes and semiconductors. Any component that can withstand more heat than the semiconductors is preferable in digital circuits, but that's only the case if those components are comparable to semiconductors in *all* other respects. Vacuum tubes can withstand more heat than semiconductors, but they're not comparable in at least one respect: their maximum current capacity falls short of that of semiconductors.

2) Look for an Obvious Inference. Vacuum tubes are not preferable to semiconductors in digital circuits because, although they have a greater heat resistivity, they aren't comparable to semiconductors in their maximum current capacity.

Choices – 1) Eliminate incorrect choices, starting with (E) (E) infers that resistance to heat is the only advantage that vacuum tubes have over semiconductors, but you don't know that to be true. It may be the only advantage *discussed*, but that doesn't mean that it's the *only* advantage. (D) infers that semiconductors will always be preferable to vacuum tubes for use in many applications other than digital circuits, but based on the information in this stimulus you can't make that inference. You can only infer which component would work better in a digital circuit, not in other circuits. (C) infers that the *only* reason vacuum tubes aren't currently used in digital circuits is that their maximum current capacity is too low. Like (E), you don't know that to be the case based on the information in the stimulus. You know that the lower maximum current capacity is a *single* reason why the vacuum tubes aren't used in digital circuits, but you don't know if there are other respects in which vacuum tubes fail to be comparable to semiconductors. (B) infers that once vacuum tubes and semiconductors have comparable maximum current capacity, vacuum tubes will be used in some digital circuits. You can't justifiably infer (B) for the same reason that (C) is incorrect; you don't know if there are other respects in addition to the maximum current capacity in which vacuum tubes and semiconductors differ. (A) infers that vacuum tubes aren't currently preferable to semiconductors for use in digital circuits, which matches the Obvious Inference. This inference is supported by the stimulus, which states that vacuum tubes are better than semiconductors in their ability to withstand heat, but that only matters if they're comparable to semiconductors in every other way. Because vacuum tubes are *not* comparable to semiconductors in at least one way (maximum current capacity), you can infer that they're not preferable for use in digital circuits.

2) Confirm. We couldn't Prove and Move because we worked through all the choices, but (A) is correct.

3.   Physics professor: Some scientists claim that superheated plasma in which electrical resistance fails is a factor in causing so-called "ball lightning." If this were so, then such lightning would emit intense light and, since plasma has gaslike properties, would rise in the air. However, the instances of ball lightning that I observed were of low intensity and floated horizontally before vanishing(**Thus,** superheated plasma with failed electrical resistance is never a factor in causing ball lightning.)

The physics professor's conclusion **follows logically if which one of the following is assumed**?

(A)   Superheated plasma in which electrical resistance fails does not cause types of lightning other than ball lightning.

(B)   The phenomena observed by the physics professor were each observed by at least one other person.

(C)   Ball lightning can occur as the result of several different factors.

(D)   Superheating of gaslike substances causes bright light to be emitted.

(E)   All types of ball lightning have the same cause.

Type: Justify
Flaw: Missing Link
Tag: Opposing View Conclusion

Stem – You're asked which choice if assumed allows the professor's conclusion to follow logically, so this is a Justify problem.

Stimulus – 1) Find the Conclusion. It comes at the end, and "thus" is a nice indicator. Superheated plasma with failed electrical resistance is never a cause of ball lightning.

2) Find the Support. Some scientists believe that superheated plasma with failed electrical resistance plays a role in causing ball lightning. If this were true, the ball lightning would be very bright and rise in the air. However, the professor has only witnessed ball lightning with low light intensity that floated horizontally, so superheated plasma with failed electrical resistance must never be a factor because this ball lightning was not intensely bright and did not rise.

3) Find the Gap. In drawing her conclusion, the professor assumes that the ball lightning she has witnessed is the same as the ball lightning that other scientists think may be caused by the specific superheated plasma. How do we know that these different instances of ball lightning are the same? Couldn't the professor's ball lightning have a different cause? These are Unlinked Concepts.

Choices – 1) Eliminate choices without both concepts. (A) talks about types of lightning other than ball lightning, but the stimulus exclusively discusses ball lightning. (B) seems to back up the professor's credibility by adding a second witness, but that doesn't have anything to do with either unlinked concept. (C) does the opposite of what we need; it tears the argument a part. In drawing her conclusion, the professor assumes that all ball lightning is the same and has the same causes. If (C) is true, then that conclusion is invalid. (D) provides additional background information that doesn't tell us anything about ball lightning. On the other hand, (E) connects the ball lightning the professor observed to the ball lightning described by other scientists. Let's get ready to confirm it.

2) Confirm: After elimination, (E) helps justify the conclusion very nicely. If all types of ball lightning – both that observed by the professor and the examples described by the scientists – have the same cause, then the professor's argument is 100% airtight. (E) is correct.

4. Two different dates have been offered as the approximate end point of the last ice age in North America. The first date was established by testing insect fragments found in samples of sediments to determine when warmth-adapted open-ground beetles replaced cold-adapted arctic beetles. The second date was established by testing pollen grains in those same samples to determine when ice masses yielded to spruce forests. The first date is more than 500 years earlier than the second.

The statements above, if true, **most strongly support which one of the following conclusions** about the last ice age and its aftermath in North America?

(A) Toward the end of the ice age, warmth-adapted open-ground beetles ceased to inhabit areas where the predominant tree cover consisted of spruce forests.

(B) Among those sediments deposited toward the end of the ice age, those found to contain cold-adapted arctic beetle fragments can also be expected to contain spruce-pollen grains.

(C) Ice masses continued to advance through North America for several hundred years after the end of the ice age.

(D) The species of cold-adapted arctic beetle that inhabited areas covered by ice masses died out toward the end of the last ice age.

(E) Toward the end of the ice age, warmth-adapted open-ground beetles colonized the new terrain opened to them faster than soil changes and seed dispersion established new spruce forests.

Type: Inference
Tags: Obvious Inference, Prove & Move

Stem – "Most strongly support which one of the following conclusions" tells you this is an Inference problem.

Stimulus – 1) Understand the facts. Using the same soil samples, scientists have come up with two different dates to approximate the end point of North America's last ice age. The first date relies on determining when warmth-adapted beetles replaced cold-adapted beetles. The second date relies on pollen grains to determine when spruce forests replaced ice masses. For some reason, these two dates are 500 years apart.

2) Look for an Obvious inference. The ice age couldn't have ended at two different times, so there must be a reason for the discrepancy. When we consider that beetles and spruce trees are very different species, we can come to a reasonable conclusion on this one. Insects have short lives and multiply quickly. On the other hand, spruce trees can live for hundreds of years. Also, a young tree will not produce pollen, so pollen will not be around until trees are mature. Beetles, by contrast, probably start having little baby beetles pretty quick. With these differences in mind, we can infer that beetles started populating the post-ice age landscape before spruce tree forests.

Choices – 1) Eliminate incorrect choices, starting with (E). (E) matches our Obvious Inference nicely. Beetles would be able to multiply faster than spruce trees could produce pollen and spread into forests, so it makes that beetles would populate the newly melted terrain faster than spruce trees. Prove and Move.

For practice, let's consider (B) and (D) – two popular choices in case you missed the obvious inference. (B) says that the sediments that contained fragments of cold-adapted beetles also contained spruce pollen. That doesn't make any sense based on the information. Warmth-adapted beetles replaced cold-adapted beetles approximately 500 years before pollen grains are present. (D) says that the cold-adapted beetle died out as the ice age was ending. The stimulus doesn't necessarily give us enough information to prove that. Those cold-adapted beetles could still be living in arctic areas even though warmth-adapted beetles replaced them in areas that melted after the ice age.

5. One child pushed another child from behind, injuring the second child. The first child clearly understands the <u>difference between right and wrong</u> (so what was done was wrong if it was <u>intended to injure</u> the second child.)

Which one of the following **principles**, if valid, most helps to **justify** the reasoning in the argument?

(A) An action that is intended to harm another person is wrong only if the person who performed the action understands the difference between right and wrong.

(B) It is wrong for a person who understands the difference between right and wrong to intentionally harm another person.

(C) Any act that is wrong is done with the intention of causing harm.

(D) An act that harms another person is wrong if the person who did it understands the difference between right and wrong and did not think about whether the act would injure the other person.

(E) A person who does not understand the difference between right and wrong does not bear any responsibility for harming another person.

Type: Justify
Flaw: Missing Link
Tags: Soft Conclusion

<u>Stem</u> – Identify the principle that allows the reasoning to be justified—that's a Justify problem stem.

<u>Stimulus</u> – 1) Find the Conclusion. Employing the indicator "so," the argument concludes that pushing the kid down was wrong if it was intended to injure the second child.

2) Find the Support. The argument states that one child pushed another. The first knows the difference between right and wrong, so what she did was wrong if it was meant to hurt the second child.

3) Find the Gap. The argument jumps from "understanding the difference between right and wrong" to "intending to injure." Yes, common sense tells us that intending to injure someone is indeed wrong, but the argument uses the two terms interchangeably. On LSAT problem, these are Unlinked Concepts.

<u>Choices</u> – In order for this reasoning to stand, the correct choice will state something to the effect of: "It is wrong for someone who knows the difference between right and wrong to purposefully act in a way that injures someone else."

1) Eliminate. (A) says that an action intended to hurt someone else is only wrong if the person who performs that action understands the difference between right and wrong. This choice doesn't fully understand the argument. The argument doesn't state that an action intended to hurt someone else is wrong *only if* the person doing the hurting knows the difference between right and wrong. Rather, it says the action was wrong if it was intended to harm someone else. (B) properly links "understands the difference between right and wrong" in a way that (A) fails to do. It states that it's wrong for someone who understands right and wrong to intentionally hurt someone else. (B) is a good plug for the gap, so hold onto it. (C) says that any act that is wrong is done with the intention of causing harm, but that's not relevant to the Unlinked Concepts. (D) says that an act that harms another person is wrong if the person doing the harming doesn't think about whether it would harm the other person. Where does that come from? There's nothing in the argument that talks about *considering* whether the act would injure the other person. (E) talks about a person who *doesn't* understand right or wrong, which is unrelated to the conclusion about people who *do* understand that difference.

2) Confirm. (B) links the Unlinked Concepts nicely, providing the support this argument needs. If you understand the difference between right and wrong, it is wrong to intentionally injure someone. (B) is correct.

6. Inez: The book we are reading, The Nature of Matter, is mistitled. A title should summarize the content of the whole book, but nearly half of this book is devoted to discussing a different, albeit closely related subject: energy.

    Antonio: I do not think that the author erred; according to modern physics, matter and energy are two facets of the same phenomenon.

    Which one of the following is **most strongly supported** by the conversation above?

    (A) Inez believes that the book should be called *The Nature of Energy.*

    (B) Antonio believes that there are no differences between matter and energy.

    (C) Inez and Antonio disagree on whether matter and energy are related.

    (D) Inez and Antonio disagree about the overall value of the book.

    (E) Inez believes that the book's title should not mention matter without mentioning energy.

Type: Inference
Tag: Prove & Move

Stem – We're asked which choice is "most strongly supported" by the stimulus, so this is an Inference problem.

Stimulus – 1) Understand the facts. Inez believes that *The Nature of Matter* is a mistitled book. She believes a book's title should summarize the content of the whole book. However, this book discusses energy almost as much as matter, so it is mistitled. Antonio disagrees with Inez because matter and energy are closely related in physics. Because matter and energy are deeply interconnected, he doesn't think the book is mistitled.

2) Look for an Obvious Inference. Nothing jumps out in particular, but we can take a few important things away from the stimulus. It's clear that Antonio and Inez disagree about how a book should be titled. Inez believes that a title must be an accurate summary of the book's content. On the other hand, Antonio believes the title is sufficient because matter and energy are so closely related that the author couldn't discuss one without the other.

Choices – 1) Eliminate choices, starting with (E). (E) looks very nice. Inez is explicit that a title should summarize the content of the whole book. Because nearly half of the book discusses energy, she believes the book is mistitled. Based on that, we can be confident that she believes the book's title must also include something about energy. If the title were *The Nature of Matter and Energy*, Inez would probably consider that an accurate summary of book and thus a fitting title for the book's content. Prove and Move.

For practice, let's look at (C), another popular choice. Antonio believes the book's title is sufficient because matter and energy are closely related. To Antonio, you can't discuss one without the other. While Inez believes that energy is a different subject, she does recognize that energy is a closely related subject to matter. Her issue isn't the inclusion of energy in the book; her concern is that the book's title does not accurately describe its content. (C) is incorrect.

7. Curator: Our museum displays only twentieth-century works, which are either on loan from private collectors or in the museum's permanent collection. Prints of all of the latter works are available in the museum store. The museum store also sells prints of some works that are not part of the museum's permanent collection, such as Hopper's Nighthawks.

If the curator's statements are true, which one of the following **must be true**?

(A) Every print in the museum store is of a work that is either on loan to the museum from a private collector or part of the museum's permanent collection.

(B) Every print that is sold in the museum store is a copy of a twentieth-century work.

(C) There are prints in the museum store of every work that is displayed in the museum and not on loan from a private collector.

(D) Hopper's Nighthawks is both a twentieth-century work and a work on loan to the museum from a private collector.

(E) Hopper's Nighthawks is not displayed in the museum.

Type: Inference
Tag: Prove & Move

Stem – You're asked which choice "must be true" based on the curator's statements. That's an Inference problem stem.

Stimulus – 1) Understand the facts. In the stimulus, we learn important criteria about the art on display in the museum and how it relates to the prints available in the museum store. First, all of the works on display are from the twentieth-century. Second, the museum displays art that is either on loan from a private collector or a part of the museum's permanent collection. The museum store sells prints of every work that is included in the permanent collection, but it also sells prints of artwork that is not a part of the permanent collection.

2) Look for an Obvious Inference. Nothing jumps out in particular. Time to work the choices.

Choices – 1) Eliminate choices, starting with (E). (E) says that Nighthawks is not on display in the museum, but we can't quite prove that. If it were on display, then it would have to be on loan from a private collector. We know that prints of every work from the permanent collection are available for sale, but we don't know if prints of some works owned by collectors are also available for sale. We don't have enough information to prove whether or not a collector owns Nighthawks, so we can't prove whether or not it fits the criteria for display. (D) is very similar. We don't really have a lot of information about the museum store. Just because prints of Nighthawks are for sale in the store doesn't necessarily mean that painting fits the criteria for display in the museum. It's not a part of the permanent collection, so it would have to be a twentieth-century work owned by a private collector if the museum displayed it. But, we don't have enough information to prove that it's on display. It could be a popular print, so the store sells it to make extra cash for the museum. On the other hand, we can prove (C) pretty nicely. If a work is displayed, it is either a part of the permanent collection or on loan from a collector. The store sells prints of every piece from the permanent collection, so the store sells prints of every work that is not owned by a private collector. Prove and Move.

Practice Set 3

Directions

- Time Limit: There is a 11 minute time limit for this Practice Set. Use a digital timer and pace with your watch. Guess on any problems you do not reach, just as you will on the official LSAT.

- Mark problems you are unsure of as you attempt the set.

- Bubble Sheet: Like all timed sets, fill in your answers in the bubble sheet for this Test Set.

- Review: Review only problems that you answered incorrectly and those that you marked as unsure. First self-review each problem, then carefully read the explanation.

1. Professor: It has been argued that freedom of thought is a precondition for intellectual progress, because freedom of thought allows thinkers to pursue their ideas, regardless of whom these ideas offend, in whatever direction they lead. However, it is clear that one must mine the full implications of interrelated ideas to make intellectual progress, and for this, thinkers need intellectual discipline. Therefore, this argument for freedom of thought fails.

The conclusion drawn by the professor follows logically if which one of the following is assumed?

(A) Thinkers who limit their line of thought to a particular orthodoxy are hindered in their intellectual progress.

(B) Thinkers can mine the full implications of interrelated ideas only in the context of a society that values intellectual progress.

(C) In societies that protect freedom of thought, thinkers invariably lack intellectual discipline.

(D) Freedom of thought engenders creativity, which aids the discovery of truth.

(E) Without intellectual discipline, thinkers can have no freedom of thought.

2. There are two kinds of horror stories: those that describe a mad scientist's experiments and those that describe a monstrous beast. In some horror stories about monstrous beasts, the monster symbolizes a psychological disturbance in the protagonist. Horror stories about mad scientists, on the other hand, typically express the author's feeling that scientific knowledge alone is not enough to guide human endeavor. However, despite these differences, both kinds of horror stories share two features: they describe violations of the laws of nature and they are intended to produce dread in the reader.

If the statements above are true, which one of the following would also have to be true?

(A) All descriptions of monstrous beasts describe violations of the laws of nature.

(B) Any story that describes a violation of a law of nature is intended to invoke dread in the reader.

(C) Horror stories of any kind usually describe characters who are psychologically disturbed.

(D) Most stories about mad scientists express the author's antiscientific views.

(E) Some stories that employ symbolism describe violations of the laws of nature.

3. Packaging is vital to a product's commercial success. For example, the maker of a popular drink introduced a "new, improved" version which succeeded in blind taste tests. However, customers did not buy the product when marketed, mainly because the can, almost identical to that used for the earlier version of the beverage, made consumers expect that the new product would share certain features of the old, an expectation not satisfied by the new product.

Which one of the following is most strongly supported by the information above?

(A) Proper product packaging is more important than the quality of the product.

(B) Products generally succeed in the market if they are packaged in a manner that accurately reflects their nature.

(C) Changing the packaging of a product will not improve the product's sales unless the product is also changed.

(D) To succeed in the market, a new product should not be packaged in a way that creates expectations that it does not meet.

(E) An improved version of an existing product will sell better than the earlier version unless the improved version is packaged like the earlier one.

4. Ethicist: Only when we know a lot about the events that led to an action are we justified in praising or blaming a person for that action—as we sometimes are. We must therefore reject Tolstoy's rash claim that if we knew a lot about the events leading up to any action, we would cease to regard that action as freely performed.

Which one of the following, if assumed, enables the conclusion of the ethicist's argument to be properly drawn?

(A) People should not be regarded as subject to praise or blame for actions that were caused by conditions beyond their control.

(B) Whether an act is one for which the person doing it is genuinely responsible is not determined by how much information others possess about that act.

(C) We can be justified in praising or blaming a person for an action only when we regard that action as freely performed.

(D) The responsibility a person bears for an action is not a matter of degree; however, our inclination to blame or praise whoever performed the action varies with the amount of information available.

(E) If we do not know much about the events leading up to any given action, we will regard that action as freely performed.

5. Members of the VideoKing Frequent Viewers club can now receive a special discount coupon. Members of the club who have rented more than ten videos in the past month can receive the discount coupon only at the VideoKing location from which the member last rented a movie. Members of the Frequent Viewers club who have not rented more than ten videos in the past month can receive the coupon only at the Main Street location. Pat, who has not rented more than ten videos in the past month, can receive the special discount coupon at the Walnut Lane location of VideoKing.

If all of the statements above are true, which one of the following must be true?

(A) The only people who can receive the special discount coupon at the Main Street location are Frequent Viewers club members who have not rented more than ten videos.

(B) Some members of the Frequent Viewers club have not rented more than ten videos.

(C) Some members of the Frequent Viewers club can receive the special discount coupon at more than one location of VideoKing.

(D) Some people who are not members of the Frequent Viewers club can receive the special discount coupon.

(E) If Pat rents a movie from the Main Street location, then she will not receive the special discount coupon.

6. It is difficult to grow cacti in a humid climate. It is difficult to raise orange trees in a cold climate. In most parts of a certain country, it is either easy to grow cacti or easy to raise orange trees.

    If the statements above are true, which one of the following must be false?

    (A) Half of the country is both humid and cold.
    (B) Most of the country is hot.
    (C) Some parts of the country are neither cold nor humid.
    (D) It is not possible to raise cacti in the country.
    (E) Most parts of the country are humid.

7. Science writer: Scientists' astounding success rate with research problems they have been called upon to solve causes the public to believe falsely that science can solve any problem. In fact, the problems scientists are called upon to solve are typically selected by scientists themselves. When the problems are instead selected by politicians or business leaders, their formulation is nevertheless guided by scientists in such a way as to make scientific solutions feasible. Scientists are almost never asked to solve problems that are not subject to such formulation.

    The science writer's statements, if true, most strongly support which one of the following?

    (A) If a problem can be formulated in such a way as to make a scientific solution feasible, scientists will usually be called upon to solve that problem.
    (B) Any problem a scientist can solve can be formulated in such a way as to make a scientific solution feasible.
    (C) Scientists would probably have a lower success rate with research problems if their grounds for selecting such problems were less narrow.
    (D) Most of the problems scientists are called upon to solve are problems that politicians and business leaders want solved, but whose formulation the scientists have helped to guide.
    (E) The only reason for the astounding success rate of science is that the problems scientists are called upon to solve are usually selected by the scientists themselves.

END OF SET

Set 3 Key & Explanations

1. C
2. E
3. D
4. C
5. D
6. A
7. C

1. Professor: It has been argued that <u>freedom of thought</u> is a precondition for intellectual progress, because freedom of thought allows thinkers to pursue their ideas, regardless of whom these ideas offend, in whatever direction they lead. However, it is clear that one must mine the full implications of interrelated ideas to make intellectual progress, and for this, thinkers need <u>intellectual discipline.</u> (**Therefore**, this argument for freedom of thought fails.)

    The conclusion drawn by the professor follows logically if which one of the following is assumed?

   (A) Thinkers who limit their line of thought to a particular orthodoxy are hindered in their intellectual progress.

   (B) Thinkers can mine the full implications of interrelated ideas only in the context of a society that values intellectual progress.

   (C) In societies that protect freedom of thought, thinkers invariably lack intellectual discipline.

    (D) Freedom of thought engenders creativity, which aids the discovery of truth.

    (E) Without intellectual discipline, thinkers can have no freedom of thought.

Type: Justify
Flaw: Missing Link
Tag: Opposing View Conclusion

<u>Stem</u> – "Follows logically" if a choice is assumed tells us this is a Justify problem.

<u>Stimulus</u> – 1) Find the Conclusion. "Therefore" is a nice indicator for the professor's Opposing View Conclusion. The argument that freedom of thought is necessary for intellectual progress fails.

2) Find the Support. Some argue that freedom of thought is necessary for intellectual progress because it allows thinkers to pursue their ideas in any direction. However, proponents of this argument forget that intellectual discipline is necessary for intellectual progress, so their argument for freedom of thought fails.

3) Find the Gap. In the professor's argument, it's pretty clear that there are two unlinked concepts: freedom of thought and intellectual discipline. The professor assumes that the two are mutually exclusive without providing any justification of that. We need a choice that tells us that freedom of thought and intellectual discipline cannot go hand in hand.

<u>Choices</u> – 1) Eliminate choices without both concepts. (A) fails to mention intellectual discipline. (B) doesn't get at either of the unlinked concepts. On the other hand, (C) mentions both, so hang onto this one. It says that thinkers lack intellectual discipline in environments that protect freedom of thought. (D) discusses freedom of thought, but it doesn't touch on intellectual discipline at all. (E) mentions both concepts, so hang onto this one, too.

2) Confirm. After elimination, (C) looks pretty good. It says that thinkers lack intellectual discipline in environments that protect freedom of thought. If thinkers lack intellectual discipline, then there cannot be intellectual progress. If we assume that freedom of thought hinders intellectual discipline, then we can conclude that freedom of thought does not promote intellectual progress. By contrast, (E) ties the unlinked concepts together in a way that tears the argument apart. It says that intellectual discipline is necessary for freedom of though, which is the opposite of the link we need. (C) is correct.

2. There are two kinds of horror stories: those that describe a mad scientist's experiments and those that describe a monstrous beast. In some horror stories about monstrous beasts, the monster symbolizes a psychological disturbance in the protagonist. Horror stories about mad scientists, on the other hand, typically express the author's feeling that scientific knowledge alone is not enough to guide human endeavor. However, despite these differences, both kinds of horror stories share two features: they describe violations of the laws of nature and they are intended to produce dread in the reader.

If the statements above are true, which one of the following would also **have to be true**?

(A)   All descriptions of monstrous beasts describe violations of the laws of nature.

(B)   Any story that describes a violation of a law of nature is intended to invoke dread in the reader.

(C)   Horror stories of any kind usually describe characters who are psychologically disturbed.

(D)   Most stories about mad scientists express the author's antiscientific views.

(E)   Some stories that employ symbolism describe violations of the laws of nature.

Type: Inference
Tag: Prove & Move

Stem – We're asked which choice must be true if the statements in the stimulus are true. That's a classic Inference problem stem.

Stimulus – 1) Understand the facts. This stem might seem a little intimidating because it's chock full of information about horror stories. Nevertheless, there is a lot of important conditional language we can pull out that could help us prove an inference. First, there are two subjects for horror stories: monstrous beasts and mad scientists' experiments. In *some* horror stories about monstrous beasts, the beast symbolizes a psychological disturbance in the story's protagonists. *Most* stories about mad scientists express the author's belief that pursuing scientific knowledge alone will not necessarily have positive consequences. Both types of horror stories share two characteristics: they describe violations of laws of nature, and the authors' intentions are to scare the reader.

2) Look for an Obvious inference: Um, there's a lot going on here. Let's work the choices.

Choices – 1) Eliminate choices, starting with (E). We can prove (E) pretty nicely with a little conditional combination. All horror stories describe violations of the laws of nature. *Some* horror stories are about monstrous beasts, and *some* of those horror stories use symbolism. Also, *some* horror stories about monstrous beasts that use symbolism represent *some* of the greater group of stories in general. Thus, *some* stories that use symbolism (*some* horror stories about monstrous beasts) describe violations of the laws of nature. Prove and Move.

For practice, let's consider (A), a popular choice on this problem. (A) is very similar to (E). All horror stories about monstrous beasts describe violations of the laws of nature because all horror stories in general describe violations of the laws of nature. However, all descriptions of monstrous beasts are not the same as all horror stories about monstrous beasts. That's an important distinction, so (A) is incorrect.

3. Packaging is vital to a product's commercial success. For example, the maker of a popular drink introduced a "new, improved" version which succeeded in blind taste tests. However, customers did not buy the product when marketed, mainly because the can, almost identical to that used for the earlier version of the beverage, made consumers expect that the new product would share certain features of the old, an expectation not satisfied by the new product.

Which one of the following is most strongly supported by the information above?

(A) Proper product packaging is more important than the quality of the product.

(B) Products generally succeed in the market if they are packaged in a manner that accurately reflects their nature.

(C) Changing the packaging of a product will not improve the product's sales unless the product is also changed.

(D) To succeed in the market, a new product should not be packaged in a way that creates expectations that it does not meet.

(E) An improved version of an existing product will sell better than the earlier version unless the improved version is packaged like the earlier one.

Type: Inference
Tags: Obvious Inference, Prove & Move

Stem – "Most strongly supported by the information above" tells you this is an Inference problem.

Stimulus – 1) Understand the facts. Packaging is vital to a product's success. The maker of a popular drink introduced a new product that succeeded in blind taste tests, but the new product was packaged in a can that was nearly identical to the older version. Because of that, customers who bought the new product thought it would share certain features of the old product, but it did not. Customers did not buy the new product as a consequence because it did not meet the expectations of the packaging, which resembled the old product.

2) Look for an Obvious Inference. In the example of the new product, what about the packaging caused the product to fail? The new product's packaging resembled the old one so much that customers expected a similar product. In a sense, the new product failed because it was packaged in a way that caused customers to have expectations that the new product could not fulfill. Let's see if that comes up in the choices.

Choices – 1) Eliminate choices, starting with (E). We can't prove (E) at all. In fact, (E) goes against the example of the new product from the stimulus. That new product failed because it was packaged like the earlier product. On the other hand, (D) matches our thinking from the stimulus nicely. The new product cannot be packaged in a way that creates expectations that the new product can't fulfill. If the new product's can looks like the old one, customers will expect the old one. If their expectations are not met, then customers will not buy the new product even if it performs better in blind tests. Prove and Move.

4. Ethicist: Only when we know a lot about the events that led to an action are we <u>justified in praising or blaming</u> a person for that action—as we sometimes are. We must **(therefore** reject Tolstoy's rash claim that if we knew a lot about the events leading up to any action, we would cease to <u>regard that action as freely performed.**)**

Which one of the following, if assumed, enables the *J* conclusion of the ethicist's argument to be properly drawn?

(A) People should not be regarded as subject to praise or blame for actions that were caused by conditions beyond their control.

(B) Whether an act is one for which the person doing it is genuinely responsible is not determined by how much information others possess about that act.

(C) We can be justified in praising or blaming a person for an action only when we regard that action as freely performed.

(D) The responsibility a person bears for an action is not a matter of degree; however, our inclination to blame or praise whoever performed the action varies with the amount of information available.

(E) If we do not know much about the events leading up to any given action, we will regard that action as freely performed.

Type: Justify
Flaw: Missing Link
Tag: Opposing View Conclusion

Stem – "If assumed" and "properly drawn" tell us this is a Justify problem.

Stimulus – 1) Find the Conclusion. "Therefore" at the beginning of the second sentence tells you that the conclusion is that the claim "if we knew a lot about the events leading up to any action, we would cease to regard that action as freely performed" is false. Pretty hefty one there.

2) Find the Support. The support is the first sentence. It helps to mentally summarize it as "you have to know about the preceding events of an action to praise or blame for it."

3) Find the Gap. Considering the density of the argument, it is surprisingly unchallenging to see which concepts are unlinked: praise or blame from the support, and regarding an action as freely performed from the conclusion.

Choices – 1) Eliminate choices without both concepts. In (A), "conditions beyond their control" ≠ "regarding an action as freely performed," so the concept from the conclusion is not here. (B) doesn't mention praise or blame. (C) has both concepts, so hold onto it. (D) doesn't mentioned freely performed, and (E) doesn't mention praise or blame.

2) Confirm. (C) is the only choice that has both concepts, so it must be correct. Seeing exactly how (C) makes the conclusion valid is challenging and not altogether necessary. That said, working it out will boost your conditional diagramming skills. Start by diagramming the support and the conclusion:

Support: praise or blame → know events

Conclusion *rejects:*

know events → not freely performed

We can link these two conditionals:

praise or blame → not freely performed

The correct choice says:

praise or blame → freely performed

So, (C) contradicts the linked conditional with Tolstoy's claim, which is what the argument's conclusion tries to do.

The fast, smooth way to solve this problem is to use process of elimination with the concepts. The linking and conditionals are here for guidance and extra teaching.

5. Members of the VideoKing Frequent Viewers club can now receive a special discount coupon. Members of the club who have rented more than ten videos in the past month can receive the discount coupon only at the VideoKing location from which the member last rented a movie. Members of the Frequent Viewers club who have not rented more than ten videos in the past month can receive the coupon only at the Main Street location. Pat, who has not rented more than ten videos in the past month, can receive the special discount coupon at the Walnut Lane location of VideoKing.

If all of the statements above are true, which one of the following **must be true**?

(A) The only people who can receive the special discount coupon at the Main Street location are Frequent Viewers club members who have not rented more than ten videos.

(B) Some members of the Frequent Viewers club have not rented more than ten videos.

(C) Some members of the Frequent Viewers club can receive the special discount coupon at more than one location of VideoKing.

(D) Some people who are not members of the Frequent Viewers club can receive the special discount coupon.

(E) If Pat rents a movie from the Main Street location, then she will not receive the special discount coupon.

Type: Inference
Tags: Obvious Inference, Prove & Move

Stem – "Must be true" indicates that this is an Inference problem stem. Understand the facts and then look for an Obvious Inference.

Stimulus – 1) Understand the facts. Members of a rental club can get a coupon at a specific location, which is dependent on their rental history. If they've fulfilled a certain amount of rentals in the past month, then they have to go where they last rented. If they haven't fulfilled that amount, they have to go to Main St. Pat didn't fulfill the amount, but she can get the coupon at Walnut Lane—which is, most notably, not Main St.

2) Look for an Obvious Inference. You know that Pat hasn't rented more than the required amount to get her coupon at the store she last rented a movie. Based on the information, that would tell you that she has to go to Main St, but then the argument says she can get the coupon on Walnut Lane—so, she must not be a member, because otherwise she would have to go to Main St (if the other statements are true, which the stem tells you they are). So, the inference here would be that non-members can get the coupon.

Choices – 1) Eliminate incorrect choices, starting with (E). (E) infers that, if Pat rents a movie from the Main St. location, she won't receive the special discount coupon. That isn't supported because the stimulus doesn't say that you have to rent a movie in order to receive the coupon. It just says that you have to go to a specific place to "receive" the coupon. (D) looks good; it infers that some people who aren't members of the Frequent Viewers club can receive the special coupons. This inference is supported because Pat doesn't fit the description for someone in the club. If she were in the club and hasn't rented more than ten videos in the past month, she would have to go to Main St. to get the coupon. But, the stimulus says she has to go to Walnut Lane, which means she must not be a member. Therefore, it follows that some people who aren't in the club (Pat, for one) can get the special coupon. (D) is proven; Prove and Move.

Let's analyze (C) for further clarification. (C) infers that some members of the Frequency Viewers club can receive the special discount coupon at more than one store location, but that isn't supported by the stimulus because the stimulus splits the Frequent Viewers category right down the middle, stating that one side has to go to a specific store, and the other has to go to a specific store. Therefore, there's no reason to believe that some people could get the coupon at more than one store.

6. It is difficult to grow cacti in a humid climate. It is difficult to raise orange trees in a cold climate. In most parts of a certain country, it is either easy to grow cacti or easy to raise orange trees.

    If the statements above are true, which one of the following **must be false**?

    (A) Half of the country is both humid and cold.
    (B) Most of the country is hot.
    (C) Some parts of the country are neither cold nor humid.
    (D) It is not possible to raise cacti in the country.
    (E) Most parts of the country are humid.

Type: Inference – EXCEPT

Stem – Everything about this stem looks like an Inference problem until the word "false." That means every choice will be possible (not necessarily proven outright, though), and the correct choice will be the only one that defies the facts in the stimulus and must be false.

Stimulus – 1) Understand the facts. It's hard to grow cacti in humidity, and it's hard to grow orange trees in cold temperatures. In most parts of a certain country, it is either easy to grow cacti or easy to grow orange trees. The either/or language is the crux of the last sentence. It's not necessarily a straight 50/50. In most of the country, you can either grow cacti easily or orange trees easily.

2) Look for an Obvious Inference. In most parts of the country, you will either be able to grow cacti or orange trees easily. Yet, the stimulus only gives us conditions under which it is difficult to grow the two plants. We don't really know what conditions will make it easy to grow the two plants. It might seem probable that the opposite of the difficult growing conditions will be the easy growing conditions, but that's not necessarily true. So, there's only one clear inference we can make: some parts of the country must not be cold, and some parts of the country must not be humid.

Choices – 1) Eliminate choices that are proven by the stimulus or that could be true, starting with (E). Even though it's difficult to grow cacti in humid climates, (E) is still possible. In most of the country, you can either grow cacti or orange trees easily. As long as some percentage of the country can grow cacti easily (> 0%), most of the country could be humid and that statement could still be true. (D) is tempting because we are told that cacti can grow easily somewhere in the country. However, "possible" and "easy" are two different adjectives. Perhaps in the parts of the country where it would be easy to grow cacti there are animals that will eat the cacti immediately, so it isn't possible to raise cacti. We can't be certain that (D) is false. (C) must be true based on the stimulus, and it matches our thinking very nicely. If you can grow either crop easily somewhere in the country, then some parts must not meet the difficult growing conditions. (B) can definitely be true. We don't know how temperature affects cacti, and we know cold temperature is bad for orange trees. On the other hand, (A) must be false.

2) Confirm. (A) says that half of the country (exactly 50%) is both humid and cold. Based on the stimulus, we know it would be difficult to grow both cacti and orange trees in such a climate. But, the stimulus tells us that, in *most* parts of the country (anything greater than 51%), it is easy to grow either of the two crops. That means that *most* parts of the country are not humid and not cold. (A) must be false, and it is the correct answer.

7. Science writer: Scientists' astounding success rate with research problems they have been called upon to solve causes the public to believe falsely that science can solve any problem. In fact, the problems scientists are called upon to solve are typically selected by scientists themselves. When the problems are instead selected by politicians or business leaders, their formulation is nevertheless guided by scientists in such a way as to make scientific solutions feasible. Scientists are almost never asked to solve problems that are not subject to such formulation.

The science writer's statements, if true, **most strongly support** which one of the following?

(A) If a problem can be formulated in such a way as to make a scientific solution feasible, scientists will usually be called upon to solve that problem.

(B) Any problem a scientist can solve can be formulated in such a way as to make a scientific solution feasible.

(C) Scientists would probably have a lower success rate with research problems if their grounds for selecting such problems were less narrow.

(D) Most of the problems scientists are called upon to solve are problems that politicians and business leaders want solved, but whose formulation the scientists have helped to guide.

(E) The only reason for the astounding success rate of science is that the problems scientists are called upon to solve are usually selected by the scientists themselves.

Type: Inference
Tags: Obvious Inference, Prove & Move

Stem – "Most strongly support" is an Inference problem stem. Understand the facts and then look for an Obvious Inference.

Stimulus – 1) Understand the facts. People believe that scientists can solve anything because they have a high rate of success in their research, but they have a high rate of success because it's scientists who decide what research to conduct. Even when they're asked to conduct research by non-scientists, those non-scientists are often guided by scientists. That stands true for most scientific studies.

2) Look for an Obvious Inference. The stimulus implies that the scientists' success rate is artificially high and that it wouldn't be as high if it weren't scientists selecting what research to conduct.

Choices – 1) Eliminate incorrect choices, starting with (E). (E) infers that the only reason for the scientists' success is that the scientists are the ones selecting the research. This choice goes beyond the stimulus, as there's no reason to believe that the *only* reason for their success is that they select the research. There are no doubt plenty of other factors that affect success. (D) infers that *most* of the problems scientists are called upon to solve are ones that business leaders and politicians want solved, which isn't supported either. You're just told that when business leaders and politicians want an issue solved, scientists are still behind that issue. Thus, you can't infer that "most" of the problems tackled by scientists are at the request of business leaders and politicians. (C) infers that scientists would have a lower success rate if their grounds for selecting problems were less narrow. This is a match for the Obvious Inference. It infers that the scientists wouldn't be as successful if they didn't have such a tailored field of research issues to choose from ("if their grounds for selecting were less narrow," i.e. if the options for research were not as controlled by the scientific community as they are). Prove and Move.

Linking Test

Complete a timed Test of Inference and Justify problems to measure your current Linking abilities. Your Tutor will use your results to measure your progress on this important Skill Group and to optimize your future Logical Reasoning prep.

Chapter Contents
Linking Skill Group Test

Linking Skill Group Test

You've finished the learning phase of the Linking Skill Group – excellent work! So far in this Module, you learned how to identify inferences, understand an argument's reasoning, and locate unlinked concepts. You also honed your skills on two important problem types: Inference and Justify.

Now, it's time to test how well you've internalized the techniques. Ahead of you is a 10-problem Linking Test, which will test all of your Linking skills. This test matches the Linking Diagnostic you took at the beginning of this Module in difficulty so it can accurately measure your improvement during the Module.

Directions

- Time Limit: Complete the 10 problems in 15 minutes. Set a digital timer and pace with your watch. Guess on any problems you do not reach, just as you will on the official LSAT.

- Mark problems you are unsure of as you attempt the set.

- Bubble Sheet: Like all timed sets, fill in your answers in the bubble sheet for this Test Set.

- Review: Review only problems that you answered incorrectly and those that you marked as unsure. For each problem, first self-review each problem, then carefully read the explanation.

The test begins on the next page.

1. Backyard gardeners who want to increase the yields of their potato plants should try growing stinging nettles alongside the plants, since stinging nettles attract insects that kill a wide array of insect pests that damage potato plants. It is true that stinging nettles also attract aphids, and that many species of aphids are harmful to potato plants, but that fact in no way contradicts this recommendation, because _____.

    Which one of the following most logically completes the argument?

    (A)   stinging nettles require little care and thus are easy to cultivate

    (B)   some types of aphids are attracted to stinging nettle plants but do not damage them

    (C)   the types of aphids that stinging nettles attract do not damage potato plants

    (D)   insect pests typically cause less damage to potato plants than other harmful organisms do

    (E)   most aphid species that are harmful to potato plants cause greater harm to other edible food plants

2. In considering the fact that many people believe that promotions are often given to undeserving employees because the employees successfully flatter their supervisors, a psychologist argued that although many people who flatter their supervisors are subsequently promoted, flattery generally is not the reason for their success, because almost all flattery is so blatant that it is obvious even to those toward whom it is directed.

    Which one of the following, if assumed, enables the psychologist's conclusion to be properly drawn?

    (A)   People in positions of responsibility expect to be flattered.

    (B)   Official guidelines for granting promotion tend to focus on merit.

    (C)   Flattery that is not noticed by the person being flattered is ineffective.

    (D)   Many people interpret insincere flattery as sincere admiration.

    (E)   Supervisors are almost never influenced by flattery when they notice it.

3. Aerobics instructor: Compared to many forms of exercise, kickboxing aerobics is highly risky. Overextending when kicking often leads to hip, knee, or lower-back injuries. Such overextension is very likely to occur when beginners try to match the high kicks of more skilled practitioners.

    Which one of the following is most strongly supported by the aerobics instructor's statements?

    (A)   Skilled practitioners of kickboxing aerobics are unlikely to experience injuries from overextending while kicking.

    (B)   To reduce the risk of injuries, beginners at kickboxing aerobics should avoid trying to match the high kicks of more skilled practitioners.

    (C)   Beginners at kickboxing aerobics will not experience injuries if they avoid trying to match the high kicks of more skilled practitioners.

    (D)   Kickboxing aerobics is more risky than forms of aerobic exercise that do not involve high kicks.

    (E)   Most beginners at kickboxing aerobics experience injuries from trying to match the high kicks of more skilled practitioners.

4. Judge: The case before me involves a plaintiff and three codefendants. The plaintiff has applied to the court for an order permitting her to question each defendant without their codefendants or their codefendants' legal counsel being present. Two of the codefendants, however, share the same legal counsel. The court will not order any codefendant to find new legal counsel. Therefore, the order requested by the plaintiff cannot be granted.

The conclusion of the judge's argument is most strongly supported if which one of the following principles is assumed to hold?

(A) A court cannot issue an order that forces legal counsel to disclose information revealed by a client.

(B) Defendants have the right to have their legal counsel present when being questioned.

(C) People being questioned in legal proceedings may refuse to answer questions that are self-incriminating.

(D) A plaintiff in a legal case should never be granted a right that is denied to a defendant.

(E) A defendant's legal counsel has the right to question the plaintiff.

5. Computer scientist: For several decades, the number of transistors on new computer microchips, and hence the microchips' computing speed, has doubled about every 18 months. However, from the mid-1990s into the next decade, each such doubling in a microchip's computing speed was accompanied by a doubling in the cost of producing that microchip.

Which one of the following can be properly inferred from the computer scientist's statements?

(A) The only effective way to double the computing speed of computer microchips is to increase the number of transistors per microchip.

(B) From the mid-1990s into the next decade, there was little if any increase in the retail cost of computers as a result of the increased number of transistors on microchips.

(C) For the last several decades, computer engineers have focused on increasing the computing speed of computer microchips without making any attempt to control the cost of producing them.

(D) From the mid-1990s into the next decade, a doubling in the cost of fabricating new computer microchips accompanied each doubling in the number of transistors on those microchips.

(E) It is unlikely that engineers will ever be able to increase the computing speed of microchips without also increasing the cost of producing them.

6. Art critic: The Woerner Journalism Award for criticism was given to Nan Paulsen for her reviews of automobiles. This is inappropriate. The criticism award should be given for criticism, which Paulsen's reviews clearly were not. After all, cars are utilitarian things, not works of art. And objects that are not works of art do not reveal important truths about the culture that produced them.

Which one of the following principles, if valid, most helps to justify the reasoning in the art critic's argument?

(A) The Woerner Journalism Award for criticism should not be given to a writer who portrays utilitarian objects as works of art.

(B) Reviews of objects cannot appropriately be considered to be criticism unless the objects reveal important truths about the culture that produced them.

(C) Unless a review is written for the purpose of revealing important truths about the writer's culture, that review should not be considered to be criticism.

(D) The Woerner Journalism Award for criticism should not be given to writers who do not consider themselves to be critics.

(E) All writing that reveals important truths about a culture should be considered to be criticism.

7. Traffic engineers have increased the capacity of the Krakkenbak Bridge to handle rush-hour traffic flow. The resultant increase in rush-hour traffic flow would not have occurred had the city not invested in computer modeling technology last year at the request of the city's mayor, and the city's financial predicament would not have been resolved if the traffic flow across the bridge during rush hour had not been increased.

Which one of the following can be properly inferred from the information above?

(A) The city's financial predicament would not have been resolved had the city chosen a competing computer modeling software package.

(B) The city's financial predicament would not have been resolved had the city not invested in computer modeling technology.

(C) On an average day, more traffic crosses the Krakkenbak Bridge this year as compared to last year.

(D) Traffic flow across the Krakkenbak Bridge during rush hour would not have increased had the city's mayor not made investing in computer modeling technology the highest budgetary priority last year.

(E) The city's mayor was a proponent of investing in computer modeling technology because of the city's need to increase traffic flow across the Krakkenbak Bridge during rush hour.

8. Ms. Sandstrom's newspaper column describing a strange natural phenomenon on the Mendels' farm led many people to trespass on and extensively damage their property. Thus, Ms. Sandstrom should pay for this damage if, as the Mendels claim, she could have reasonably expected that the column would lead people to damage the Mendels' farm.

The argument's conclusion can be properly inferred if which one of the following is assumed?

(A) One should pay for any damage that one's action leads other people to cause if one could have reasonably expected that the action would lead other people to cause damage.

(B) One should pay for damage that one's action leads other people to cause only if, prior to the action, one expected that the action would lead other people to cause that damage.

(C) It is unlikely that the people who trespassed on and caused the damage to the Mendels' property would themselves pay for the damage they caused.

(D) Ms. Sandstrom knew that her column could incite trespassing that could result in damage to the Mendels' farm.

(E) The Mendels believe that Ms. Sandstrom is able to form reasonable expectations about the consequences of her actions.

9. Council member: The profits of downtown businesses will increase if more consumers live in the downtown area, and a decrease in the cost of living in the downtown area will guarantee that the number of consumers living there will increase. However, the profits of downtown businesses will not increase unless downtown traffic congestion decreases.

If all the council member's statements are true, which one of the following must be true?

(A) If downtown traffic congestion decreases, the number of consumers living in the downtown area will increase.

(B) If the cost of living in the downtown area decreases, the profits of downtown businesses will increase.

(C) If downtown traffic congestion decreases, the cost of living in the downtown area will increase.

(D) If downtown traffic congestion decreases, the cost of living in the downtown area will decrease.

(E) If the profits of downtown businesses increase, the number of consumers living in the downtown area will increase.

10. Activist: Any member of the city council ought either to vote against the proposal or to abstain. But if all the members abstain, the matter will be decided by the city's voters. So at least one member of the city council should vote against the proposal.

The conclusion of the activist's argument follows logically if which one of the following is assumed?

(A) If all the members of the city council abstain in the vote on the proposal, the city's voters will definitely decide in favor of the proposal.

(B) The proposal should not be decided by the city's voters.

(C) No members of the city council will vote in favor of the proposal.

(D) If not every member of the city council abstains in the vote on the proposal, the matter will not be decided by the city's voters.

(E) If one member of the city council ought to vote against the proposal, the other members should abstain in the vote on the proposal.

END OF SET

Linking Test Answer Key

1. C
2. E
3. B
4. B
5. D
6. B
7. B
8. A
9. B
10. B

Linking Test Explanations

1. Backyard gardeners who want to increase the yields of their potato plants should try growing stinging nettles alongside the plants, since stinging nettles attract insects that kill a wide array of insect pests that damage potato plants. It is true that stinging nettles also attract aphids, and that many species of aphids are harmful to potato plants, but that fact in no way contradicts this recommendation, because _____.

   Which one of the following most **logically completes** the argument?

   (A) stinging nettles require little care and thus are easy to cultivate

   (B) some types of aphids are attracted to stinging nettle plants but do not damage them

   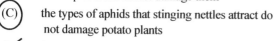(C) the types of aphids that stinging nettles attract do not damage potato plants

   (D) insect pests typically cause less damage to potato plants than other harmful organisms do

   (E) most aphid species that are harmful to potato plants cause greater harm to other edible food plants

Type: Inference
Tags: Logically Completes Subtype, Prove & Move

Stem – "Logically completes" tells you this is a Logically Completes type of Inference problem. "Fact group proves correct choice" is your core focus.

Stimulus – 1) Understand the facts. Stinging nettles attract insects that kill other insects harmful to potato plants. However, the nettles attract aphids, many species of which harm potatoes, but that's not an issue because… Can you see why?

2) Obvious Inference: Well, you know the nettles attract aphids, many of which are bad for potato plants, and you also know that these aphids aren't an issue. How could that be? You're told that "many species of aphids are harmful to potato plants," but "many" implies "not all." Maybe the species of aphids attracted by nettle plants aren't harmful to potatoes. That would make the aphid attraction a non-issue as the stimulus says is the case.

Choices – The correct answer should describe how it could be that it isn't a bad thing for the potato plants that the nettles should attract aphids.

1) Eliminate choices, starting with (E). (E) talks about how aphid species are harmful to other plants, but you don't need to know about how they affect *other* plants, you need some more information about the aphids as they interact with potato plants. (D) is like (E); it talks about other *organisms* that affect potato plants, but you need a choice that talks about aphids affecting potato plants. (E) and (D) are classic half-baked choices, talking about only one side of a two-part system. Both choices also introduce some new info that you don't need to know anything about and that doesn't affect the stimulus at all, much less logically completes it. (C), on the other hand, talks about both aphids and potato plants. It says that the type of aphid stinging nettles attract doesn't hurt potato plants. That logically completes the stimulus because it describes how it could be the case that the nettles attract aphids—many of which are bad for potato plants—yet this aphid attraction is not an issue. (C) is correct, so go ahead and Prove and Move even though it's a rare approach to a Logically Completes Subtype..

2. In considering the fact that many people believe that promotions are often given to undeserving employees because the employees successfully flatter their supervisors, a psychologist argued that although many people who flatter their supervisors are subsequently promoted,(flattery generally is <u>not the reason</u> for their success) because almost all flattery is so blatant that it is <u>obvious</u> even to those toward whom it is directed.

J   Which one of the following, **if assumed, enables** the psychologist's **conclusion** to be **properly drawn**?

    (A) People in positions of responsibility expect to be flattered.

    (B) Official guidelines for granting promotion tend to focus on merit.

    (C) Flattery that is not noticed by the person being flattered is ineffective.

    (D) Many people interpret insincere flattery as sincere admiration.

    (E) Supervisors are almost never influenced by flattery when they notice it.

Type: Justify

Stem – The stem here asks which choice allows the conclusion to be properly drawn—a classic Justify problem stem. Find the gap!

Stimulus – 1) Find the Conclusion. The psychologist concludes that flattery tends not to be the reason people are promoted.

2) Find the Support. As reasoning for his conclusion, the psychologist states that almost all flattery is blatant to the point that it's obvious to the person who's being flattered.

3) Find the Gap. The conclusion states flattery tends not to be the reason people are promoted on the basis of the flattery being too obvious. But just because flattery is obvious, does that mean it can't be the reason for these people being promoted? Maybe the boss likes to be flattered, whether she's aware of it or not. There's no reason to assume—and no statement in the argument to support the idea—that obvious flattery is not the reason for these people being promoted. There's your gap in the argument.

Choices – The correct answer will fill the gap: it will state the assumption that if a person is obviously being flattered, the boss won't promote the person flattering them just on the basis of that flattery. Basically, it will state that the people being flattered are immune to flattery (when it comes to handing out promotions, that is).

1) Eliminate. (A) says people in positions of responsibility expect to be flattered, but it doesn't matter whether or not they expect it. You need a choice that talks about them *recognizing* the flattery and not being influenced by it. (B) says that the official guidelines for promotions are merit-based, which is wrong for the same reasons as (A). It doesn't plug the gap between obvious flattery and promotions. (C) says flattery that isn't noticed by the person who's being flattered is ineffective flattery—that just describes what makes flattery "effective." But you don't need to worry about effective or ineffective flattery, you're looking for a description of how obvious flattery does not influence a boss' to hand out promotions. (D) says many people think insincere flattery is admiration, which is irrelevant. It doesn't matter how they interpret the insincere flattery, and that doesn't tell you anything about promotions.

2) Confirm. The only choice left is (E), and it looks good. If supervisors are almost never influenced by obvious flattery, then that connects the two sides of the gap: "obvious flattery" and the doc's conclusion that flattery tends not to be the reason people get a promotion. If they're not influenced by obvious flattery, then it makes sense that flattery is generally not the reason for a promotion. (E) is correct.

3. Aerobics instructor: Compared to many forms of exercise, kickboxing aerobics is highly risky. Overextending when kicking often leads to hip, knee, or lower-back injuries. Such overextension is very likely to occur when beginners try to match the high kicks of more skilled practitioners.

Which one of the following is **most strongly supported** by the aerobics instructor's statements?

(A) Skilled practitioners of kickboxing aerobics are unlikely to experience injuries from overextending while kicking.

(B) To reduce the risk of injuries, beginners at kickboxing aerobics should avoid trying to match the high kicks of more skilled practitioners.

(C) Beginners at kickboxing aerobics will not experience injuries if they avoid trying to match the high kicks of more skilled practitioners.

(D) Kickboxing aerobics is more risky than forms of aerobic exercise that do not involve high kicks.

(E) Most beginners at kickboxing aerobics experience injuries from trying to match the high kicks of more skilled practitioners.

Type: Inference
Tags: Obvious Inference, Prove & Move

Stem – "Most strongly supported" is an Inference problem stem.

Stimulus – 1) Understand the facts. Kickboxing aerobics is risky because beginners are prone to overextending, which leads to injuries of the hip, knee, or back. But, that happens when they try to match the high kicks of skilled practitioners.

2) Look for an Obvious Inference. Beginners shouldn't try to match the high kicks of skilled practitioners because that's when they get injured.

Choices – 1) Eliminate choices, starting with (E). (E) infers that "most beginners" experience injuries, but that's not supported because the stimulus only says that kickboxing is "highly risky." It certainly doesn't say that "most" beginners get hurt. (D) infers that kickboxing is more risky than other forms of aerobic exercise that don't have high kicks, but you don't know that to be the case. The stimulus only talks about kickboxing, not about other forms of exercise. (C) infers that beginners won't get hurt if they don't try to kick high like the experienced practitioners. Again, you don't know that to be the case—you only know that overextending a high kick is *one way* the beginners can get hurt. The stimulus doesn't say it's the *only* way they get injured, though. (B) infers that, to reduce injuries, beginners should avoid trying to match the high kicks of more skilled practitioners. That matches the Obvious Inference, and it's supported because the stimulus says that the overextension that leads to injury happens "when beginners try to match" high kicks. So, don't match the high kicks, they won't overextend and they'll reduce the risk of injury. (B) is proven, so move on.

4.   Judge: The case before me involves a plaintiff and three codefendants. The plaintiff has applied to the court for an order permitting her to (question each defendant without their codefendants or their codefendants' legal counsel being present.) Two of the codefendants, however, share the same legal counsel. The court will not order any codefendant to find new legal counsel. (**Therefore**, the order requested by the plaintiff cannot be granted.)

The conclusion of the judge's argument is most strongly supported if which one of the following principles is assumed to hold?

(A)   A court cannot issue an order that forces legal counsel to disclose information revealed by a client.

(B)   Defendants have the right to have their legal counsel present when being questioned.

(C)   People being questioned in legal proceedings may refuse to answer questions that are self-incriminating.

(D)   A plaintiff in a legal case should never be granted a right that is denied to a defendant.

(E)   A defendant's legal counsel has the right to question the plaintiff.

Type: Justify
Tag: Referential Conclusion

Stem – The stem is a little unusual for a Justify problem because it doesn't contain the word "justify" or directly talk about the conclusion being properly inferred. However, it asks you to strengthen the conclusion using a principle, which means it is a Justify problem.

Stimulus – 1) Find the Conclusion. The indicator word "therefore" helps us see that the conclusion is the final sentence: the order to question one defendant without their codefendants or their codefendants legal-council present cannot be granted. This is a Referential Conclusion because the content of the order is mentioned early in the stimulus.

2) Find the Support. Because two of the codefendants have the same legal counsel, the order thus asks that two of the defendants be questioned without *their own legal counsel* because their council would count as a codefendant's counsel as well. This is a key concept to understand for this problem.

3) Find the Gap. There is no link between why the order cannot be granted and the fact that two of the codefendants would be questioned without their own legal counsel. The correct answer will provide just that link.

Choices – 1) Eliminate: (A) talks about disclosing legal information, which doesn't touch on the concept of questioning the defendants without appropriate counsel. (B) gives a reason why the defendants cannot be questioned without their counsel. This is the link we need, so keep it. (C) is off topic because nothing in the stimulus talks about self-incriminating questions. (D) – We don't know what rights the plaintiff has, so this choice does not provide any new link. (E), like (D), talks about questioning the *plaintiff*, but the conclusion is about questioning the defendants.

2) Confirm. (B) supports the conclusion by explaining that the order, if granted, would take away a right that defendants must have, the right to have their legal counsel present when questioned. So, the order cannot be granted. This provides the Missing Link. (B) is correct.

5. Computer scientist: For several decades, the number of transistors on new computer microchips, and hence the microchips' computing speed, has doubled about every 18 months. However, from the mid-1990s into the next decade, each such doubling in a microchip's computing speed was accompanied by a doubling in the cost of producing that microchip.

l Which one of the following can be properly **inferred** from the computer scientist's statements?

(A) The only effective way to double the computing speed of computer microchips is to increase the number of transistors per microchip.

(B) From the mid-1990s into the next decade, there was little if any increase in the retail cost of computers as a result of the increased number of transistors on microchips.

(C) For the last several decades, computer engineers have focused on increasing the computing speed of computer microchips without making any attempt to control the cost of producing them.

(D) From the mid-1990s into the next decade, a doubling in the cost of fabricating new computer microchips accompanied each doubling in the number of transistors on those microchips.

(E) It is unlikely that engineers will ever be able to increase the computing speed of microchips without also increasing the cost of producing them.

Type: Inference
Tags: Obvious Inference, Prove & Move, Logic Chain

Stem – "Properly inferred" is an Inference problem stem.

Stimulus – 1) Understand the facts. As computer technology advances with new changes rolling out each 18 months, the number of transistors doubles with each new rollout, and consequently so too does the computer speed. Another factor in the mix, of course, is the cost, which also doubles with every new tech rollout.

2) Look for an Obvious Inference. You've got a pretty straightforward Logic Chain here: 2x the transistors leads to 2x the computer speed leads to 2x the cost of production. When you connect the two ends of the chain, doubling the amount of *transistors* on a microchip has led to a doubling in the *cost* of producing new microchips with each new chip that comes out.

Choices – The correct choice will describe an inference like that identified in the Obvious Inference.

1) Eliminate choices, starting with (E). (E) infers that it's unlikely engineers will ever be able to increase the computing speed without also increasing the cost of production of microchips, but just because that's been the trend of the past few decades doesn't mean it will continue to be an unwavering rule of advancement in the future. (D) looks just like the Obvious Inference; it connects both ends of the Logic Chain, stating that a doubling in the cost of fabricating new computer microchips accompanied every doubling in the number of transistors on the chips. That's supported by the stimulus, which links doubling transistors with doubling microchip speed, which is linked with doubling in cost. (D) is supported. Prove and Move to the next problem.

6. Art critic: (The Woerner Journalism Award for criticism was given to Nan Paulsen for her reviews of automobiles. This is inappropriate.) The criticism award should be given for criticism, which Paulsen's reviews clearly were not. After all, cars are utilitarian things, not works of art. And objects that are not works of art do not reveal important truths about the culture that produced them.

Which one of the following **principles**, if valid, most helps to **justify** the reasoning in the art critic's argument?

(A) The Woerner Journalism Award for criticism should not be given to a writer who portrays utilitarian objects as works of art.

(B) Reviews of objects cannot appropriately be considered to be criticism unless the objects reveal important truths about the culture that produced them.

(C) Unless a review is written for the purpose of revealing important truths about the writer's culture, that review should not be considered to be criticism.

(D) The Woerner Journalism Award for criticism should not be given to writers who do not consider themselves to be critics.

(E) All writing that reveals important truths about a culture should be considered to be criticism.

Type: Justify
Tag: Referential Conclusion

Stem – You are asked which principle most helps to justify the argument, so you know that this is a Justify problem.

Stimulus – 1) Find the Conclusion. It was inappropriate that Paulsen received the Woerner Journalism Award.

2) Find the Support: There are two pieces here: Paulsen's reviews were not criticism, and cars do not reveal important truths about the culture that produced them.

3) Find the Gap. There is no link between the nature of criticism and objects that reveal important truths about the culture that created them. The correct answer will tie these two together.

Choices – 1) Eliminate. (A) does not talk about either unlinked concept. (B) gives a requirement for a review of an object to be criticism, so keep it. (C) jumbles up the link we need. It is the object the review is written about that needs to reveal an important truth about the culture that produced it, not the review itself. (D) talks about whether Paulsen considers herself to be a critic, something we don't know anything about. The argument does not consider her to be a critic, which is what matters here. (E) makes the same mistake as (C), talking about writing that reveals important truths.

2) Confirm. (B) provides the link we need because it ties the reviewing of objects that reveal important truths directly to the definition of criticism. Diagram:

Review is criticism → object reveals truths

(B) is correct.

7. Traffic engineers have increased the capacity of the Krakkenbak Bridge to handle rush-hour traffic flow. The resultant increase in rush-hour traffic flow would not have occurred had the city not invested in computer modeling technology last year at the request of the city's mayor, and the city's financial predicament would not have been resolved if the traffic flow across the bridge during rush hour had not been increased.

Which one of the following can be **properly inferred** from the information above?

(A) The city's financial predicament would not have been resolved had the city chosen a competing computer modeling software package.

(B) The city's financial predicament would not have been resolved had the city not invested in computer modeling technology.

(C) On an average day, more traffic crosses the Krakkenbak Bridge this year as compared to last year.

(D) Traffic flow across the Krakkenbak Bridge during rush hour would not have increased had the city's mayor not made investing in computer modeling technology the highest budgetary priority last year.

(E) The city's mayor was a proponent of investing in computer modeling technology because of the city's need to increase traffic flow across the Krakkenbak Bridge during rush hour.

Type: Inference
Tags: Obvious Link, Logic Chain, Prove & Move

Stem – "Properly inferred" is an Inference problem stem. First understand the facts and then look for an Obvious Inference.

Stimulus – 1) Understand the facts. There are a number of facts in this stimulus. The way the stimulus is constructed, one fact leads to the other, stating that X wouldn't have happened if not for Y, and Y wouldn't have happened if not for Z. Let's take stock of the facts. Traffic has been alleviated, which was caused by an investment in computer modeling, and the fact that traffic was alleviated made the city's finances better. So, putting this in sequential order: the computer model led to the alleviated traffic, and the alleviated traffic led to the improved city financials.

2) Look for an Obvious Inference. Because this is a cause-and-effect Logic Chain where one thing leads to another, which leads to another, you can infer that the initial cause was ultimately responsible for the final effect: the investment in computer modeling improved the city's finances.

Choices – 1) Eliminate choices, starting with (E). (E) talks about why the city's mayor wanted to invest in the computer modeling, which doesn't look like the Obvious Inference that the computer modeling lead to improved city finances. (D) also fails to match the Obvious Inference, and it doesn't even mention the improvement to the city's finances. (C) talks about the average traffic on the bridge, which is not an inference supported by the stimulus. Just because the rate of traffic flow has increased doesn't mean you can infer that more or fewer cars go over the bridge. Maybe the bridge has the same number of cars go over it, just at a faster rate of flow. (B) connects the city's resolved financial predicament to the investment in computer modeling technology, which exactly matches the Logic Chain inference that the initial cause in fact produced the final effect. We can prove (B). Prove and Move.

8. Ms. Sandstrom's newspaper column describing a strange natural phenomenon on the Mendels' farm led many people to trespass on and extensively damage their property (**Thus**, Ms. Sandstrom should <u>pay for this damage</u> if, as the Mendels claim, she could have <u>reasonably expected</u> that the column would lead people to damage the Mendels' farm.)

The argument's **conclusion can be properly inferred** if which one of the following is assumed?

 (A) One should pay for any damage that one's action leads other people to cause if one could have reasonably expected that the action would lead other people to cause damage.

 (B) One should pay for damage that one's action leads other people to cause only if, prior to the action, one expected that the action would lead other people to cause that damage.

 (C) It is unlikely that the people who trespassed on and caused the damage to the Mendels' property would themselves pay for the damage they caused.

 (D) Ms. Sandstrom knew that her column could incite trespassing that could result in damage to the Mendels' farm.

 (E) The Mendels believe that Ms. Sandstrom is able to form reasonable expectations about the consequences of her actions.

Type: Justify
Tags: Soft Conclusion

<u>Stem</u> – "Conclusion... properly inferred" = a Justify problem.

<u>Stimulus</u> – 1) Find the Conclusion. This is a Soft Conclusion, signaled by "thus." Ms. Sandstrom should pay for the damage *if* she could have anticipated that the column would lead to the damage.

2) Find the Support. The soft part of the conclusion is actually the support. Ms. Sandstrom could have reasonably suspected that the column would lead people to damage the farm.

3) Find the Gap. There is a Missing Link between Ms. Sandstrom's ability to suspect that the column would have that impact and her paying for the damages to the farm. The correct choice will link these two concepts.

<u>Choices</u> – 1) Eliminate. (A) mentions both concepts—paying for the damage and the idea of reasonably expecting the action could lead to the damage—so keep it. (B) is similar, but it tells about requirement for paying for the damage, not something that is sufficient for it. So, it does not provide the link, despite mentioning both concepts. (C) might strengthen the conclusion, but it does not link the concepts to make the argument valid. (D) does not mention the concept of her needing to pay for the damage, so it doesn't link the concepts. (D) moves beyond the hypothetical nature of the Soft Conclusion and says that Ms. Sandstrom knew that the column could result in damage. This does not link the concepts nor does it make the conclusion valid. (E) is similar to (D); it provides more detailed information about Ms. Sandstroms knowledge and abilities without linking the concepts.

2) Confirm: (A) provides the needed link. Here's the diagram:

Reasonably expect → pay for damage

This link makes the conclusion valid. (A) is correct.

9. Council member: The profits of downtown businesses will increase if more consumers live in the downtown area, and a decrease in the cost of living in the downtown area will guarantee that the number of consumers living there will increase. However, the profits of downtown businesses will not increase unless downtown traffic congestion decreases.

   If all the council member's statements are true, which one of the following **must be true**?

   (A)   If downtown traffic congestion decreases, the number of consumers living in the downtown area will increase.

   (B)   If the cost of living in the downtown area decreases, the profits of downtown businesses will increase.

   (C)   If downtown traffic congestion decreases, the cost of living in the downtown area will increase.

   (D)   If downtown traffic congestion decreases, the cost of living in the downtown area will decrease.

   (E)   If the profits of downtown businesses increase, the number of consumers living in the downtown area will increase.

Type: Inference
Tags: Obvious Inference, Prove & Move, Logic Chain

Stem – "Must be true" is an Inference problem stem.

Stimulus – 1) Understand the facts. Profit increases in downtown businesses will occur if more consumers live there, and a decrease in the cost of living in the downtown area will guarantee that more consumers live there. Yet, downtown profits won't increase unless traffic decreases. To put it in straightforward terms, if there's a decrease in the cost of living, more consumers will live downtown, and the more consumers that live downtown, the higher profits will rise in downtown businesses. So, when cost of living goes down, consumers downtown go up, and profits go up. But if traffic doesn't go down, then the profits won't go up. So, traffic is one limiting factor, but it's not connected to people living downtown (at least not by the stimulus).

2) Look for an Obvious Inference. You have a Logic Chain connecting a decreased cost of living to more consumers living downtown to an increase in downtown profits. Thus, you can look for a choice that simply links the two ends of the Logic Chain, stating that, when the cost of living goes down, profits go up.

Choices – 1) Eliminate choices, starting with (E). (E) infers that, as profits go up, the number of people living downtown will go up, but that's backwards. you know that more consumers living downtown will cause profits to go up, but that doesn't mean that, if profits go up, it was necessarily caused by more consumers living downtown. Consumers living downtown is a condition sufficient to grant an increase in profits, not one that's necessary for downtown businesses to see profit. (D) infers that, if traffic goes down, the cost of living will go down, but traffic isn't actually connected to anything in the Logic Chain. You can't make an Inference based on traffic. (C) infers that if traffic goes down, cost of living will go up. That's the opposite of (D), but it's incorrect for the same reason. (B) infers that, if the cost of living downtown goes down, the profits of downtown businesses will go up. That is the Obvious Inference linking the two ends of the Logic Chain. It's supported by the stimulus, which tells you that a decrease in the cost of living downtown will lead to more consumers living downtown, which will lead to an increase in profits of downtown businesses. That's your Prove—(B) is correct—so go ahead and Move.

An important note, the final sentence of the stimulus may make (B) look unappealing because it gives a *requirement* for the profits of downtown businesses to increase (downtown traffic congestion must decrease). However, when something is said to be sufficient for an outcome, then you know that all requirements are met and the outcome occurs. More consumers living in the downtown area is sufficient to increase the profits of the downtown businesses, which means it must meet whatever requirements there are for the profits to increase. In this situation, you can assume that more consumers in the downtown area somehow reduce the downtown traffic congestion. This may sound a little strange, but it is the case.

10. Activist: Any member of the city council ought either to vote against the proposal or to abstain. But if all the members abstain, the matter will be <u>decided by the city's voters</u>. (**So** at least one member of the city council should <u>vote against the proposal</u>.)

    The **conclusion** of the activist's argument **follows logically** if which one of the following is assumed?

    (A) If all the members of the city council abstain in the vote on the proposal, the city's voters will definitely decide in favor of the proposal.

    (B) The proposal should not be decided by the city's voters.

    (C) No members of the city council will vote in favor of the proposal.

    (D) If not every member of the city council abstains in the vote on the proposal, the matter will not be decided by the city's voters.

    (E) If one member of the city council ought to vote against the proposal, the other members should abstain in the vote on the proposal.

Type: Justify
Flaw: Missing Link

Stem – You're asked to find the answer that allows the conclusion to follow logically from the reasoning. That's a Justify problem stem.

Stimulus – 1) Find the Conclusion. Marked by the indicator, "so," the conclusion comes at the end of the stimulus. At least one member of the city council should vote against the proposal.

2) Find the Support. As support for this conclusion, the argument states that any member of the city council must either vote against the proposal or abstain from voting—no one should vote for it. If all of the city council members abstain from voting, then the decision will be left up to the city's voters, so the argument concludes that at least one member should vote against the proposal. That means that the conclusion argues to not allow the vote to go to the city's voters.

3) Find the Gap. There's a Concept Jump in the way the conclusion—"at least one member should vote against the proposal"—matches up with the support piece, "if all the members abstain, the matter will be decided by the city's voters." Why does that conclusion follow logically from this reasoning? It doesn't really, which means you're looking at the gap in the argument. The argument apparently thinks that the city's voters should not be allowed to decide the fate of this proposal, but it never states that belief. The conclusion doesn't follow.

Choices – The correct answer will state a link for these Unlinked Concepts; something along the lines of "we shouldn't let the city's voters decide the fate of the proposal."

1) Eliminate. (A) says what the city's voters will do if they're given the chance to vote on the proposal, which does not link the voters deciding on the matter with the members of the board not allowing that to happen. (B) does link those concepts however. Hold onto it. (C) says what members of the city council will do and specifically that none will vote for it. That doesn't offer any helpful information in the case of this Missing Link. (D) tries to trick you with some wonky "not" usage. Basically, it says that, if at least one member does not abstain, the city's voters won't decide the matter. That just states a logical deduction from information in the argument, not something that fixes the Missing Link. (E) says what the other members should do if one member votes against the proposal, but that doesn't really matter for the outcome (the vote still stays with the councilmembers). It also doesn't talk about not allowing the city's voters to decide on the issue.

2) Confirm. You're left with (B), which says that the proposal shouldn't be decided by the city's voters. This link justifies the conclusion that at least one member should vote against the proposal, which would ensure that the vote stays within the council and not go to the city's voters. (B) is correct.

39628267R00163

Made in the USA
Lexington, KY
03 March 2015